40.00

D1715217

# SOFTWARE RELIABILITY

# TRW Series
# of Software Technology

VOLUME 2

NORTH-HOLLAND PUBLISHING COMPANY – AMSTERDAM •NEW YORK•OXFORD

# SOFTWARE RELIABILITY

## A Study of Large Project Reality

THOMAS A. THAYER
MYRON LIPOW
and
ELDRED C. NELSON

*TRW Systems and Energy, Inc.*
*Redondo Beach, California*

1978

NORTH-HOLLAND PUBLISHING COMPANY – AMSTERDAM•NEW YORK•OXFORD

ISBN: 0 444 85217 4

*Published by:*
NORTH-HOLLAND PUBLISHING COMPANY – AMSTERDAM•NEW YORK•OXFORD




*Sole distributors for the U.S.A. and Canada:*
ELSEVIER NORTH-HOLLAND PUBLISHING COMPANY, INC.
52 VANDERBILT AVENUE
NEW YORK, N.Y. 10017




Library of Congress Cataloging in Publication Data
Thayer, Thomas A
   Software reliability.

   (TRW series of software technology ; v. 2)
   Bibliography:  p.
   1.  Computer programs--Reliability.  I.  Lipow,
Myron, joint author.  II.  Nelson, Eldred Carlyle,
1917-    III.  Title.  IV.  Series.
QA76.6.T445     001.6'42      78-12388
ISBN 0-444-85217-4

PRINTED IN THE NETHERLANDS

ABSTRACT

This document is the final technical report for the Software Reliability Study, performed by TRW for the Rome Air Development Center. It presents results of a study of data, principally error data, collected from four software development projects. These data were analyzed to determine what might be learned about various types of errors in the software; the effectiveness of the development and test strategies in preventing and detecting errors, respectively; and the reliability of the software itself.

This report also provides guidelines for data collection and analysis on other projects: data that are generally available, how project data were collected in this study, and some observed realities concerning the data collection and analysis processes.

Finally, the most recent work on TRW's Mathematical Theory of Software Reliability (MTSR), the Nelson model, is presented. This is complemented by a survey of software reliability models currently available in the software community.

# ACKNOWLEDGEMENTS

Software development projects have a potential for creating tremendous amounts of data, not all of which are recognized as being valuable at the outset of a study such as this. In some instances, analysis of the data is best accomplished with assistance from those who created the data; they alone are able to provide interpretation.

For their genuine interest and efforts in providing data and helping with the analysis, the authors would like to thank the following people:

| | |
|---|---|
| D. H. Barakat | W. L. Hetrick |
| B. T. Carnovale | F. S. Ingrassia |
| M. G. Calhoun | A. S. Liddle |
| C. D. Calvin | J. H. Petersen |
| G. R. Craig | R. N. Schreiner |
| T. P. Dillon | B. R. Seefeldt |
| K. F. Fischer | L. F. Summerill |
| M. A. Florczyk | P. N. Taylor |
| L. E. Frey | L. R. Vallembois |
| A. L. Green | C. E. White |
| D. L. Harris | J. A. Whited |
| H. W. Hawthorne | J. A. Yoxtheimer |
| D. E. Heine | |

# TABLE OF CONTENTS

TABLE OF CONTENTS (Continued)

TABLE OF CONTENTS (Continued)

TABLE OF CONTENTS (Continued)

TABLE OF CONTENTS (Continued)

LIST OF ILLUSTRATIONS

LIST OF ILLUSTRATIONS (Continued)

LIST OF ILLUSTRATIONS (Continued)

LIST OF TABLES

LIST OF TABLES (Continued)

# 1.0 INTRODUCTION

## 1.1 Study Objectives

The objectives of the Software Reliability Study (often abbreviated to "S.R.S." in this report) may be summarized by the following:

- Determine what software structural and development characteristics are available for analysis and which of these characteristics are relevant to the description (or prediction) of software reliability.

- Define improved methods for collecting reliability data.

- Based on error histories seen in the data, define sets of error categories, both causative and symptomatic, to be applied in the analysis of software problem reports and their closures.

- Recommend changes in: 1) development techniques to enhance the error-freeness (reliability) of the coded product and 2) test techniques to make it possible to find more errors earlier.

- Perform a survey of existing software reliability models.

- Extend Nelson's Mathematical Theory of Software Reliability (MTSR) and apply it to data collected on an ongoing software development project.

These objectives are achieved principally through analysis of empirical data collected during software testing, although as the reader will note in subsequent sections, what we see in testing is largely determined by what occurs in the preceding phases of the software development cycle, i.e. during the requirements analysis, design, and coding phases. Therefore, when necessary (and possible) this study has examined other software development disciplines, too.

## 1.2 Background

The driving force behind this study is the idea that much can be said about the quality and reliability of software from the software's error history. This idea is a popular one and one which serves as a central theme in this study.

Although the term "software reliability" is defined in Sections 5.0 and 6.0 in conjunction with software reliability models, a more general

definition for purposes of the analysis of empirical error data is in
order. The definition chosen is the one offered in Reference 1.

> Software possesses reliability to the extent that it
> can be expected to perform its intended functions
> satisfactorily.

Assuming that documented errors represent an inability to perform intended
functions satisfactorily, error-free software would be reliable software.
This assumption is made in the investigation of errors and other software
characteristics.

In the definition above, the word "satisfactorily" also needs definition. A universally applicable quantitative definition does not presently
exist; however, in the world of software problem reports mere creation of
the report registers some dissatisfaction with performance, whether the
report documents a real problem, a need for software enhancement, or what
turns out to be no problem at all.

Using the definition given above, the number of errors documented on
problem reports can be used as an indicator of software reliability. However, raw counts of errors don't tell the whole story and can be misleading.
Therefore, further analysis is necessary to determine the types of errors,
when and where they were introduced, how they were detected, and their
impact on the operation of the software system.

## 1.3  Approach

The fundamental approach taken in this study has been to base analysis on real data gathered from four large software projects:  two command
and control systems, a data management system, and a highly analytical
real-time system.  An attempt has been made to quantify the various characteristics of the software, the development program that produced the
software, the test program that detected the errors, and finally, the
errors themselves.

The study was conducted in two parts.  The first part consisted of
collecting and analyzing data from two completed projects (three projects
were actually used) to get a better picture of data availability in order
to determine what parameters were generally available and meaningful to
analyze.  Analysis techniques were also developed during the first part
of the study.  The second part of the study called for an application of
findings and techniques identified during the first part of the study to
a fourth, ongoing project.

Also in the last part of the study work was done to expand and
evaluate the Mathematical Theory of Software Reliability (MTSR).  This
software reliability model is particularly noteworthy since it addresses
data and the functional characteristics of the software in its assessment
of reliability.

Details of specific approaches taken in the analysis of data and
expansion of MTSR are given throughout the remainder of this document.

## 1.4 Terminology

Although a glossary of terms is presented in Appendix A, several general terms need definition to familiarize the reader with what follows in this document. These are terms used by TRW and some of its customers, and as such, may not be commonly understood.

Project – The end product of a project is the software and its documentation. The project itself is the combination of development activities, personnel, material resources, schedules, etc., required to produce the software and its documentation. In this study we talk about four projects, and since they have provided data for analysis, we call them source projects.

Programmer – For the projects under study a programmer is the individual who creates the software product and documentation. Sometimes called a developer or programmer/analyst, he designs, codes, and tests the portion of the end product for which he is responsible. He doesn't just code.

Tester – In this study a tester, or test analyst, is an individual who accepts delivery of the software from the developers and executes it to verify that it performs its intended functions correctly. He prepares test plans and procedures, executes the test procedures, analyzes test results, and documents problems. He is independent of the developers in the sense that he does not create the product. He is, however, required to work with the developers to verify that corrections to the software work properly through retesting. The term tester is also given to the system integration contractor personnel and customer people involved in test activities.

Problem/Error – A problem is a user oriented registration of dissatisfaction which is documented on a form we generically call a problem report. It can be either symptomatic or causative and need not be the result of an execution of the software (e.g., code inspections can result in the detection of problems). In this report we use the terms problem and error synonymously, although we recognize that they should be different. This is a concession made necessary by the fact that we have used real data from large projects, and it has not been possible to retrace each problem report to determine the original error.

Ideally, an error would be defined as a causative act producing a fault* in the software which, if evoked, would result in a symptomatic execution failure.

The assumption made in this study is that one problem report documents one error or, more accurately, one fault. Of course, this is not always the case. We therefore work with "actual" problems or "actual" errors, i.e., those problems that required a change in the code to affect corrective action. By considering only the code change problems and performing analyses at the routine level, the inaccuracies of the above assumption are minimized.

---

*Some people call these "bugs."

## 1.5  Suggestions on Reading This Document

This document presents the results of the Software Reliability Study
in seven major sections.  As might be imagined, there is some diverseness
between the essentially theoretical work concerning software reliability
models and the work connected with collecting and analyzing real data.
Also, since the Software Reliability Study had few precedents to follow,
results included many lessons learned about collecting data and methods
of analysis which should be valuable to those who attempt similar studies
in the future.  Parts of this document will hold varying importance for
different readers.  Therefore, this document has been organized in such a
way that topics of data description, data collection, results of analysis,
and reliability modeling appear in separate sections.  And, it's not
imperative that sections be read sequentially.  Lessons learned and results
are presented as part of each section.

In our previous study of empirical data, work done in support of the
CCIP-85 study group [5], our recommendation to the reader who was tempted
to further analyze data included in the final report was "don't."  This was
due to the quality of data, collected and analyzed retrospectively, and the
lack of supporting information to explain the error data.  Here our suggestion
to the same reader is "go ahead."  Although we haven't presented the sheer
volume of raw data that was in the previous study, the quality of data presented in this document is much better, and supporting information to explain
trends and statistical "outliers" is available.

There is, however, one fairly significant *caveat*.  Our experience in
this study has shown that there can be tremendous variabilities from one
project to the next, and for that matter, between different portions of the
same project.  What is true for one project may not be true for the next,
even when the project performers are essentially the same people.  So, the
reader is cautioned to view findings presented here and any he may conclude
from his own analyses with caution in an application to other projects.

The following paragraphs briefly discuss contents of the remainder of
this document.

Section 2.0 contains a description of the four source projects and
the data provided by these projects.  Although not strictly necessary
reading, it provides a background for Section 4.0, which contains the
results of analysis.

Section 3.0 specifically addresses the categorization of software
errors.  It discusses a method for generating categories and recommends
methods for increasing the quality of data collected.  It also offers a
brief history of category lists used in TRW's experience.

Section 4.0 contains the results of analyses performed during the
study.  An attempt has been made in this section to define the data, conditions, qualifiers, and assumptions made concerning each investigation.

Section 5.0 presents a summary of software reliability models presently available in the industry.

Section 6.0 presents work accomplished on the Mathematical Theory of Software Reliability and, to the extent possible, work done in evaluating this model.

Section 7.0 presents observed realities and lessons learned about data collection.

Finally, Section 8.0 summarizes major study conclusions.

## 2.0 DATA DESCRIPTION

In this section we will describe the data that are available for study. Data were taken from four software projects which, for purposes of anonymity, have been assigned names other than their real project designators. Table 2-1, below, lists the categories of data which are generally available from software development projects and the projects for which each category is available. Each of these categories will be described in detail.

## 2.1 General Project Descriptions

The four subject projects all represent major software development activities. One of them, Project 3, involves a co-contractor other than ·TRW producing some subset of the total software package. Specific findings traceable to the interface or differing development techniques are being analyzed, recognizing characteristics of the multi-contractor relationship. Although this multi-contractor relationship is believed to be extremely important to the analysis, review of the data includes a "one contractor" survey as well.

Table 2-1.  Data Availability

| Data Category | Project 2 | Project 3 | Project 4 | Project 5 |
|---|---|---|---|---|
| 1) General Project Descriptions | X | X | X | X |
| 2) Design Problem Data | | X | | |
| 3) Problem Report (Error) Data | X | X | X | X |
| 4) Software Characteristics | X | X | X* | X* |
| 5) Testing Data | X | X | | X |
| 6) Personnel Data | | X | | |
| 7) Computer Usage Data | | X | | |

*Detail of software characteristics for these projects is comparatively less than that which is available for Projects 2 and 3 due to the unavailability of automated tools.

## 2.1.1 Project 2

Project 2* is the Project B mentioned in Reference 5. Data available for this project was collected during four major modifications to the Final Operating Configuration (FOC) version of that software. These modifications are identified as MOD1A, MOD1B, MOD1BR, and MOD2 and are considered generally as separate development packages (in fact, separate projects), each with its own cycle of design, coding, debug, and formal test activities.

The software itself is a command and control software system written in JOVIAL J4. Only the applications software is considered in this study, although error data for the operating system (SYMON) and its system support software was sought in the course of data collection. OS software was virtually error free for this project and Project 3.

A majority of the errors for Project 2 was detected during formal test cycles composed of validation, acceptance, and integration testing (See Section 4.2.2). As with the FOC version, validation and acceptance tests were conducted by TRW, while a separate contractor performed the system integration tests. No operational demonstrations were conducted prior to delivery of the software to the customer, however.

Software Development for each modification was governed by formally specified and approved requirements, and it was these requirements that formal validation and acceptance tests were designed to demonstrate. System integration testing, on the other hand, was directed at verifying compatibility of the applications software with the operating system environment.

Structurally, the smallest compilable unit of source code was the routine. Routines were joined to form functions, functions were joined to form subsystems, and finally the system was comprised of several subsystems. This structure, which was also maintained for Project 3, was produced by a project organization based on the function. That is, a work unit (a group of developers or testers) was responsible for one or more whole functions, a relation that has proved helpful in the analysis.

## 2.1.2 Project 3

Project 3 represents an initial delivery of a large command and control software package. The applications software is written in JOVIAL J4 and is compatible with the SYMON operating system.

As with Project 2, the majority of errors analyzed were detected during formal testing; however, operational data for Project 3 spanning a period of approximately one year was also analyzed. In other respects the development and test characteristics are quite similar to those for Project 2, Table 2-2. As was mentioned earlier, TRW was not the sole

---

*Project 1 corresponds to Project A mentioned in Reference 5. It is not referenced in this study.

Table 2-2. General Project Characteristics

| | Project 2 | Project 3 | Project 4 | Project 5 |
|---|---|---|---|---|
| Size (total source statements) | 96,931 | 115,346 | ---* | 11,105**<br>17,459 MLI |
| Number of routines | 173 | 249 | 190 | 531 |
| Language | JOVIAL J4 | JOVIAL J4 | PWS | FORTRAN and Assembly |
| Formal Requirements | To function level | To function level | To software system level | To routine level |
| Documentation Standard | SSD Exhibit 61-47B | SSD Exhibit 61-47B | TRW Standards | MIL STD 490 |
| Co-contractor (routines) | No | Yes (77) | No | No |
| Operating Mode | Batch | Batch | On-line or batch | Real time and batch |
| Formal Testing (descending in order of occurrence) | • Validation<br>• Acceptance<br>• Integration | • Validation<br>• Acceptance<br>• Integration<br>• Operational Demonstration | --- | • Routine Development<br>• Routine Integration<br>• Process Integration<br>• Performance Evaluation<br>• Operational Demonstration |

contractor writing applications software, but data resulting from both contractors was available through a common configuration management source. Some data, e.g., personnel characteristics and computer time usage, are available only for the TRW portion of the software.

---
*PWS macros not measurable in comparable units.
**Project 5 size here in measured in executable source statements for FORTRAN code and in machine language instructions for assembly language code.

### 2.1.3 Project 4

Project 4 is a generalized information processing system written in a specially designed macro language called Program Word Structure or PWS. This system, with data storage, retrieval, and reporting capabilities, is highly flexible in that it can easily be tailored to suit a user's requirements through use of an English-like language.

The Project 4 structure begins with the subroutine as the smallest compilable unit of code. These are nestable and can call other subroutines or themselves. Subroutines group to form modes and modes are grouped to form decks. Decks are link edited to form pages.

It is important to note that all Project 4 data is representative of operational software. No data for the Project 4 development period was available.

### 2.1.4 Project 5

Project 5 is the on-going software development project which was selected to serve as a test bed for evaluation of early S.R.S. data collection and analysis techniques. It was chosen because of its schedule, the availability of development and test tools, and the fact that it is producing state-of-the-art realtime software using top-down structured programming. Software being produced on Project 5 includes a realtime data processor (the applications software), a realtime operating system, a realtime simulator to simulate the external hardware and operational environments, and support software, both batch and realtime, to support construction, testing, and configuration management of the software system.

Not all of the Project 5 code was used for study, however. We analyzed data from the applications, simulator, and operating system software, all of which is realtime code, and the batch mode Product Assurance tools, including a dynamic path analyzer, a code auditor, and a code structure analyzer.

Development and test techniques being used on Project 5 make it particularly attractive as an object of study. First of all, true top-down incremental development is being followed. That is to say, critical portions of the software are developed and tested in a series of "increments" and less critical portions are simulated using stubs (dummy elements). Each increment is a complete development cycle in itself, consisting of design coding, and testing phases. And, each successive increment adds more of the total system capability by replacing stubs with deliverable code. In this manner risk can be assessed early and critical algorithms analyzed thoroughly before large portions of programs have been committed to code. The degree of breakage or recoding on Project 5 is minimized in this manner and flexibility is maintained until optimum design solutions are achieved. As the critical algorithms and routines are shown to work successfully, lower levels of

subroutines are developed and the total system is integrated and
tested. Other projects in the study were developed in a one-time,
all-at-once traditional development cycle.

Project 5 is also being developed under rigorously enforced standards
and procedures. The size and duration of the project, coupled with
inherent turnover of personnel dictated that a consistent set of coding
standards be developed. During the contract definition phase a Software
Standards and Procedures Manual was developed. This manual contains
thirty-two (32) discrete standards dealing with the following major areas:

- Number of executable statements
- Flow charting
- Nomenclature or naming conventions
- Preface and inline comments
- Structured Programming
- Statements Labels

The standards and procedures are enforced by a product assurance
group utilizing an automated test tool entitled "Code Auditor" which
operates on routines and programs to check compliance for 32 individual
coding instructions.

Project 5 is also attractive from a testing standpoint since considerable emphasis is placed on unit or routine level testing. A project
standard calls for exercise of all executable statements and branch
points during unit testing, and for the realtime applications software
there is a requirement to execute all paths* at the unit level.

### 2.1.5 Summary of General Project Descriptions

Individual project characteristics may best be displayed in tabular
form in relation to similar characteristics for the other subject projects,
Table 2-2. When, in the course of analysis, project-specific characteristics are germane to results, these will be identified and contrasted with
the similar (or dissimilar) characteristics from other projects.

### 2.2 Design Problem Data

To date, very little has been done to analyze design problems
uncovered in the formal reviews of the preliminary and detailed design.
This is mentioned since these reviews, typically designated the PDR and
CDR, respectively, produce a significant amount of data critiquing the

---

*Paths through loops are defined to be at least one traversal of the loop,
although more traversals typically occur.

basic design. This information is easily collected, but never used.

In fact, the design problem report (DPR) is difficult to analyze in its present form because it is written without benefit of guidelines, and the important parameters are not presently defined or known. This wealth of information (Project 3 produced 5619 such reports!), some of it describing acute problems resulting from the design process, faces the same need for organization that the software problem report has required.

The extent to which the Project 3 DPR's will be used is limited. A raw count of total occurrences by routine is being used <u>only</u> to get a feel for the amount of review each routine received. (See Section 4.5.4.)

## 2.3  Problem Report (Error) Data

The software problem report (SPR) and the closure report (MTM)* form the backbone of data for this study. It is from the combination of these reports that the error category is determined. For each of the subject projects the SPR/MTM pair provided the vehicles for opening and closing a problem.

Every SPR required at least one MTM, whether the problem was a real one or not. An SPR could be written against a routine, the data base, the COMPOOL (in the case of Projects 2 and 3), a document, a test case, or just to ask a question. It was also used to place product improvements on the CM records for future software updates. From the SPR the following may be determined.

- The subject of the problem (routine, data base, etc.)

- When it was discovered

- The test case that pointed out the problem

- The software configuration when the problem was found

- A description of the problem.

The MTM closes the problem by 1) delivering a new modification to the software, 2) delivering a change to the data base (values) or COMPOOL (definitions), or by demonstrating that the problem is not a problem, i.e., an explanatory closure. It also indicates whether the SPR was written against the right subject. The key information on the MTM, however, is the explanation of the problem and the fix. For Projects 4

---

*Modification Transmittal Memorandum, Projects 2 and 3, Project 4 and Project 5 used only one form, the SPR and Discrepancy Report (DR), respectively.

and 5 the software problem report was used, as a single piece of paper, to both open and close the problem.  See Appendix B for sample problem reports.

Totals of SPR's analyzed for the source projects are presented throughout this document for each individual investigation of errors. This is because, depending on the investigation, the total number of documented problem reports may not have been used.

## 2.4  Software Characteristics

As might be imagined, the characteristics of the software come in two forms:  those that can be quantitatively measured and those that require some subjective evaluation.  In this study both are considered important.  Both are needed to explain errors.  Both are needed to under-stand the background against which the software is designed, coded, and tested; this need carries into the operational environment, too.  Examples of both types are presented in Table 2-3.

## 2.4.1  Software Structural Characteristics

Structural characteristics are measurable.  They quantify the soft-ware size, interface descriptions, use of the data base, and use of various language elements.  The approach taken in the initial planning of the S.R.S. data collection task was to provide as much quantitative detail as possible.  Several automated tools were available to aid in this task.

## 2.4.1.1  'TMETRIC Language Analyzer

'TMETRIC is a utility routine which statically analyzes JOVIAL J4 source code, breaking this code down into its component language elements. This analysis is done at the routine level.  Figure 2-1 presents sample output for a routine called COMP012.  The principal output of 'TMETRIC is the total size in source code statements, the number of logic branches, and the distinction between executable and non-executable statements. Comments are distinguished from statements.

In an effort to tie specific types of problems (Section 4.3) to types of routines and, finally, types of code within a routine, four generic types of executable code have been arbitrarily defined.

I/O            - I/O refers to JOVIAL defined and SYSTEM defined input and output statements.  JOVIAL I/O state-ments include FORMIN, FORMOUT, DECODE and ENCODE. SYSTEM DISC I/O includes 'SDAHA and its various entrances.  Examples of SYSTEM TAPE I/O are 'CWRITE, 'WEOF and 'REWIND.

COMPUTATIONAL - These are statements expressing equations contain-ing arithmetic operators.

Example:  AA = BB*CC**2/DD $

COMP012   CUSRT • • • • • • • • • • • • • • • • • • • • • • • • • • • • • • • • • • • • • • • • • • • • • • • • • • • • • •

| | NO. | PERCENT OF TOTAL | PERCENT OF EXECUTABLE | PERCENT OF I/O | PERCENT OF SYSTEM | | | | | |
|---|---|---|---|---|---|---|---|---|---|---|
| TOTAL STATEMENTS | 2300 | | | | | | | | | |
| EXECUTABLE | 1477 | 63.97 | | | | | | | | |
| I/O | 39 | 1.69 | 2.64 | | | | | | | |
| JOVIAL | 21 | 0.91 | 1.42 | 53.85 | | | | | | |
| SYSTEM | 18 | 0.78 | 1.22 | 46.15 | | | | | | |
| DISC | 18 | 0.78 | 1.22 | 46.15 | 100.00 | | | | | |
| TAPE | 0 | 0.00 | 0.00 | 0.00 | 0.00 | | | | | |
| COMPUTATIONAL | 201 | 8.71 | 13.61 | | | | | | | |
| DATA HANDLING | 592 | 25.64 | 40.08 | | | | | | | |
| LOGICAL | 336 | 14.55 | 22.75 | PERCENT OF LOGICAL | | | | | | |
| IF | 278 | 11.95 | 18.69 | 82.14 | L1= 149 | L2= 83 | L3= 48 | L4= 11 | L5= 0 | |
| IFEITH | 4 | 0.17 | 0.27 | 1.19 | | | | | | |
| CRIF | 8 | 0.35 | 0.54 | 2.38 | | | | | | |
| FOR | 45 | 1.95 | 3.05 | 13.39 | N1= 26 | N2= 16 | N3= 3 | N4= 0 | N5= 0 | |
| | | | | | P2= 0 | P3= 0 | P4= 0 | P5= 0 | | |
| GOTO SWITCH | 3 | 0.13 | 0.20 | 0.89 | | | | | | |
| PROC CALL | 120 | 5.20 | 8.12 | | | | | | | |
| PROGRAM EXIT | 15 | 0.65 | 1.02 | | | | | | | |
| GOTO | 101 | 4.37 | 6.84 | | | | | | | |
| TEST | 55 | 2.38 | 3.72 | | | | | | | |
| RETURN | 18 | 0.78 | 1.22 | | | | | | | |
| NON-EXECUTABLE | 932 | 36.03 | PERCENT OF NON-EXECUTABLE | PERCENT OF DECLARATION | | | | | | |
| DECLARATION | 239 | 10.35 | 28.79 | | | | | | | |
| ITEM | 199 | 8.43 | 23.68 | 87.43 | | | | | | |
| TABLE | 3 | 0.13 | 0.38 | 1.26 | | | | | | |
| ARRAY | 24 | 1.04 | 2.88 | 10.04 | | | | | | |
| OVERLAY | 0 | 0.00 | 0.00 | 0.00 | | | | | | |
| SWITCH | 3 | 0.13 | 0.38 | 1.26 | R1= 0 | R2= 0 | R3= 0 | R4= 0 | R5= 1 | |
| REFINE | 2 | 0.09 | 0.24 | 0.84 | | | | | | |
| NONE | 0 | 0.00 | 0.00 | 0.00 | | | | | | |
| PROC | 9 | 0.39 | 1.08 | 3.77 | | | | | | |
| CLOSE | 0 | 0.00 | 0.00 | 0.00 | | | | | | |
| ENTRANCE | 0 | 0.00 | 0.00 | 0.00 | | | | | | |
| SUBR | 1 | 0.04 | 0.12 | 0.42 | | | | | | |
| LABEL | 85 | 3.68 | 10.22 | | | | | | | |
| RECTN | 252 | 10.91 | 30.20 | | | | | | | |
| ENC | 256 | 11.09 | 30.77 | | | | | | | |
| TOTAL BRANCHES | 103 | | | | | | | | | |
| TOTAL COMMENTS | 1-39 | | | | | | | | | |

Figure 2-1.   Sample 'TMETRIC Output

DATA HANDLING  – These statements effect a simple data transfer (equality) from one variable to another and are distinguished from computational statements.

Examples: XX=YY $, AA($BB+2, DD$) = 'PR $.

LOGICAL  – Logical statements establish branches in the code and include the IF, IFEITH, ORIF, FOR and GOTO SWITCH statements.

Additional considerations in the 'TMETRIC output are as follows:

● EXECUTABLE statements are distinguished from NON-EXECUTABLE data declarations, procedure declarations, etc.

● L1=, L2=, etc., refer to the number of IF, IFEITH, and ORIF statements indentured 1 level, 2 levels, etc. LL= includes levels of indenture of 5 or greater.

● N1=, N2=, etc., refer to the number of FOR loop statements nested 1 deep, 2 deep, etc. NN includes depths of nesting of 5 or greater.

● PROC CALL includes internal and external (SUBR) procedure calls.

● B1=, B2=, etc., refer to the number of SWITCH declarations that contain 1 branch, 2 branches, etc. BB includes SWITCH branches of 5 or greater.

● TOTAL BRANCHES includes all possible logical branches, resulting from IF, IFEITH, ORIF and GOTO-SWITCH name statements. This does not reflect the actual number of logical branches the program will make when it executes.

The four code types described above appear to be general enough to be applicable to Projects 4 and 5, but two code types were added to cover the PWS language of Project 4:

● Information and program format control statements

● Instrumentation statements for compilation and identification.

The macros in the PWS language have been classified according to the four generic types and the two additional types given above. Project 4 diagnostics output routine usage of the PWS macros. From this a breakdown of code type by routine can be determined.

## 2.4.1.2  Interface Definitions

Routine/routine and routine/data base interface descriptions are generally available from system utility or construct routines. To this can be added details of the individual interface, e.g., number of arguments in the calling sequence, the type of interface (applications, system,

user, data base) and the format of information passed (see Table 2-3).
The level of embedment of the "distance from the executive" can be determined and may give us a clue to why routines are used incorrectly or why
some routines suffer from a large number of inaccurately written SPRs.

## 2.4.2 Subjective Characteristics

These characteristics provide the background necessary for understanding the software problems. Here again the approach was to collect
any information that wasn't nailed down; however, in the course of defining
common questions that could be asked of each developer, the term "difficulty"
kept cropping up. When asked to describe a routine's complexity we typically describe its type (e.g., a utility routine) and quickly launch into
a description of how difficult it is, was, or will be to produce. Ask the
same question of a tester or maintainer of software and the response is
likely to be the same. The point to be made here is that we don't know
how to describe software complexity. We do have a pretty good and remark-
ably universal understanding of what makes a routine "difficult." Therefore, questions related to subjective routine characteristics were limited
to asking about routine type and difficulty. Work unit managers were
requested to assign difficulty ratings to each of the following disciplines;
they were also asked to provide additional comment concerning the routine
and the difficulty encountered during development and test:

- Design — preliminary and detailed design work, the design reviews,
  requirements definition and, all work done prior to coding.

- Coding — the process of transferring the flow documented in the
  detailed design documentation into source code.

- Checkout — debug, checkout, and development testing of the
  routine, including preparation of special test drivers and
  debug code.

- Implementation — work necessary to make the routine interface
  with other routines, the OS, and the COMPOOL; effort required
  to provide data base inputs; the human interfaces with other
  developers, the test group, configuration management, etc.

- Documentation — preparation of all documents related to the
  routine, excluding status reports.

Routine type is assigned according to the primary function of the routine.
These are given below.

- CON — control or executive routine

- INP — input routine

- SET — setup or initialization routine

Table 2-3.   Available Parameters

---

Routine Structural Characteristics

- Routine size

  - Total source code statements
  - Executable statements
  - Non-executable statements
  - Machine dependent number of instructions

- Number of branches

- Number of direct interfaces

  - With other applications routines
  - With operating system routines

- Number of arguments in interface calls

- Data interfaces

  - Number of global data blocks
  - Number of internal data variables

- Number of procedures

- Number of entry points

- Number of exit points

- Routine code type

  - % computational
  - % logical
  - % data handling
  - % I/O

- Loop and nesting levels

- Branch statement (IF) nesting levels

- Number of comments

- Pages of documentation

- Computer time (clock time, not CPU time)

  - Development time
  - Test time

Table 2-3.  Available Parameters (continued)

<u>Subjective Characteristics</u>

- Routine difficulty at preliminary design

- Routine difficulty after formal test and delivery

  - Design
  - Code
  - Debug/checkout
  - Implementation
  - Documentation

- Routine type

  - Executive
  - Control
  - Setup
  - Input
  - Computational
  - Post processing
  - Output

- Personnel data

  - Number of people working on routine
  - Load factor on each programmer
  - Programmer rating
  - Programmer/job evaluation

- P/C — primarily computational routine

- P/P — post-processing routine

- OUT — output routine

- UTL — utility routine

A near similar rating of difficulty for Project 3 routines is available from the pre-detailed design period. Comparison will be made to the post-delivery difficulty rating to investigate differences and any possible relation to the types of problems encountered.

## 2.5 Test Characteristics for Projects 2, 3, 4 and 5

This source of information, believed to be essential to the study of software reliability, has proved to be a major disappointment in that test data of the required detail is not available for Projects 2, 3, and 4. Although information about numbers of tests, the type of test, and how many problems each uncovered is available and will be examined for Project 3, a quantitative measure of how much of the software was tested is not available. That is, we cannot determine how much stress the test program put the software through.* Aside from being a disappointment to the S.R.S. this lack of information is really a fundamental criticism of the test program since it is key to the question of determining how much testing is "enough." When formal testing was over it could be said that all the requirements were satisfied, a "large" number of the additional software capabilities were demonstrated, and when exercised in the operational environment, the software correctly processed operational-like data within the allotted time limit. It is impossible, however, to say what percentage of the code was exercised.

Testing for Projects 2 and 3 was conducted in five distinct test periods, each with a general test goal.** These periods are described in the following paragraphs.

No test data were available for Project 4 since it is an operational program.

---

*Measures of stress other than the amount of code exercised are 1) computer time used for testing, see Section 4.0, 2) number of test executions, and 3) number of analysts available to review test results. Item 2), although available, is considered a poor parameter because test reruns generally did not execute new code. Item 3) is also available and may help to explain both the number and type of SPRs generated.

**Project 2 actually employed four of these, eliminating the operational demonstration because Project 2 is operational software under frequent update.

## 2.5.1  Development Test

Test cases, formal only to the extent that they were documented, were written and executed by the development personnel.  The goal during this test period was to demonstrate specific functional capabilities, test data extremes and singularities, trigger output of all error messages, test the operator interface, and produce all output formats in the appropriate media. Use of special drivers, debug code, and instrumentation techniques was practiced.  This testing was begun after a routine was compiled and debugged, i.e., the routine would load and cycle.  Tests were structured in a bottom-up fashion; once routines were sufficiently tested, they were grouped and tested as functions.  Functions were grouped for the subsystem tests.

## 2.5.2  Validation Test and Acceptance Test

Validation testing was begun after a batch delivery of the software at an event called "internal delivery."  At this point an independent test group took delivery of the software and began formal testing with a goal of demonstrating the approved software performance and design requirements.  An additional goal was to demonstrate selected software capabilities agreed upon by the customer and the test group.  These included use of operationally oriented unique data sets, selected limits tests, and use of operational scenarios. Key to the conduct of validation and acceptance testing was the fact that all testing was performed on a master configuration and no alteration of the code was allowed; even addition of diagnostic code was not allowed.

Validation and acceptance tests were run at the subsystem level through the main subsystem entrance but were designed to examine performance at the routine, function, subsystem, and system levels.

Acceptance testing consisted of a rerun of a subset of validation tests, those that specifically demonstrated the software requirements.  Customer acceptance of the software hinged on successful completion of these tests.

## 2.5.3  Integration Test

This test period was conducted by an independent integrating contractor whose responsibility it was to demonstrate that the applications software interfaced correctly with the operating system and the system support software.  Additional goals were to test the following:

●  the software/operator interface

●  all listable, card, and tape outputs

●  out of bounds input conditions

Tests conducted during this period were similar in structure and formality to the validation and acceptance tests.

## 2.5.4 Operational Demonstration

The operational demonstration (OD) was a short period of testing which followed an operational timeline and used an operational data base. The goal during this period was to demonstrate the software in the operational environment.

## 2.5.5 Project 5 Testing

The Project 5 test program differs primarily in that the development test period is conducted in a more formal fashion. More specifically, the goals of the development test period are to 1) demonstrate requirements allocated to the routine level, 2) exercise all code, and 3) demonstrate an extensive list of functional capabilities in formal test cases. Extensive low level interface testing is an additional goal. Development tests are conducted at the routine and task (analogous to the function of Project 3) levels, calling for drivers to be built to do this early integration testing.

Following this period is a process integration test period during which formal tests are executed to demonstrate interfaces between tasks making up subprocesses and between subprocesses making up the various realtime processes. This test phase is conducted by an independent test team and is the period which produces the problem reports, called discrepancy reports, used in this study. This testing is actually system level testing because the entire software system*, interfacing with the realtime simulator, is exercised.

Although no measure of test thoroughness was possible at the process or system level of testing**, test thoroughness was determinable at the routine level through use of a dynamic path analysis tool. This allowed development testers to assure that all executable code had been tested and that, in a select portion of the system's applications software, all paths had been tested. This was coupled with use of an operational-like test data base during early routine level testing. The effectiveness of this test thoroughness will be discussed in Section 4.7.4.

---

*To the extent possible with each successive iteration of the top-down approach.

**Automated tools available for measuring test thoroughness ran out of core at the system level.

## 2.6  Personnel Data

Evaluation of personnel performance was limited to TRW programmers
for Project 3 up to product delivery at the end of the operational demonstration.  Once again this was done because of the incompleteness of the
Project 3 data set, coupled with the subjective nature of the parameters.
Evaluation of test personnel was considered as a possible avenue of investigation but was discarded due to our inability to quantitatively evaluate
individual test cases.*  Incidentally, evaluation criteria proposed below
would work equally well for the test group.

Selection of parameters was based on several observations.

- Programmer experience, both in years of industry experience and
  years of experience in a specific environment, was not considered
  important.

- Development schedules were tight, manpower sometimes limited,
  and crises frequent.

- All software was delivered on schedule and was accepted by the
  customer.

Given these observations, two general measures relating to programmer performance were considered important:  1) programmer-specific criteria
and 2) assignment or job-specific criteria.  And, since these measures
are not believed to be independent, a programmer/job evaluation parameter
was devised.  Table 2-4 presents parameters considered in the study of
programmer characteristics relative to software quality.  From these
parameters the following may be determined.

PROGRAMMER RATING = (KNOWLEDGE) + (INTELLIGENCE) + (INITIATIVE)

+ (RESPONSIBILITY)

PROGRAMMER/JOB EVALUATION = (2.0 - LOAD FACTOR) (PROGRAMMER RATING)

Evaluation was made for 76 TRW programmers who worked directly
on and were responsible for the Project 3 software.  This evaluation is
being done by the programmer's line management after project completion.

---

*Note:   Evaluation of test personnel performance is a particularly attrac-
         tive idea since, as we shall see in Section 4.5.5, the programmers
         and the independent test group for Project 3 formed two distinct
         colonies of data.

Table 2-4. Personnel Evaluation Parameters

| | | Parameter | Range | Based on |
|---|---|---|---|---|
| Programmer Specific Parameters | Technical Capability* | KNOWLEDGE | 1-5 | Familiarity with language and machines<br>Familiarity with engineering concepts<br>Familiarity with processing concepts |
| | | INTELLIGENCE | 1-5 | Problem-solving abilities<br>Creativity<br>Mental acuity |
| | | INITIATIVE | 1-5 | Recognition of tasks required<br>Attack of problems and interfaces<br>Effective utilization of time |
| | Work Habits | RESPONSIBILITY | 1-5 | Concentration on job<br>Commitment to doing job well<br>Working extra hours if required |
| Job Specific Parameters | | WORK LOAD FACTOR | 0.5-1.5 | Estimated relationship of actual work load to normal full work load (0.5 to 1.5) |

*Notes: 1) Technical capability not related to years of experience.

2) Rating scale for programmer specific parameters:

1 - Inadequate
2 - Adequate
3 - Average
4 - Excellent
5 - Superior

## 2.7  Computer Usage Data

Information concerning the amount of computer time used during formal testing, although not in units of CPU time, is available for Project 3. Clock on and off times were recorded for every TRW run made during the development and test periods.  Analysis of development and test computer usage consistent with documented problems discovered during testing is presented in Section 4.5.5.

The subject of machine time and the number of problems encountered during that time is cause for lengthy and often heated discussion.  In any event, one thing is clear from this study; if we are to investigate the matter, we must have accurate records of wall clock and CPU times and be able to tie them to specific runs of the software.

## 3.0  ERROR DATA CATEGORIZATION

This section discusses classification or categorization of software errors.  Category lists generated and used during performance of the Software Reliability Study are the principal object of discussion, although general comments and recommendations concerning error categorization are also presented.

### 3.1  Error Categories

For purposes of this report an error category is defined as a generic description of error type.  The source materials used in categorizing an error are the problem report and the closure report, both of which are necessary for accurate error categorization.  Reasons for such a general definition will become apparent from the following sections, which address three aspects of dealing with categorization of software problems:  1) generation of categories,  2) assignment of categories to problem reports, and  3) analysis of results.

### 3.1.1  Generation of Error Categories for Projects 2, 3, and 4

The approach taken in generating the error categories (failure categories, error codes, or defect categories, as they are sometimes called) was to base results on an analysis of the SPRs and MTM's rather than to draw up a list a priori.  This was done for two reasons; existing lists tended to be rather long (the longest presenting over 400 categories) and the fact that more than one project was being examined, each with its own characteristics.  Problem reports and closures varied in information content, too.

Since Project 3 represents the largest source of error information, a pilot study was conducted on a sample of 600 SPRs to generate a list of error categories.  The sample was selected from the mid-validation test phase of Project 3 to take advantage of SPRs which were written after the initial test personnel learning period.  Once a list was consolidated, SPRs from Projects 2, 3, and 4 were categorized according to the list.  Additions and refinements to this list were encouraged, but the resulting alterations were surprisingly minimal.  Major changes consisted of a regrouping of existing categories.*  Twenty-six new categories were added as a result of Project 4.  Thirteen of these were added because Project 4 is an operational system with many user requested changes, and the remaining 13 were added to provide greater detail for existing categories or to establish Project 4-specific categories.

It should also be noted here that, although major groupings tend to be argumentative, they were selected to be as compatible as possible with techniques available for determining routine characteristics and code type, Section 2.0.

---

*Changes to this list were forbidden after analysis of Project 5 error data began.

Table 3-1 presents the 169 error categories under 20 major headings or groups. Total numbers of occurrence for each category are also given for each project and for the four modifications to Project 2 being considered in this study. Detailed analysis is presented in Section 4.2.1.

Note that the level of detail provided by a category is indicated by the level of indenture for the category number. Major headings, e.g., AA000, are considered categories, but most problems were assigned to categories at a greater level of indenture (detail).

A brief description of each of the 20 major groups is given below. Explanation of selected categories within each group is also provided, where necessary.

### 3.1.1.1 Computation Errors

Computation errors were errors in or resulting from coded equations. These equations fell generally into two categories, those that produced values directly related to the physical problem being solved by the software (algorithms, vector algebra, modeling code, etc.) and equations used in a bookkeeping sense (computation of indices, record numbers, entry numbers, etc.). Categories worthy of special mention are as follows:

AA040 - This category covers coded equations which were of the wrong form, missing terms, or based on the wrong physical convention. A special case in this category is AA041, which indicates an inaccuracy in a mathematical model.

AA050 - This category was assigned to errors found through comparison of output to results from manual calculations or previously validated sources. It is a highly symptomatic category resulting from non-specific SPR and MTM documentation.

AA070 - Time calculation errors were peculiar to Projects 2 and 3 and occurred frequently enough to generate three categories. In general, these were modeling problems.

### 3.1.1.2 Logic Errors

In generating the logic error categories an attempt was made to tie errors to existing logical code or the need for logical code. Categories in this group tend to be highly symptomatic.

Table 3-1.  Error Categories and Frequency of Occurrence for Subject Projects

| CATEGORY ID | CATEGORIES | PROJECT 2 | | | | | PROJECT 3 | PROJECT 4 |
|---|---|---|---|---|---|---|---|---|
| | | MOD1A | MOD1B | MOD1BR | MOD2 | TOTAL | | |
| AA000 | COMPUTATIONAL ERRORS | | | | | | | |
| AA010 | Total number of entries computed incorrectly | 0 | 0 | 0 | 0 | 0 | 0 | 0 |
| AA020 | Physical or logical entry number computed incorrectly | 8 | 6 | 2 | 21 | 37 | 19 | 0 |
| AA030 | Index computation error | 2 | 7 | 1 | 17 | 27 | 27 | 0 |
| AA040 | Wrong equation or convention used | 3 | 6 | 4 | 11 | 24 | 31 | 4 |
| AA041 | Mathematical modeling problem | 0 | 0 | 0 | 1 | 1 | 57 | 0 |
| AA050 | Results of arithmetic calculation inaccurate/not as expected | 0 | 0 | 2 | 5 | 7 | 7 | 0 |
| AA060 | Mixed mode arithmetic error | 0 | 0 | 0 | 0 | 0 | 74 | 2 |
| AA070 | Time calculation error | 2 | 1 | 5 | 13 | 21 | 36 | 0 |
| AA071 | Time conversion error | 0 | 0 | 0 | 0 | 0 | 7 | 0 |
| AA072 | Time truncation/rounding error | 1 | 0 | 1 | 2 | 4 | 2 | 0 |
| AA080 | Sign convention error | 0 | 2 | 0 | 5 | 7 | 16 | 0 |
| AA090 | Units conversion error | 1 | 0 | 2 | 15 | 18 | 28 | 1 |
| AA100 | Vector calculation error | 1 | 0 | 0 | 0 | 1 | 13 | 0 |
| AA110 | Calculation fails to converge | 0 | 0 | 3 | 2 | 5 | 4 | 0 |
| AA120 | Quantization/truncation error | 1 | 4 | 1 | 4 | 10 | 32 | 0 |
| | **TOTALS** | 19 | 26 | 21 | 96 | 162 | 353 | 7 |
| BB000 | LOGIC ERRORS | | | | | | | |
| BB010 | Limit determination error | 0 | 0 | 0 | 0 | 0 | 0 | 0 |
| BB020 | Wrong logic branch taken | 2 | 5 | 4 | 5 | 16 | 37 | 1 |
| BB030 | Loop exited on wrong cycle | 1 | 4 | 1 | 5 | 11 | 49 | 0 |
| BB040 | Incomplete processing | 0 | 0 | 0 | 0 | 0 | 0 | 0 |
| BB050 | Endless loop during routine operation | 4 | 2 | 4 | 10 | 20 | 58 | 0 |
| BB060 | Missing logic or condition test | 1 | 4 | 1 | 0 | 6 | 35 | 72 |
| BB061 | Index not checked | 6 | 9 | 8 | 26 | 49 | 233 | 0 |
| BB062 | Flag or specific data value not tested | 2 | 0 | 0 | 1 | 3 | 59 | 0 |
| BB070 | Incorrect logic | 5 | 4 | 8 | 34 | 51 | 139 | 57 |
| BB080 | Sequence of activities wrong | 0 | 0 | 0 | 0 | 0 | 0 | 3 |
| BB090 | Filtering error | 4 | 7 | 2 | 18 | 31 | 57 | 1 |
| BB100 | Status check/propagation error | 1 | 3 | 0 | 4 | 8 | 7 | 0 |
| BB110 | Iteration step size incorrectly determined | 6 | 3 | 1 | 2 | 12 | 103 | 1 |
| BB120 | Logical code produced wrong results | 0 | 0 | 0 | 0 | 0 | 0 | 0 |
| BB130 | Logic on wrong routine | 3 | 5 | 0 | 19 | 27 | 39 | 0 |
| BB140 | Physical characteristics of problem to be solved, overlooked, or misunderstood | 0 | 0 | 0 | 2 | 2 | 6 | 2 |
| BB150 | Logic needlessly complex | 1 | 1 | 0 | 0 | 2 | 64 | 0 |
| BB160 | Inefficient logic | 0 | 1 | 1 | 2 | 4 | 7 | 2 |
| BB170 | Excessive logic | 1 | 3 | 1 | 9 | 14 | 26 | 1 |
| BB180 | Storage reference error (software problem) | 0 | 0 | 0 | 0 | 0 | 18 | 0 |
| | **TOTALS** | 37 | 51 | 31 | 137 | 256 | 937 | 140 |

Table 3-1. Error Categories and Frequency of Occurrence for Subject Projects (Continued)

| CATEGORY ID | CATEGORIES | PROJECT 2 | | | | | PROJECT 3 | PROJECT 4 |
|---|---|---|---|---|---|---|---|---|
| | | MOD1A | MOD1B | MOD1BR | MOD2 | TOTAL | | |
| CC000 | I/O ERRORS | | | | | | | |
| CC010 | Missing output | 0 | 0 | 0 | 0 | 0 | 0 | 0 |
| CC020 | Output missing data entries | 3 | 1 | 0 | 5 | 9 | 92 | 4 |
| CC030 | Error message not output | 2 | 6 | 0 | 0 | 8 | 49 | 0 |
| CC040 | Error message garbled | 1 | 4 | 1 | 1 | 7 | 38 | 0 |
| CC050 | Output or error message not compatible with design documentation (including garbled output) | 9 | 5 | 3 | 6 | 23 | 42 | 19 |
| CC060 | Misleading or inaccurate error message text | 0 | 0 | 0 | 0 | 0 | 147 | 1 |
| CC070 | Output format error (including wrong location) | 3 | 4 | 0 | 6 | 13 | 12 | 0 |
| CC080 | Duplicate or excessive output | 10 | 9 | 3 | 16 | 38 | 41 | 2 |
| CC090 | Output field size inadequate | 2 | 2 | 1 | 9 | 14 | 77 | 2 |
| CC100 | Debug output problem (relative to design documentation) | 1 | 0 | 0 | 0 | 1 | 29 | 0 |
| CC101 | Lack of debug output | 0 | 1 | 0 | 0 | 1 | 3 | 4 |
| CC102 | Too much debug | 0 | 1 | 2 | 4 | 7 | 27 | 0 |
| CC110 | Header output problem | 3 | 4 | 0 | 1 | 8 | 15 | 0 |
| CC120 | Output tape format error | 1 | 0 | 0 | 0 | 1 | 64 | 0 |
| CC130 | Output card format error | 0 | 1 | 0 | 2 | 3 | 5 | 2 |
| CC140 | Error in printer control | 0 | 1 | 0 | 1 | 2 | 3 | 0 |
| CC150 | Line count/page eject error | 0 | 0 | 0 | 0 | 0 | 1 | 0 |
| CC160 | Needed output not provided in design | 3 | 2 | 1 | 15 | 21 | 32 | 2 |
| CC161 | Insufficient output options | 0 | 0 | 0 | 0 | 0 | 42 | 1 |
| | TOTALS | 38 | 41 | 11 | 66 | 156 | 719 | 36 |
| DD000 | DATA HANDLING ERRORS | | | | | | | |
| DD010 | Valid input data improperly set/used | 9 | 2 | 7 | 15 | 33 | 79 | 31 |
| DD020 | Data written in or read from wrong disk location | 7 | 0 | 0 | 1 | 8 | 11 | 8 |
| DD030 | Data lost/not stored | 5 | 9 | 3 | 12 | 29 | 51 | 2 |
| DD040 | Data, index, or flag not set or set/initialized incorrectly | 9 | 3 | 8 | 9 | 29 | 144 | 37 |
| DD041 | Number of entries set incorrectly | 0 | 2 | 2 | 4 | 8 | 22 | 0 |
| DD050 | Data, index, or flag modified or updated incorrectly | 0 | 2 | 0 | 11 | 13 | 68 | 15 |
| DD051 | Number of entries updated incorrectly | 2 | 1 | 3 | 0 | 6 | 2 | 0 |
| DD060 | Extraneous entries generated (table, array, etc.) | 1 | 0 | 0 | 1 | 2 | 28 | 0 |
| DD070 | Bit manipulation error | 0 | 0 | 0 | 1 | 1 | 22 | 0 |
| DD071 | Error using bit modifier | 0 | 0 | 0 | 0 | 0 | 1 | 0 |
| DD080 | Floating point/integer conversion error | 0 | 1 | 0 | 0 | 1 | 3 | 2 |
| DD090 | Internal variable error (definition or set/use) | 0 | 0 | 0 | 0 | 0 | 6 | 0 |
| DD100 | Data packing/unpacking error | 1 | 0 | 0 | 6 | 7 | 5 | 0 |
| DD110 | Routine looking for data in non-existent record | 0 | 1 | 0 | 0 | 1 | 19 | 0 |
| DD120 | Bounds violation | 3 | 0 | 1 | 1 | 5 | 23 | 0 |
| DD130 | Data chaining error | 1 | 4 | 0 | 0 | 5 | 5 | 0 |
| DD140 | Data overflow or overflow processing error | 0 | 0 | 0 | 2 | 2 | 46 | 0 |
| DD150 | Read error | 1 | 0 | 1 | 5 | 7 | 8 | 13 |
| DD151 | All available data not read | 0 | 0 | 0 | 0 | 0 | 3 | 0 |
| DD160 | Long literal processing error | 1 | 0 | 0 | 0 | 1 | 8 | 0 |
| DD170 | Sort error | 0 | 0 | 1 | 3 | 4 | 55 | 0 |
| DD180 | Overlay error | 0 | 0 | 0 | 2 | 2 | 4 | 0 |
| DD190 | Subscripting convention error | 0 | 0 | 0 | 0 | 0 | 0 | 0 |
| DD200 | Double buffering error | 0 | 0 | 0 | 0 | 0 | 0 | 1 |
| | TOTALS | 40 | 25 | 26 | 73 | 164 | 613 | 110 |

Table 3-1.  Error Categories and Frequency of Occurrence for Subject Projects (Continued)

| CATEGORY ID | CATEGORIES | PROJECT 2 | | | | | PROJECT 3 | PROJECT 4 |
|---|---|---|---|---|---|---|---|---|
| | | MOD1A | MOD1B | MOD1BR | MOD2 | TOTAL | | |
| EE000 | OPERATING SYSTEM/SYSTEM SUPPORT SOFTWARE ERRORS | | | | | | | |
| EE010 | JOVIAL produces erroneous machine code | 0 | 0 | 0 | 0 | 0 | 3 | 0 |
| EE020 | OS missing needed capability | 0 | 0 | 1 | 0 | 1 | 1 | 0 |
| | TOTALS | 0 | 0 | 1 | 0 | 1 | 4 | 0 |
| FF000 | CONFIGURATION ERRORS | | | | | | | |
| FF010 | Compilation error | 5 | 4 | 0 | 4 | 13 | 47 | 0 |
| FF011 | Segmentation Problem | 0 | 0 | 0 | 0 | 0 | 7 | 0 |
| FF020 | Illegal instruction | 0 | 0 | 3 | 0 | 3 | 11 | 0 |
| FF030 | Unexplainable program halt | 0 | 0 | 0 | 0 | 0 | 18 | 0 |
| | TOTALS | 5 | 4 | 3 | 4 | 16 | 83 | 0 |
| GG000 | ROUTINE/ROUTINE INTERFACE ERRORS | | | | | | | |
| GG010 | Routine passing incorrect amount of data (insufficient or too much) | 1 | 0 | 0 | 0 | 1 | 24 | 0 |
| GG020 | Routine passing wrong parameters or units | 1 | 1 | 1 | 4 | 6 | 57 | 0 |
| GG030 | Routine expecting wrong parameters | 2 | 1 | 0 | 6 | 9 | 24 | 7 |
| GG040 | Routine fails to use available data | 5 | 0 | 0 | 1 | 6 | 19 | 0 |
| GG050 | Routine sensitive to input data order | 2 | 0 | 0 | 2 | 4 | 0 | 2 |
| GG060 | Calling sequence or routine/routine initialization error | 0 | 8 | 3 | 21 | 32 | 105 | 22 |
| GG070 | Routines communicating through wrong data block | 0 | 2 | 0 | 0 | 2 | 17 | 1 |
| GG080 | Routine used outside design limitation | 0 | 0 | 0 | 7 | 7 | 0 | 1 |
| GG090 | Routine won't load (routine incompatibility) | 1 | 0 | 0 | 0 | 1 | 3 | 0 |
| GG100 | Routine overflows core when loaded | 0 | 0 | 1 | 0 | 1 | 1 | 0 |
| | TOTALS | 12 | 11 | 5 | 41 | 69 | 250 | 33 |
| HH000 | ROUTINE/SYSTEM SOFTWARE INTERFACE ERRORS | | | | | | | |
| HH010 | OS interface error (calling sequence or initialization) | 0 | 0 | 0 | 0 | 0 | 20 | 0 |
| HH020 | Routine uses existing system support software incorrectly | 0 | 0 | 0 | 4 | 4 | 1 | 0 |
| HH030 | Routine uses sense/jump switch improperly | 0 | 0 | 0 | 1 | 1 | 7 | 0 |
| | TOTALS | 0 | 0 | 0 | 5 | 5 | 28 | 0 |
| II000 | TAPE PROCESSING INTERFACE ERROR | | | | | | | |
| II010 | Tape unit equipment check not made | 0 | 0 | 0 | 0 | 0 | 0 | 2 |
| II020 | Routine fails to read continuation tape | 0 | 0 | 0 | 0 | 0 | 0 | 1 |
| II030 | Routine fails to unload tape after completion | 0 | 0 | 0 | 0 | 0 | 0 | 2 |
| II040 | Erroneous input tape format | 0 | 0 | 0 | 1 | 1 | 9 | 4 |
| | TOTALS | 0 | 0 | 0 | 1 | 1 | 9 | 9 |

Table 3-1. Error Categories and Frequency of Occurrence for Subject Projects (Continued)

| CATEGORY ID | CATEGORIES | PROJECT 2 MOD1A | PROJECT 2 MOD1B | PROJECT 2 MOD1BR | PROJECT 2 MOD2 | PROJECT 2 TOTAL | PROJECT 3 | PROJECT 4 |
|---|---|---|---|---|---|---|---|---|
| JJ000 | USER INTERFACE ERRORS | | | | | | | |
| JJ010 | Operations request or data card/routine incompatibility | 0 | 0 | 0 | 0 | 0 | 0 | 0 |
| JJ020 | Multiple physical card/logical card processing error | 0 | 0 | 0 | 0 | 0 | 8 | 0 |
| JJ030 | Input data interpreted incorrectly by routine | 1 | 2 | 1 | 5 | 9 | 3 | 0 |
| JJ040 | Valid input data rejected or not used by routine | 2 | 0 | 2 | 0 | 4 | 29 | 3 |
| JJ050 | Input data rejected but not used | 0 | 0 | 0 | 0 | 0 | 96 | 0 |
| JJ060 | Input data read but not used | 0 | 2 | 2 | 1 | 5 | 4 | 0 |
| JJ070 | Illegal input data accepted and processed | 6 | 8 | 0 | 1 | 15 | 15 | 0 |
| JJ080 | Legal input data processed incorrectly | 1 | 2 | 0 | 2 | 5 | 61 | 19 |
| JJ090 | Poor design in operator interface | 11 | 30 | 10 | 25 | 76 | 58 | 6 |
| JJ100 | Inadequate interrupt and restart capability | 0 | 0 | 0 | 0 | 0 | 60 | 6 |
| | TOTALS | 21 | 44 | 15 | 34 | 114 | 334 | 34 |
| KK000 | DATA BASE INTERFACE ERRORS | | | | | | | |
| KK010 | Routine/data base incompatibility | 4 | 0 | 2 | 0 | 6 | 0 | 0 |
| KK011 | Uncoordinated use of data elements by more than one user | 0 | 1 | 0 | 3 | 4 | 21 | 15 |
| | TOTALS | 4 | 1 | 2 | 3 | 10 | 21 | 15 |
| LL000 | USER REQUESTED CHANGES | | | | | | | |
| LL010 | Simplified interface and/or convenience | 0 | 0 | 0 | 0 | 0 | 0 | 0 |
| LL020 | New and/or enhanced functions | 0 | 0 | 0 | 0 | 0 | 0 | 39 |
| LL021 | CPU | 0 | 0 | 0 | 0 | 0 | 0 | 11 |
| LL022 | Disk | 0 | 0 | 0 | 0 | 0 | 0 | 3 |
| LL023 | Tape | 0 | 0 | 0 | 0 | 0 | 0 | 3 |
| LL024 | I/O | 0 | 0 | 0 | 0 | 0 | 0 | 11 |
| LL025 | Core | 0 | 0 | 0 | 0 | 0 | 0 | 3 |
| LL030 | Security | 0 | 0 | 0 | 0 | 0 | 0 | 8 |
| LL040 | New hardware/OS capability | 0 | 0 | 0 | 0 | 0 | 0 | 2 |
| LL050 | Instrumentation | 0 | 0 | 0 | 0 | 0 | 0 | 12 |
| LL060 | Capacity | 0 | 0 | 0 | 0 | 0 | 0 | 1 |
| LL070 | Data base management and integrity | 0 | 0 | 0 | 0 | 0 | 0 | 15 |
| LL080 | External program interface | 0 | 0 | 0 | 0 | 0 | 0 | 2 |
| | TOTALS | 0 | 0 | 0 | 0 | 0 | 0 | 111 |
| MM000 | PRESET DATA BASE ERRORS | | | | | | | |
| MM010 | Data or operations request card descriptions | 6 | 12 | 4 | 32 | 54 | 32 | 4 |
| MM020 | Error message text | 0 | 4 | 0 | 0 | 4 | 114 | 0 |
| MM030 | Nominal, default, legal, max/min values | 5 | 5 | 5 | 16 | 31 | 66 | 0 |
| MM040 | Physical constants and modeling parameters | 1 | 4 | 0 | 2 | 7 | 23 | 4 |
| MM041 | Ephemeris parameters | 0 | 0 | 0 | 1 | 1 | 2 | 0 |
| MM050 | Dictionary (bit string) parameters | 0 | 0 | 3 | 4 | 7 | 105 | 0 |
| MM060 | Missing data base settings | 2 | 0 | 0 | 5 | 7 | 28 | 1 |

Table 3-1. Error Categories and Frequency of Occurrence for Subject Projects (Continued)

| CATEGORY ID | CATEGORIES | PROJECT 2 | | | | | PROJECT 3 | PROJECT 4 |
|---|---|---|---|---|---|---|---|---|
| | | MOD1A | MOD1B | MOD1BR | MOD2 | TOTAL | | |
| NN000 | GLOBAL VARIABLE/COMPOOL DEFINITION ERRORS | | | | | | | |
| NN010 | Items in wrong location (wrong data block) | 0 | 0 | 0 | 0 | 0 | 0 | 0 |
| NN011 | Definition sequence error | 0 | 0 | 0 | 0 | 0 | 3 | 0 |
| NN020 | Data definition error | 0 | 0 | 0 | 1 | 1 | 0 | 0 |
| NN021 | Table definition incorrect | 5 | 3 | 1 | 10 | 19 | 33 | 11 |
| NN030 | Length of definition incorrect | 0 | 0 | 0 | 0 | 0 | 0 | 1 |
| NN040 | Comments error | 1 | 4 | 1 | 7 | 13 | 7 | 0 |
| NN050 | Delete unneeded definitions | 4 | 9 | 2 | 8 | 23 | 7 | 0 |
| | **TOTALS** | 10 | 16 | 4 | 26 | 56 | 50 | 12 |
| PP000 | RECURRENT ERRORS | | | | | | | |
| PP010 | Problem report reopened | 6 | 3 | 1 | 7 | 17 | 69 | 0 |
| PP020 | Problem report a duplicate of previous report | 1 | 4 | 1 | 1 | 7 | 11 | 0 |
| | **TOTALS** | 7 | 7 | 2 | 8 | 24 | 80 | 0 |
| QQ000 | DOCUMENTATION ERRORS | | | | | | | |
| QQ010 | Routine limitation | 5 | 16 | 5 | 15 | 41 | 39 | 0 |
| QQ020 | Operating procedures | 0 | 0 | 0 | 0 | 0 | 3 | 0 |
| QQ030 | Difference between flow chart and code | 8 | 5 | 1 | 7 | 21 | 34 | 5 |
| QQ040 | Tape format | 0 | 0 | 0 | 0 | 0 | 4 | 1 |
| QQ050 | Data card/operation request card format | 5 | 8 | 1 | 2 | 16 | 23 | 0 |
| QQ060 | Error message | 3 | 6 | 1 | 10 | 20 | 17 | 0 |
| QQ070 | Routine's functional description | 4 | 19 | 0 | 19 | 42 | 38 | 0 |
| QQ080 | Output format | 2 | 2 | 0 | 1 | 5 | 10 | 0 |
| QQ090 | Documentation not clear/not complete | 3 | 11 | 3 | 4 | 21 | 11 | 16 |
| QQ100 | Test case documentation | 0 | 0 | 0 | 0 | 0 | 4 | 0 |
| QQ110 | Operating system documentation | 0 | 0 | 0 | 0 | 0 | 0 | 1 |
| QQ120 | Typo/editorial error/cosmetic change | 0 | 1 | 0 | 5 | 6 | 13 | 0 |
| | **TOTALS** | 30 | 68 | 11 | 63 | 172 | 196 | 23 |
| RR000 | REQUIREMENTS COMPLIANCE ERRORS | | | | | | | |
| RR010 | Excessive run time | 0 | 1 | 0 | 3 | 4 | 4 | 0 |
| RR020 | Required capability overlooked or not delivered at time of report | 2 | 1 | 0 | 3 | 6 | 43 | 0 |
| | **TOTALS** | 2 | 2 | 0 | 6 | 10 | 47 | 0 |

Table 3-1. Error Categories and Frequency of Occurrence for Subject Projects (Continued)

| CATEGORY ID | CATEGORIES | PROJECT 2 | | | | | PROJECT 3 | PROJECT 4 |
|---|---|---|---|---|---|---|---|---|
| | | MOD1A | MOD1B | MOD1BR | MOD2 | TOTAL | | |
| SS000 | UNIDENTIFIED ERRORS | 5 | 16 | 9 | 50 | 80 | 178 | 0 |
| | TOTALS | 5 | 16 | 9 | 50 | 80 | 178* | 0 |
| TT000 | OPERATOR ERROR | | | | | | | |
| TT010 | Test execution error | 1 | 0 | 0 | 1 | 2 | 1 | 0 |
| TT020 | Routine compiled against wrong Compool/Master Common | 18 | 15 | 0 | 23 | 56 | 97 | 0 |
| TT030 | Wrong data base used | 1 | 0 | 0 | 1 | 2 | 7 | 0 |
| TT040 | Wrong master configuration used | 0 | 0 | 0 | 0 | 0 | 6 | 0 |
| TT050 | Wrong tape(s) used | 1 | 5 | 1 | 19 | 26 | 7 | 0 |
| | TOTALS | 21 | 20 | 1 | 44 | 86 | 118 | 0 |
| UU000 | QUESTIONS | | | | | | | |
| UU010 | Data base | 0 | 0 | 0 | 0 | 0 | 0 | 0 |
| UU020 | Master configuration | 0 | 2 | 0 | 3 | 5 | 8 | 0 |
| UU030 | Routine | 0 | 0 | 0 | 0 | 0 | 23 | 0 |
| | TOTALS | 0 | 2 | 0 | 3 | 5 | 49 | 0 |

BB060 - Missing logic or condition tests was a major problem. These
were errors resulting from a lack of code to perform some
logical function; specific sub-categories involved failure
to check indices, number of entries, flags, and singularity
values of data items.

BB070 - This category was added for Project 4 and is the equivalent
of BB120 for Projects 2 and 3. In effect these categories
point to errors in the logical code but as a result of
problem documentation provide no further detail. The
categories remain separate because of Project 4's operational
status while BB120 errors were uncovered as a result of
formal pre delivery testing.

BB100 - Projects 2 and 3 both dealt with data items which were set
initially and updated periodically. Status of settings and
the propogation of values was monitored. Logic designed
to handle this was error prone.

BB140 - This category represents logical modeling problems (to be
distinguished from computational modeling problems).

BB150
BB160 -
BB170
These categories criticize the logic design. It is important
to note that this criticism comes from review after the
logic has been coded, not from a design review based on
documentation only.

BB180 - This category, a storage reference error, deserves special
mention since it was a software error which produced results
looking like a hardware error. It is the only category
of this nature in the list.

## 3.1.1.3  I/O Errors

An attempt was made to limit categories in this group to errors
resulting from I/O code and to distinguish them from interface or other
error categories. This turned out to be very difficult since the physical
manifestations that are usually labeled I/O are generally symptomatic of
other errors. For example, CC020 (output missing data entries) could
be symptomatic of a loop processing or logic error. The goal, however,
was to establish categories relating to output format, position,
completeness, field size, and control. Categories in this group are
believed to be self-explanatory.

### 3.1.1.4  Data Handling Errors

This group of categories covers errors made in reading, writing, moving, storing, and modifying data.  An attempt was made here to limit these errors to those occurring wholly within a routine and not those occurring across an interface.  Categories needing additional description are as follows:

> DD070 - Bit manipulation errors in Project 3 were common.  These were generally encountered when a packed data item required reformatting.

> DD120 - Bounds violations occurred when a routine tried to access an area outside its allocated core environment.

### 3.1.1.5  Operating System/System Support Software Errors

These categories list errors discovered in the operating system (OS) software, the compiler, the assembler, and the system support or specialized utility software.  The OS and system support software for Projects 2 and 3 were the same and virtually error free.  No OS problems were encountered in the Project 4 data.

### 3.1.1.6  Configuration Errors

Configuration errors were the catastrophic problems encountered when the software, after undergoing some sort of modification (usually to fix a problem), failed to be compatible with operating system or remaining applications software.  These errors, for the most part, were the product of a tight schedule and a failure to adhere to rigorous configuration management techniques.  That is, in the real world of delivering software under pressure, errors which should have been caught by existing CM procedures were not noted, usually resulting in software that wouldn't load.

Also in this group is the unexplainable program halt (FF030), which is not covered by the paragraph above.  This category was assigned to non-repeatable halts.  Although possibly a hardware problem, documentation did not identify the problem source, and it should be noted that none of these produced alteration of the software.

### 3.1.1.7  Interface Errors

Interface errors have been grouped into five major headings.

- Routine/routine interface errors - This group contains error categories at the interfaces between applications software routines.

- Routine/system software interface errors - These are errors resulting from the interface between an applications routine and an operating system or system utility routine.

- Tape processing interface errors - These are errors in handling magnetic tapes.

- User interface errors - This group contains errors at the user interface, including the machine operator, manual or data card inputs, tape inputs, etc.  In this group the term "input data" is used to include all sources at the user level.

- Data base interface errors - This group contains categories which describe incompatibilities between the data base structure and a setting or using routine(s).

Categories in these groups are generally self-explanatory.

### 3.1.1.8  User Requested Changes

This group of categories was established as a result of the fact that Project 4 was operational, and the problem report was used to request changes and enhancements of capability based on usage of the delivered software.

### 3.1.1.9  Preset Data Base Errors

These categories were assigned to SPRs written directly against preset or constant data* in the data base.

MM010 - Data and operation request card formats were described in the data base for Projects 2 and 3.  Generalized free and fixed field card processing utility routines used these descriptions.

MM020 - Information and error message text was specified in the data base for a generalized message processor for Projects 2 and 3.

*NOTE:  Preset data is generated by the user and remains constant or serves as an initial setting to be updated or modified by a routine.

### 3.1.1.10  Global Variable/COMPOOL Definition Errors

This group includes categories defining errors in the specification of global variables or constants, i.e., data defined for use by interfacing routines. In the environment of Projects 2 and 3 these amount to COMPOOL definition errors. These variables are to be distinguished from internal or local variables used only within a single routine.

### 3.1.1.11  Recurrent Errors

Establishment of this group was an attempt to assess the number of problems that were reopened (the fix did not work when retested in the master configuration) and duplicates of previous SPRs.

### 3.1.1.12  Documentation Errors

This group is possible because the SPR was used to flag documentation problems. In the environment of Projects 2 and 3 the approved (code to) design document is part of the deliverable product and is maintained rigorously. Later, the document is updated to reflect validation and acceptance test results and represents the "as-built" design. This concept of the documentation being the design is an important one and one which allows us to quantitatively determine the source of an error, as we shall see in Section 4.2.3.

### 3.1.1.13  Requirements Compliance Errors

These categories resulted directly from the fact that the software failed to provide a capability specified by the requirements document. This does not, however, say that the design overlooked the requirement. A thorough review of the design against the requirements was carried out for Project 2 and 3 prior to the initiation of coding. Therefore, these categories point to the fact that supposed "full capability" code was not in compliance with the requirements at the time the SPR was written*.

It should be noted here that no SPRs were written against the software requirements; these were baselined and not a subject for change in the formal test phases for Projects 2 and 3.

### 3.1.1.14.  Unidentified Errors

This group recognizes that all problem reports and closures do not supply sufficient information for analysis. SPRs in this group and their closures provided so little information that no error category could be assigned. (From Table 4-1 it can be seen that occurrence of these ran as high as 6.9 percent for one modification of Project 2 and 4.0 percent for Project 3. Project 5 had no occurrences due to the real-time nature of the data collection process.)

---

*Note:  By the end of acceptance testing, which is requirements oriented, all requirements were satisfied by the software.

### 3.1.1.15  Operator Errors

Operator errors were assigned when the problem was due to machine operator, developer, or tester error.  An attempt was made to separate these errors from those where the operator's error was due to a problem with the user interface, i.e., an error in the user interface design.

### 3.1.1.16  Questions

The final group was generated to accommodate the fact that the SPR was used as a vehicle for asking questions and guaranteeing an answer.

### 3.2.  Observations on Category Generation

The approach recommended in generating error category lists is basically the one suggested in the June 1973 report by MITRE entitled "A Software Error Classification Methodology".* Attempts to generate these lists should be open-ended in order to encompass specific characteristics of the data being analyzed.  However, the principal problem encountered in such an approach is the tendency to create a category for each error analyzed. This one-for-one phenomenon also occurs when categories are generated through speculative techniques.  The obvious result is very few occurrences per category, and any attempt to relate category frequency of occurrence to software characteristics proves inconclusive.

Once the open-ended list is established, there is a tendency to condense the list by combining several detailed categories into a single more general category.  The danger here, of course, is in changing the nature of the error category to the point where some of the categories making up the new category are no longer accurately identified by that new category.

As the industry gains experience in first recognizing the significant characteristics of various types of software and then generating category lists, definition techniques will be refined and the more universal lists will surface.

### 3.3  Recommendations on Category Generation

To anyone preparing to generate an error category list the recommendation is to plan to do the job at least twice.  The first attempt should result in a fairly detailed list; any consolidation of categories should be accompanied by a second pass through the data to evaluate the new categories.  This is an iterative business.

---

*Reference 3.

The reader will note that error categories (Table 3-1) fall into
two groups, symptomatic categories and categories which identify the cause
of the error. For example, I/O error CC020 (Output missing data entries)
is a symptom which could have been caused by improper definition of a loop
variable, a table initialization error, etc. Computational error AA080
(Sign convention error) points to the cause of the error. Whether the cause
is evident depends on the information content of the problem closure report.
Symptoms are generally well documented on the problem report. An accurate
statement of cause was not guaranteed in the available data. This symptom/
cause situation prompted the general description of an error category offered earlier.

The experience of generating error categories leads the analysts to
conclude that two lists are actually possible, one for the symptom and one
for the specific cause of that symptom at the code level. We can speculate
on the eventual application of such lists. A purely symptomatic list could
be useful to test groups as an aid in knowing what symptoms to look for.
Code level errors (causes) could aid in generation of automated development
and test tools, improvement of languages, etc.

The observation that symptomatic and causative lists are possible
and the suggestion that there may be a predictable relation between the two
is a subject addressed in Section 4.4.

## 3.4  Assignment of Error Categories

Assignment of error categories from data in the archives is something
of an art, even when a problem is well documented. In this study the approach was to read the problem report and the closure report, reconstructing
the error from available information and assigning an error category. In
this after-the-fact analysis it was obvious that a familiarity with the
project and the conditions under which problem reports were generated is
essential. Categorization of the 7910 problem reports used in this study
was done by analysts who performed on the subject projects.

It is important to note that all problem reports were assigned to a
category, regardless of whether the problem was a real one or not. If not
a real problem, i.e., an exploratory closure, the SPR symptoms were categorized. The thinking behind this approach was 1) to gain insight into the
analyst's understanding of the situation at the time he documented the
problem (some categories suffered a higher percentage of "no problem"
responses than other categories), and 2) to recognize the fact that all
problem reports, whether actual problems or not, required effort on the
part of a programmer to effect a problem closure.

## Observations on Category Assignment

The following is apparent from the work done in this study:

- The fixer of the problem should be the source of the code level error category assignment. He alone is close enough to the problem to define it in non-symptomatic terms.

- Error categorization should be done at the time the problem is closed, not after the fact.

- Assignment of categories should be based on the problem report and the closure report.

- Long category lists with fine granularity are hard to use and require practice to use effectively.

- A change in data collection philosophy is necessary to guarantee collection of reliability-related data at the time it is available while satisfying configuration management data requirements. Not only are changes in the collection forms necessary, but the authors of the various forms need to be fully aware of the objectives of the data collection effort.

## 3.5 Development of Project 5 Error Categories

With the experience of creating error categories for Projects 2, 3, and 4 behind us we set about creating a list to be used on Project 5. Our goals, in order of importance, were to create a list that,

- Fixers of errors would use,

- Would be causative in nature,

- Would provide information on each error's origin

- Would be similar enough to existing lists at the major category level to allow comparison of results.

Since the list had to recognize project peculiarities, assistance in refining the categories was sought from Project 5 performers. Early attempts at generating such a list produced a very long list, containing 435 detailed categories, which was eventually discarded as being impractical and counterproductive in a real world software development environment.* What error data were available at that time were also used to generate the list.

---

*Comments from the potential users indicated that the list's length was antagonizing, too.

The resultant list is presented in Table 3-2. Note that there is a blank character in the five character, alpha-numeric error category designator. This blank is for the error's source. Once the fix was made and tested, the responsible programmer was asked to select an error category that most accurately described the cause of the problem. As in the previous list, indenture denoted a level of categorization detail, and programmers were instructed to assign categories only to the level of detail they felt was accurate. The remaining information needed was the error's source, which is defined in the following:

| Source ID | Problem Source | Description |
|---|---|---|
| 0 | Design | The source of the problem was in the preliminary or detailed design. |
| 1 | Coding | The source of the problem was an error made in implementing the design as code. |
| 2 | Requirements | The source of the problem was a changing, ill conceived, or poorly stated requirement. |
| 3 | Maintenance | The source of the problem was an error introduced in the process of trying to fix a previous error. |
| 4 | Not Known | Source of error not known. |

As an example of categorization with the Project 5 list, A2300 would be a sign convention computational error traceable to an origin in the software requirements.

Referring back to Table 3-2, note that there still remain some symptomatic categories. A completely causative list makes for many categories, and shortness was mandatory.

Categories themselves are, with some exceptions, self-explanatory. Noteworthy exceptions are as follows:

I_100      (Operating system error). This category was provided because the real time operating system was an addition to a vendor supplied basic operating system. This category applied only to this basic operating system.

J_100 } J_200 }      (Time and core limits exceeded). These categories are particularly important to real time software systems where there may be no error per se. The problem in these cases is a potential one, that the system may be too slow.

X0005        (Problem report deferred). Provision for this was necessitated by the multiple build, top-down approach being taken in the Project 5 environment. In many cases authors of problem reports are able to foresee problems with future iterations of the development cycle. This category made it possible to identify these and track their closure at a future date, an important feature of a thorough configuration management discipline of a top-down approach.

As with the preceding error category lists, not all Project 5 problem reports document errors, an error being something requiring corrective action in the form of a change to the software (source code or data base) or its documentation. Detailed analysis of the frequency of occurrence of various types of errors is presented in Section 4.2.1 for each of the source projects. In that section particular emphasis is placed on the errors which produced a change in the code or in the data base. These we termed code change errors or "actual" problems.

Table 3-2.  Project 5 Error Categories

| A_000 | COMPUTATIONAL ERRORS |
|---|---|
| A_100 | Incorrect operand in equation |
| A_200 | Incorrect use of parenthesis |
| A_300 | Sign convention error |
| A_400 | Units or data conversion error |
| A_500 | Computation produces an over/under flow |
| A_600 | Incorrect/inaccurate equation used |
| A_700 | Precision loss due to mixed mode |
| A_800 | Missing computation |
| A_900 | Rounding or truncation error |
| B_000 | LOGIC ERRORS |
| B_100 | Incorrect operand in logical expression |
| B_200 | Logic activities out of sequence |
| B_300 | Wrong variable being checked |
| B_400 | Missing logic or condition tests |
| B_500 | Too many/few statements in loop |
| B_600 | Loop iterated incorrect number of times (including endless loop) |
| B_700 | Duplicate logic |
| C_000 | DATA INPUT ERRORS |
| C_100 | Invalid input read from correct data file |
| C_200 | Input read from incorrect data file |
| C_300 | Incorrect input format |
| C_400 | Incorrect format statement referenced |
| C_500 | End of file encountered prematurely |
| C_600 | End of file missing |
| D_000 | DATA HANDLING ERRORS |
| D_050 | Data file not rewound before reading |
| D_100 | Data initialization not done |
| D_200 | Data initialization done improperly |
| D_300 | Variable used as a flag or index not set properly |
| D_400 | Variable referred to by the wrong name |
| D_500 | Bit manipulation done incorrectly |
| D_600 | Incorrect variable type |
| D_700 | Data packing/unpacking error |
| D_800 | Sort error |
| D_900 | Subscripting error |

Table 3-2.  Project 5 Error Categories (Continued)

| | |
|---|---|
| E_000 | DATA OUTPUT ERRORS |
| E_100 | Data written on wrong file |
| E_200 | Data written according to the wrong format statement |
| E_300 | Data written in wrong format |
| E_400 | Data written with wrong carriage control |
| E_500 | Incomplete or missing output |
| E_600 | Output field size too small |
| E_700 | Line count or page eject problem |
| E_800 | Output garbled or misleading |
| F_000 | INTERFACE ERRORS |
| F_100 | Wrong subroutine called |
| F_200 | Call to subroutine not made or made in wrong place |
| F_300 | Subroutine arguments not consistent in type, units, order, etc. |
| F_400 | Subroutine called is nonexistent |
| F_500 | Software/data base interface error |
| F_600 | Software user interface error |
| F_700 | Software/software interface error |
| G_000 | DATA DEFINITION ERRORS |
| G_100 | Data not properly defined/dimensioned |
| G_200 | Data referenced out of bounds |
| G_300 | Data being referenced at incorrect location |
| G_400 | Data pointers not incremented properly |
| H_000 | DATA BASE ERRORS |
| H_100 | Data not initialized in data base |
| H_200 | Data initialized to incorrect value |
| H_300 | Data units are incorrect |
| I_000 | OPERATION ERRORS |
| I_100 | Operating system error (vendor supplied) |
| I_200 | Hardware error |
| I_300 | Operator error |
| I_400 | Test execution error |
| I_500 | User misunderstanding/error |
| I_600 | Configuration control error |

Table 3-2.  Project 5 Error Categories (Continued)

| | |
|---|---|
| J_000 | OTHER |
| | |
| J_100 | Time limit exceeded |
| J_200 | Core storage limit exceeded |
| J_300 | Output line limit exceeded |
| J_400 | Compilation error |
| J_500 | Code or design inefficient/not necessary |
| J_600 | User/programmer requested enhancement |
| J_700 | Design nonresponsive to requirements |
| J_800 | Code delivery or redelivery |
| J_900 | Software not compatible with project standards |
| | |
| K_000 | DOCUMENTATION ERRORS |
| | |
| K_100 | User manual |
| K_200 | Interface specification |
| K_300 | Design specification |
| K_400 | Requirements specification |
| K_500 | Test documentation |
| | |
| X0000 | PROBLEM REPORT REJECTION |
| | |
| X0001 | No problem |
| X0002 | Void/withdrawn |
| X0003 | Out of scope — not part of approved design |
| X0004 | Duplicates another problem report |
| X0005 | Deferred |

## 3.6  History of Error Category Lists

It is instructive to summarize our various attempts to create error category lists because it helps to put some of our problems, at least those related to list length, in perspective.  Such a summary is presented in Table 3-3 below.  These range from early (circa 1971) work done in support of CCIP-85 to current work done on this study.

Table 3-3.  History of Error Category Lists

| Major Categories | Detailed Categories | Iteration | Comments |
|---|---|---|---|
| 13 | 0 | Study done in support of CCIP-85 | ● Entirely symptomatic |
| 13 | 224 | Post-CCIP-85 in-house work | ● Greater emphasis on cause<br>● Failed to recognize code types |
| 20 | 164 | Interim technical report for Software Reliability Study (Table 3-1) | ● Predominately symptomatic<br>● Recognized types of code<br>● Assignment not by problem fixer |
| 25 | 435 | Early causative work | ● Generated by speculation<br>● Long with redundancies<br>● Hard to use |
| 12 | 79 | Final causative list (Table 3-2) | ● Comprehensive but short<br>● Easy to use<br>● Problem fixer assigns categories |

   Note that the length of these lists has progressed from the very short,
when software problems were not fully understood, to the very long, when the
interest in detail overshadowed all other considerations, back to a relatively short list, which is comprehensive and informative but recognizes
the need for ease of use in any attempt to collect accurate error data.

   The question of universality* of these lists is one for which we
have only limited answers.  The list used for Project 5 is, in many respects,
similar to the one used for Project 3.  This was by design.  The major categories, e.g., logical, computational, interface errors etc., appear to be
quite universal in their applicability.  The detailed categories, however,
are less universal and suffer in applicability due to differences in language, development philosophy, software type, etc.  When data are collected
may also have a bearing on applicability to some software test environments.
For Project 5 the list used was apparently adequate for the real time applications and simulator software, as well as the Product Assurance tools.
However, there was criticism concerning applicability of detailed categories
to the real time operating system software** problems.  No attempt was made
to identify specific deficiencies because, even with the instructions to
categorize only to an accurate level, i.e., stick to the major categories,
the detailed categories were used, and checks of assignments showed them
to be appropriate.

---

*Applicability to more than one project.

**This software is written in assembly language; all other software is in
FORTRAN.

## 4.0 ANALYSIS OF ERROR DATA

This section contains the bulk of analysis of data collected from the four source projects. The principal object of this analysis has been software error data collected during testing and operational usage. However, where other information has been available it too has been used to aid in the analysis of error data.

In Section 7.0, Data Collection, we point out that software projects have a potential for creating a tremendous amount of data.* Our experience, when confronted with data from four projects, was much like the first trip to a candy store, i.e., where do we start and how much do we consume? We quickly realized that to deal with all the data would be, in a practical sense, impossible. It also became obvious that data collected after the fact leaves much to question in terms of accuracy and completeness, as well as availability on other projects. A third early lesson was that promising results on one project may not be borne out by similar investigations on other projects. Therefore, a decision was made to work principally with projects for which data were most current and complete, and to follow avenues of investigation believed to be most productive in terms of useful results. The result has been that, although findings from all four source projects are presented, Projects 3 and 5 are most thoroughly represented by this section, and by the remainder of this report. Project 3 provided the most complete (and final) data set and Project 5, an on-going project, provided an opportunity to tailor data collection activities to study needs.

### 4.1 Approaches to Analysis and Background Information

Two basic approaches were taken in analyzing the error data. The first was to examine the raw problem reports or empirical data to learn as much as possible about the types of errors, how and when they were detected, and to identify trends. Results are presented in Section 4.2. Specific questions asked during the course of analysis were as follows:

- What was the error type or category?
- When was the error detected?
- Should the error have been detected earlier?
- When was the error introduced?
- How critical was the error to successful software operation?
- How long did it take to fix the error?

---

*Project 3 alone produced 5619 design problem reports; 4521 software problem reports; cost, schedule, manpower, and personnel data for 76 programmers; and software structural information for 115,346 source statements forming 249 routines.

As part of the error categorization process, it was noted in Section 3.4 that error categories can be causative or symptomatic, depending on the viewpoint of the test analyst. That is, the finder and fixer of an error often view the error differently. The finder sees symptoms, while the fixer thinks in terms of cause. A brief analysis of the relation between symptoms and causes is presented in Section 4.4.

The second approach to analysis was termed the phenomenological approach. Statistical in nature, this approach investigates the relation of software attributes and metrics* to error histories. A detailed description of this approach and results of analysis are presented in Section 4.3.

Finally, in conjunction with this examination of error data, a number of ancillary investigations using other available empirical data were performed. Results of these investigations are presented in Section 4.5.

Before proceeding, one piece of information concerning software structure is germane to the understanding of results presented throughout this section. It is also useful information to anyone planning to analyze empirical data on other projects. It will be noted that the unit of software modularization varies depending on the particular investigation being pursued. In some instances for Project 3, results are presented at the routine level, i.e., one data point per routine. In other instances results are presented at the function or subsystem levels, where routines are grouped to perform a single function or a number of related functions, respectively. This is because not all trends were observable at the routine level. Some trends that were obscure at the routine level became well correlated when routines were grouped functionally (e.g., data base management function) or according to purpose (e.g., computational routines). That groupings by purpose produced well correlated results (in some cases) is not particularly surprising.** Results from functional groupings are not so surprising either, once one realizes that routines in the same function tended to have the same schedule, manpower, and implementation problems. In fact, Project 3 management was set up in conjunction with the software structure so that personnel assigned to one work unit, ranging in size from 5 to 15 programmers, produced all the software in one or more of the functions. Also, software requirements allocated to a function were all of equivalent detail and represented similar problems to the function developers. The Project 3 structure is presented in Figure 4-0.

Although the other projects had functionally oriented architectural structures,*** Project 3 is the only one with results presented in this form. Project 4 results are presented for the project as a whole, and Project 5 results are presented according to applications, simulator, operating system, and software tools. Since each of these Project 5 groupings is so large, both in software size and in development organization size, each is considered as a separate project.

---

*Attributes identify specific software characteristics, such as size, complexity, and readability, and metrics quantify these attributes.
**See Section 4.3.
***Project 2's was nearly identical, with functions and subsystems performing in very similar generic functions.

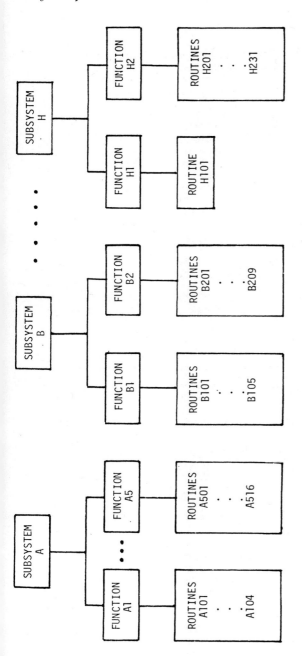

**Figure 4-0. Project 3 Software System Structure**

## 4.2  Analysis of Empirical Data

This section contains results of our analysis of software errors, how many there were, what type they were, when they were found, and their origin in the development cycle. Where necessary (and possible) supporting information is drawn into the analysis to explain trends.

### 4.2.1  Error Types and Frequency of Occurrence

Using the error category lists described in Section 3.0, we attempted to answer the questions "what were the types of errors?" and "how many of each type were there?" Our analysis of the number of occurrences of each type took place on two levels; first, at the major category level, and second, at the detailed category level. And, as was explained earlier, particular emphasis was placed on "actual" problems or the errors which required an alteration to the code or data base to effect corrective action; although all documented problems were tracked and are represented at the major category level of analysis.

Data from all four source projects are presented. As a refresher, the following table summarizes project characteristics again. Note that the Project 5 software is broken down into its component portions; each of these portions (there are others on this large project) is essentially a project all by itself because of differences in language, development personnel, software requirements, etc.

|  | Software Type | Operating Mode | Language | Development Approach |
|---|---|---|---|---|
| Project 2 | Command and Control | Batch | JOVIAL J4 | Single Increment* |
| Project 3 | Command and Control | Batch | JOVIAL J4 | Single Increment* |
| Project 4 | Data Management | Time Critical Batch | PWS MACRO | Operational |
| Project 5 | Applications S/W | Real-Time | FORTRAN | Top-Down Multiple Increment |
|  | Simulator S/W | Real-Time | FORTRAN | Top-Down Multiple Increment |
|  | Operating System | Real-Time | Assembly | Top-Down Multiple Increment |
|  | PA Tools | Batch | FORTRAN | Single Increment* |

*"Single increment" refers to a typical development cycle where each development phase is performed only once. This is in contrast to the top-down, multiple increment approach where the cycle is repeated several times, first for a system of stubs and subsequently for replacement of stubs with deliverable software.

It should also be restated that available error data for the four
source projects do not come from the same type of testing. However, the
levels of testing (subsystem and system) are similar. That is, the software under test or operation* was being exercised as a system or major subsystem. Therefore, even though Project 5 data come from integration testing, the applications software, the operating system, and the simulator are
operating as a system with a near-operational** data base.

Occurrences of Errors for Projects 2, 3, and 4
=====================

Figure 4-1, presents a percentage breakdown by major category for the
four modifications to Project 2***, the initial development of Project 3,
and the results of operational errors for Project 4. Raw data are presented
in Section 3.1 along with the description of Project 3 detailed error categories. Table 4-1 presents raw data at the major category level.

Percentage breakdowns are what might be expected, given the types of
software and the test environments. For example, Project 4 had virtually
no computational errors (<1.3%) because there is very little computational
code in this data management system, the bulk of the code being logical or
data handling in nature. Percentages for these categories reflect this
fact at 26.0 and 20.4 percent, respectively.

Similarities between the various updates of Project 2 and Project 3
show up in Figure 4-1 also. For these systems the percentage mix of errors
is roughly the same for a given major category. Variations which do exist,
e.g., the differences in the percentage of data handling errors between
modifications MOD1B and MOD1BR of Project 2, can be explained by a close
look at the type of code being added in the modification or created in the
initial development. That is, if data handling code is the largest component of the change, the percentage of data handling errors can be expected
to be large compared to percentages for other types of code†. In this
example MOD1BR, a single purposed new capability, was predominantly addition of logical and data handling code. It was a small update with only
one new routine added, therefore there was only one new routine/routine
interface. However, there was an added demand placed on the user at the
user interface. The effects of each of these may be seen in Figure 4-1
by a comparison to other updates to Project 2. MOD1B, on the other hand,
was a fairly substantial update with additions and changes representing
virtually all code types and significant interface alterations, resulting
in a spreading of error occurrences to more categories.

---

*Project 4.

**To the extent possible at the current point in the development cycle.

***MOD1A, MOD1B, MOD1BR, and MOD2.

†This relationship is quantitatively explored in Section 4.3.

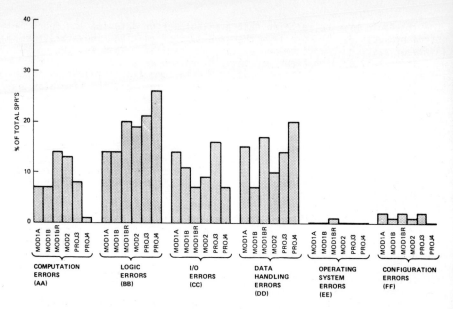

Figure 4-1. Percentage Occurrence of Error Category Groups

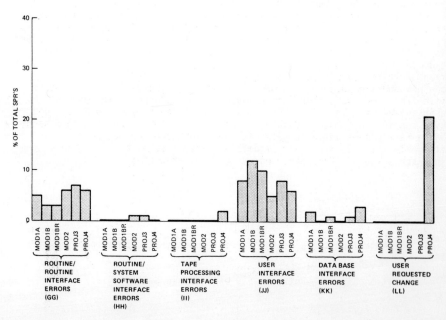

Figure 4-1. Percentage Occurrence of Error Category Groups (Continued)

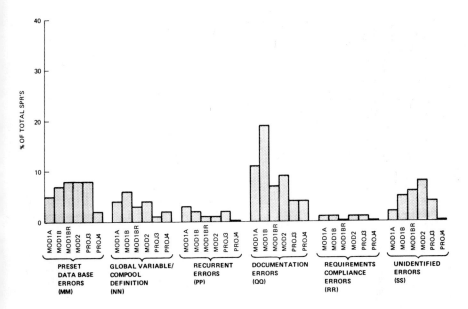

Figure 4-1. Percentage Occurrence of Error Category Groups (Continued)

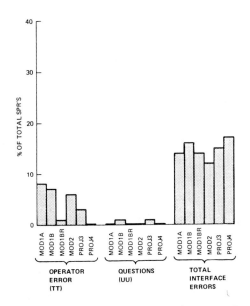

Figure 4-1. Percentage Occurrence of Error Category Groups (Continued)

Table 4-1.  Percentage Occurrence of Major Categories by Project

| CATEGORY GROUP | | MOD1A SPRs | MOD1A % | MOD1B SPRs | MOD1B % | MOD1BR SPRs | MOD1BR % | MOD2 SPRs | MOD2 % | PROJECT 2 TOTALS | PROJECT 3 SPRs | PROJECT 3 % | PROJECT 4 SPRs | PROJECT 4 % |
|---|---|---|---|---|---|---|---|---|---|---|---|---|---|---|
| COMPUTATIONAL | (AA) | 19 | 7.2 | 26 | 7.2 | 21 | 13.7 | 96 | 13.3 | 162 | 353 | 8.0 | 7 | 1.3 |
| LOGIC | (BB) | 37 | 14.0 | 51 | 14.2 | 31 | 20.2 | 137 | 19.1 | 256 | 937 | 21.1 | 140 | 26.0 |
| I/O | (CC) | 38 | 14.3 | 41 | 11.4 | 11 | 7.2 | 66 | 9.2 | 156 | 719 | 16.2 | 36 | 6.7 |
| DATA HANDLING | (DD) | 40 | 15.1 | 25 | 7.0 | 26 | 16.9 | 73 | 10.1 | 164 | 613 | 13.8 | 110 | 20.4 |
| OPERATING SYSTEM/SYSTEM SUPPORT SOFTWARE | (EE) | 0 | 0 | 0 | 0 | 1 | 0.6 | 0 | 0 | 1 | 4 | 0.1 | 0 | 0 |
| CONFIGURATION | (FF) | 5 | 1.9 | 4 | 1.0 | 3 | 1.9 | 4 | 0.6 | 16 | 83 | 1.9 | 0 | 0 |
| ROUTINE/ROUTINE INTERFACE | (GG) | 12 | 4.5 | 11 | 3.1 | 5 | 3.2 | 41 | 5.7 | 69 | 250 | 5.6 | 33 | 6.1 |
| ROUTINE/SYSTEM SOFTWARE INTERFACE | (HH) | 0 | 0 | 0 | 0 | 0 | 0 | 5 | 0.7 | 5 | 28 | 0.6 | 0 | 0 |
| TAPE PROCESSING INTERFACE | (II) | 0 | 0 | 0 | 0 | 0 | 0 | 1 | 0.1 | 1 | 9 | 0.2 | 9 | 1.7 |
| USER INTERFACE | (JJ) | 21 | 7.9 | 44 | 12.3 | 15 | 9.7 | 34 | 4.7 | 114 | 334 | 7.5 | 34 | 6.3 |
| DATA BASE INTERFACE | (KK) | 4 | 1.5 | 1 | 0.3 | 2 | 1.3 | 3 | 0.4 | 10 | 21 | 0.5 | 15 | 2.8 |
| USER REQUESTED CHANGE | (LL) | 0 | 0 | 0 | 0 | 0 | 0 | 0 | 0 | 0 | 0 | 0 | 111 | 20.6 |
| PRESET DATA BASE | (MM) | 14 | 5.3 | 25 | 7.0 | 12 | 7.8 | 60 | 8.3 | 111 | 370 | 8.3 | 9 | 1.7 |
| GLOBAL VARIABLE/COMPOOL DEFINITION | (NN) | 10 | 3.8 | 16 | 4.5 | 4 | 2.6 | 26 | 3.6 | 56 | 50 | 1.1 | 12 | 2.2 |
| RECURRENT | (PP) | 7 | 2.6 | 7 | 1.9 | 2 | 1.3 | 8 | 1.1 | 24 | 80 | 1.8 | 0 | 0 |
| DOCUMENTATION | (QQ) | 30 | 11.3 | 68 | 18.9 | 11 | 7.2 | 63 | 8.8 | 172 | 196 | 4.4 | 23 | 4.2 |
| REQUIREMENTS COMPLIANCE | (RR) | 2 | 0.8 | 2 | 0.6 | 0 | 0 | 6 | 0.8 | 10 | 47 | 1.1 | 0 | 0 |
| UNIDENTIFIED | (SS) | 5 | 1.9 | 16 | 4.5 | 9 | 5.8 | 50 | 6.9 | 80 | 178 | 4.0 | 0 | 0 |
| OPERATOR | (TT) | 21 | 7.9 | 20 | 5.5 | 1 | 0.6 | 44 | 6.2 | 86 | 118 | 2.7 | 0 | 0 |
| QUESTIONS | (UU) | 0 | 0 | 2 | 0.6 | 0 | 0 | 3 | 0.4 | 5 | 49 | 1.1 | 0 | 0 |
| TOTALS | | 265 | | 359 | | 154 | | 720 | | 1498 | 4439 | | 539 | |

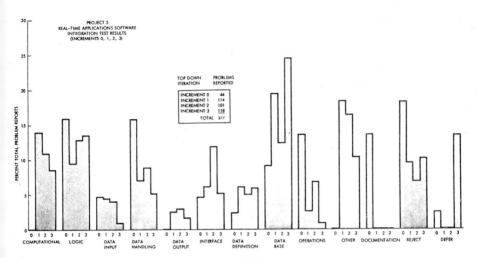

Figure 4-2.
Project 5 Integration Test Results for the Real-Time Applications Software

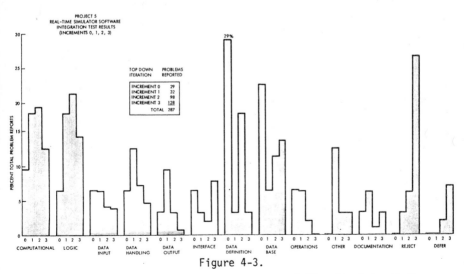

Figure 4-3.
Project 5 Integration Test Results for the Real-Time Simulator Software

Other points of interest in Table 4-1 are listed below.

- Very few operating system and system support errors were documented for any of the source projects. With the exception of update MOD1BR for Project 2, only the "tried and true" operating system and system support capabilities were used. MOD1BR utilized OS software service capabilities not commonly used, and use of these services uncovered some errors. The operating system in each of these software system environments could be considered error-free in each case.

- Although percentages for interface errors varied from project to project, a total of all interface errors* was nearly constant for all three projects, ranging from a low of 11.6 percent to a high of 15.7 percent of the total errors. No specific reason can be given for this phenomenon, however.

- Configuration errors, where the configuration control procedures broke down under the pressure of implementing fixes to errors, was a fairly constant percentage for each project in the Project 2 and Project 3 environment. A low of 0.6 percent and a high of 1.9 percent was observed. Note that in the lower pressure Project 4 operational maintenance environment no such errors were encountered.

A more detailed examination of these data are presented in subsequent paragraphs of Section 4.2.

## Occurrences of Errors for Project 5 Applications Software

Figures 4-2 and 4-3 present the percentage breakdown by major category for the Project 5 real-time applications software and simulator software, respectively. These histograms present four entries for each major category, one for each "increment" in the top-down approach. Increments are identified as 0, 1, 2, and 3, where increment 0 was a system made up of stubs or dummies and subsequent increments have added needed system capability by successively replacing stubs and dummy software with real code. Data for the real-time operating system and product assurance tools are not presented here due to the fact that data cannot be considered complete.

Our principal purpose in presenting the data by increment was to show any variations in the mix of errors over time as a result of the top-down approach. In Figure 4-2, total problems for the applications software, there appear to be some increment dependent variations. Increment 0, the

---

*Composed of routine/routine, routine/system software, tape processing, data base, and user interface errors.

dummy processor, was composed of very little computational code, and data output code was of the debug variety, i.e., to be replaced with deliverable code. It is not surprising that there were no errors in these two major categc ᵉs during Increment 0. Data input code was part of the Increment 0 software, and the data show a corresponding presence of data input errors in Increment 0.

The trends for some categories in Figure 4-2 appear to be tapering off while others are rising. For example, in Increments 1 and 2 most of the computational code was added to the applications software. Most of the data handling code was created in the early increments also. As a result, per- centages for both of these categories have dropped in the later increments, presumably because the earlier code has been tested and errors removed, while lesser amounts of code in these categories is being added in the later increments. Interfaces have increased with each increment and there has been a corresponding rise in the number of interface errors, although there appears to be a decline in the percentage of interface errors for Incre- ment 3*, which is consistent with the fact that fewer interfaces were added than in Increment 2. Logical and data definition error percentages appear to be remaining relatively constant, regardless of increment.

Finally, one very positive observation that can be made in Figure 4-2 is the relatively large and increasing percentage of data base value "errors". Use of an operational data base during integration testing is being encouraged partly to create and tune an operational data base in order to avoid the risk of waiting until just prior to format system test- ing to attempt creating such a data base. In the main, these are not neces- sarily errors but alterations in data values made necessary by tuning for best operational performance. As the top-down approach progresses through the increments, the data base category takes on an increasing percentage of errors, even though, as is indicated in Figure 4-2, the number of errors per increment is essentially constant.

## Occurrences of Errors for Project 5 Simulator Software

Variations in the percentage mix of errors for the four increments of the simulator software are not obvious, although some similarities to the applications software results may be seen in Figure 4-3. For instance, there is a build up and eventual tailoff in the percentage of computational and data output errors. The trend of data input errors is also similar to that experienced for the applications software. Logical and data handling errors, however, differ in their variation over a period of four increments, possibly because of the early introduction of computational code in the simulator software. Note that the percentage of data base errors, as for the applications software, is significant, again demonstrating the impor- tance of preparing an operational data base early in the development cycle.

--------

*
Available data show that the percentage increase in the number of inter- face errors is not proportional to the number of new interfaces being added by each increment. We hypothesized that the smaller routines made necessary by Project 5 size standards would result in a proportionally greater number of interface errors. However, these preliminary data indicate no penalty in terms of interface errors and that our hypothesis was not correct.

Our findings that the occurrences of problem reports are related to the predominant type of code is not a surprising one, and is a relationship that we will pursue in greater detail in Section 4.3. In the next paragraph we will look in greater detail at the code and data base change errors in major categories for each of the source projects and then we will look at the occurrences of errors in the most prevalent detailed categories.

## Comparison of Projects' Major Error Categories

Table 4-2 presents a percentage breakdown of errors by major category for errors which resulted in a code change. In this table data from Projects 3 and 4 have been regrouped to be compatible with the more accurately collected Project 5 data*. Note that for each of the subject projects code change errors tended to fall primarily into the following four major categories: logic, data handling, data I/O, and interfaces. If data input and output categories are lumped together, as is the case with Project 3, and the category called "Other Errors" is not considered, the order of importance based on relative percentage magnitude is surprisingly similar in some respects and understandably different in others, Table 4-3.

It is significant that logical errors ranked high for each project, regardless of software type, language, operating mode, or other project differences. It is also significant that data handling errors ranked a close second for all projects except the highly analytical applications and simulator portions of Project 5, which experienced computational errors in place of the data handling errors. As for the computational category on the other projects, its relatively low position in the order of precedence was due to a thorough understanding of algorithms in Project 3 and the fact that computational code did not form a very large part of the software on Project 4.

In Table 4-4 the percentages are given for each major category as a function of increment to show changes due to the top-down approach.

## Occurrences of Detailed Errors

Having examined the major categories and found some similarities between projects, the next step was to examine the detailed error categories to determine the predominant detailed categories within the major categories. Again this investigation centered only on those documented problems which caused a change to the code, i.e., the actual errors.

---

*Project 2 is not considered here because data come from successive updates to an existing system rather than from an initial development. Even so, as we have seen, results are much like Project 3 results.

Table 4-2. Percentage Breakdown of Code Change Errors Into Major Error Categories

| Project 5 Major Error Categories | Project 3 (%) | Project 4 (%) | Project 5 | | | | Total |
|---|---|---|---|---|---|---|---|
| | | | Applications Software (%) | Simulator Software (%) | Operating System (%) | PA Tools (%) | |
| Computational (A) | 9.0 | 1.7 | 13.5 | 19.6 | 2.5 | 0 | |
| Logic (B) | 26.0 | 34.5 | 17.1 | 20.9 | 34.6 | 43.5 | |
| Data Input (C) | 16.4 | 8.9 | 7.3 | 9.3 | 8.6 | 5.5 | |
| Data Output (E) | | | | | | | |
| Data Handling (D) | 18.2 | 27.2 | 10.9 | 8.4 | 21.0 | 9.3 | |
| Interface (F) | 17.0 | 22.5 | 9.8 | 6.7 | 7.4 | 0 | |
| Data Definition (G) | 0.8 | 3.0 | 7.3 | 13.8 | 7.4 | 3.7 | |
| Data Base (H) | 4.1 | 2.2 | 24.7 | 16.4 | 4.9 | 2.8 | |
| Other (J) | 8.5 | 0 | 9.4 | 4.9 | 13.6 | 35.2 | |
| Code Change Problem Reports | 2019 | 405 | 275 | 225 | 81 | 108 | 3113 |

Table 4-3.  Order of Precedence for Major Error Categories

| | Project 3 | Project 4 | Project 5 (Applications) | Project 5 (Simulator) | Project 5 (OS) | Project 5 (Tools) |
|---|---|---|---|---|---|---|
| 1 | Logic | Logic | Data Base | Logic | Logic | Logic |
| 2 | Data Handling | Data Handling | Logic | Computational | Data Handling | Data Handling |
| 3 | Interface | Interface | Computational | Data Base | I/O | I/O |
| 4 | I/O | I/O | Data Handling | Data Definition | Interface | Data Definition |
| 5 | Computational | Data Definition | Interface | I/O | Data Definition | Data Base |
| 6 | Data Base | Data Base | I/O | Data Handling | Data Base | Interface |
| 7 | Data Definition | Computational | Data Definition | Interface | Computational | Computational |

Table 4-4. Percentage Breakdown of Code Change Errors into Major Error Categories by Increment

| Project 5 Major Error Categories | Project 5 (%) | | | | | | | | | |
|---|---|---|---|---|---|---|---|---|---|---|
| | Application S/W | | | | Simulator S/W | | | | Operating System | PA Tools |
| | Incr. 0 | Incr. 1 | Incr. 2 | Incr. 3 | Incr. 0 | Incr. 1 | Incr. 2 | Incr. 3 | | |
| Computational (A) | 0 | 18.8 | 14.1 | 11.2 | 10.7 | 20.7 | 21.8 | 19.8 | 2.5 | 0 |
| Logic (B) | 30.4 | 12.9 | 16.7 | 18.1 | 7.1 | 20.7 | 24.2 | 22.2 | 34.6 | 43.5 |
| Data Input (C) | 8.8 | 5.7 | 5.1 | 1.1 | 7.1 | 6.9 | 4.6 | 6.2 | 3.7 | 3.7 |
| Data Output (E) | 0 | 3.5 | 3.8 | 2.2 | 3.7 | 10.3 | 3.5 | 1.2 | 4.9 | 1.8 |
| Data Handling (D) | 30.4 | 9.4 | 11.5 | 6.7 | 7.1 | 13.9 | 8.1 | 7.5 | 21.0 | 9.3 |
| Interface (F) | 8.7 | 8.2 | 15.4 | 6.7 | 7.1 | 3.4 | 2.3 | 12.3 | 7.4 | 0 |
| Data Definition (G) | 4.3 | 8.2 | 6.4 | 7.9 | 32.1 | 3.4 | 19.5 | 4.9 | 7.4 | 3.7 |
| Data Base (H) | 17.4 | 25.9 | 16.7 | 32.6 | 25.1 | 6.9 | 12.6 | 21.0 | 4.9 | 2.8 |
| Other (J) | 0 | 7.1 | 10.3 | 13.5 | 0 | 13.8 | 3.4 | 4.9 | 13.6 | 35.2 |

Direct comparison of detailed error categories between Project 3 and Project 5 is made difficult by the fact that the error category list used for Project 5 differs from that used in analyzing data from other projects.* Therefore, results are presented separately, but to make the comparison easier, detailed categories for Projects 3 and 4 have been grouped where similarities warrant such grouping. These results appear in Table 4-5 where entries are percentages of the major category. Table 4-6 presents a similar percentage breakdown of Project 5 major categories for each of the four portions of the Project 5 software being studied. It will be noted in Table 4-6 that not all detailed categories are represented. In this table only those categories representing a significant, greater than 5 percent, portion of the major category for at least one portion of the Project 5 software are presented.**

For both Projects 3 and 4 the highest occurrences of computational errors were in computing entry numbers, indices, and flag settings. Percentages ran 26.3 and 57.1 percent, respectively. None of the portions of Project 5 experienced this type of error, possibly due to the detailed routine level testing done before integration testing. Sign convention errors ranged from 2.7 percent to 9.1 percent in the Project 5 data and were at 5.0 percent for Project 3. Project 4 had no occurrences. Units conversion error percentages were surprisingly similar at 8.1, 8.3, and 9.3 percent for the analytical Projects 3 and 5 and 14.3 percent for Project 4. The highest percentages of computational errors, however, fell in the incorrect or inaccurate equation categories.

Logical errors, the major category with the most occurrences for all projects, fell predominantly in the missing logic or condition test detailed category for all projects. Percentages ranged from 39.6 percent for the Project 5 simulator software to 76.6 percent for the Project 5 Product Assurance tools. Of all the errors encountered this one represents the most significant found in the whole study. Incorrect logic (logical results were wrong) or incorrect logical sequence activities were next most important for all projects. Combined, these ranged from 14.9 to 45.0 percent of the logical category. Surprisingly, errors involving loops and endless loops were not very common, representing only 5.2 percent of the Project 3 logical errors and even less for the other projects.

For all projects the predominant input/output detailed error categories had to do with incorrect formats and output that was either garbled or didn't correspond with the design specification. Missing output and output missing entries were also common in the I/O major category.

---

*
As mentioned in Section 3, this was done 1) to simplify the categorization process in order to make it acceptable to project performers, and 2) to make it as causative as possible. The Project 5 error categories did evolve from the Project 3 list, however, and common categories do exist at both the major and detailed levels.
**
This was done to cut down on the number of zero and near zero entries.

Data handling errors, next to logical errors in occurrences, were predominantly errors in initializing and updating data. Occurrences in these categories formed 65.7 and 77.3 percent of the major category for Projects 3 and 4, respectively, and ranged from 26.3 percent for the simulator software to 82.3 percent for the operating system software for Project 5. Errors in initialization of flags and indices were a large problem on all of the source projects.

Similarities between projects in the interface categories are harder to find because of the differences between category lists.* However, from Tables 4-4, 4-5 and 4-6, it can be seen that routine/routine calling sequence (argument) errors and errors in data compatability were most common.

For Project 5 tape processing is not a very significant activity. For Projects 3 and 4, however, tape handling was a significant task. Why all Project 3 errors fell in one detailed category is a mystery.

Remaining detailed categories exhibit percentage breakdowns that aren't so comparable. But these unique data are useful by themselves along with other error percentages in defining tools and techniques to improve the development and test processes (see Section 4.7).

---

*One of the major simplifying concessions made on the Project 5 list was in the area of interfaces.

Table 4-5. Detailed Error Category Breakdown for Projects 3 and 4

| Grouped Detailed Error Categories | | Percent of Major Category | |
|---|---|---|---|
| | | Project 3 | Project 4 |
| COMPUTATIONAL ERRORS | | | |
| A010 A020 A030 | Errors in computing entry numbers, indices, and flag settings | 26.3 | 57.1 |
| A040 A041 | Incorrect/inaccurate equation used | 18.6 | 0 |
| A050 | Results of equation wrong | 16.5 | 0 |
| A060 | Mixed mode arithmetic errors | 0 | 28.6 |
| A070 A071 A072 | Time calculation/conversion errors | 8.3 | 0 |
| A080 | Sign convention errors | 5.0 | 0 |
| A090 | Units conversion errors | 9.3 | 14.3 |
| A100 | Vector calculation errors | 5.0 | 0 |
| A120 | Quantization/truncation errors | 11.0 | 0 |

Table 4-5. Detailed Error Category Breakdown for Projects 3 and 4 (Continued)

| | Grouped Detailed Error Categories | Percent of Major Category | |
|---|---|---|---|
| | | Project 3 | Project 4 |
| **LOGIC ERRORS** | | | |
| B010 | Limit determination error | 4.0 | 0.7 |
| B030 B050 | Loop exited at wrong point or endless loop | 5.2 | 1.4 |
| B040 | Incomplete processing | 7.0 | 0 |
| B060 B061 B062 | Missing logic or condition test | 47.6 | 51.4 |
| B020 B070 B120 B130 B140 | Incorrect logic | 14.5 | 42.9 |
| B080 | Logic activities out of sequence | 6.1 | 2.1 |
| B090 | Filtering error | 1.3 | 0.7 |
| B100 | Status check/propagation error | 9.5 | 0 |
| B150 B160 B170 | Logic inefficient | 4.8 | 0.7 |

Table 4-5.  Detailed Error Category Breakdown for Projects 3 and 4 (Continued)

| Grouped Detailed Error Categories | | Percent of Major Category | |
|---|---|---|---|
| | | Project 3 | Project 4 |
| INPUT/OUTPUT ERRORS | | | |
| C010 C030 | Missing output | 16.6 | 11.1 |
| C020 | Output missing entries | 4.8 | 0 |
| C040 C050 | Output garbled or not compatible with design specification | 21.1 | 52.8 |
| C070 C090 C110 C120 C130 | I/O format error | 26.5 | 5.6 |
| C080 | Duplicate/excessive output | 10.2 | 5.6 |
| C100 C101 C102 | Debug output error | 10.9 | 11.1 |
| C140 C150 | Printer control error | 4.8 | 8.2 |
| C60 C160 C161 | Insufficient output to support operations | 5.1 | 5.6 |

Table 4-5. Detailed Error Category Breakdown for Projects 3 and 4 (Continued)

| Grouped Detailed Error Categories | | Percent of Major Category | |
|---|---|---|---|
| | | Project 3 | Project 4 |
| **DATA HANDLING ERRORS** | | | |
| D010 D030 D040 D041 D050 D051 D090 D100 | Data initialization/setting error | 65.7 | 77.3 |
| D020 D110 D120 D150 D151 | Data location error | 12.0 | 7.3 |
| D070 D071 D130 D190 D200 | Data and bit manipulation error | 4.8 | 1.8 |
| D080 | Integer to floating point conversion error | 0.3 | 1.8 |
| D060 D140 | Overflow/overflow processing error | 9.8 | 11.8 |
| D160 | Long literal processing error | 1.1 | 0 |
| D170 | Sort error | 6.3 | 0 |

Table 4-5. Detailed Error Category Breakdown for Projects 3 and 4 (Continued)

| Grouped Detailed Error Categories | Percent of Major Category | |
|---|---|---|
| | Project 3 | Project 4 |
| **ROUTINE/ROUTINE INTERFACE ERRORS** | | |
| G010 G020 G030 G040 G050 G070 — Errors in communication of data | 49.7 | 30.3 |
| G060 H010 — Calling sequence errors | 44.9 | 66.7 |
| G090 H100 — Routine/routine incompatibility forces loading problems | 2.2 | 0 |
| H030 — Sense switch usage error | 3.2 | 0 |
| G080 — Routine used outside of design | 0 | 3.0 |
| **TAPE PROCESSING INTERFACE ERRORS** | | |
| I010 — Equipment check not made | 0 | 22.2 |
| I020 — Routine fails to read continuation tape | 0 | 11.1 |
| I030 — Routine fails to unload tape | 0 | 22.2 |
| I040 — Erroneous input tape format | 100.0 | 44.4 |

Table 4-5. Detailed Error Category Breakdown for Projects 3 and 4 (Continued)

| Grouped Detailed Error Categories | Percent of Major Category | |
|---|---|---|
| | Project 3 | Project 4 |
| **USER INTERFACE ERRORS** | | |
| J010 ) J020 )   Card related errors | 2.3 | 0 |
| J030 J040 J050 J060 J070 J080   Data related errors | 87.3 | 64.7 |
| J090   Interface design poor | 10.4 | 35.3 |
| **ROUTINE/DATA BASE INTERFACE ERRORS** | | |
| K010   Routine data element incompatability | 100.0 | 0 |
| K011   Uncoordinated use of data base elements | 0 | 100.0 |
| **PRESET DATA BASE ERRORS** | | |
| M010   Card parameters | 4.9 | 0 |
| M020   Error messages | 40.3 | 0 |

Table 4-5. Detailed Error Category Breakdown for Projects 3 and 4 (Continued)

| Grouped Detailed Error Categories | Percent of Major Category | |
|---|---|---|
| | Project 3 | Project 4 |
| PRESET DATA BASE ERRORS (Continued) | | |
| M000 M030 M040 M041 } Nominal constants | 37.8 | 88.9 |
| M050 Bit strings | 8.5 | 0 |
| M060 Data should have been initialized but wasn't | 8.5 | 11.1 |
| GLOBAL VARIABLE DEFINITION ERRORS | | |
| N010 Definition placement error | 6.3 | 0 |
| N020 N030 N050 } Definition incorrect | 93.7 | 100.0 |

Table 4-6. Project 5 Detailed Error Category Breakdown

| Detailed Error Categories | Percent of Major Category | | | |
|---|---|---|---|---|
| | Applications S/W | Simulator S/W | Operating System S/W | PA Tools |
| A-000 COMPUTATIONAL ERRORS | 0 | 20.4 | 50.0 | 0 |
| A-100 Incorrect operand in equation | 37.8 | 27.3 | 50.0 | 0 |
| A-300 Sign convention error | 2.7 | 9.1 | 0 | 0 |
| A-400 Units or data conversion error | 8.1 | 9.1 | 0 | 0 |
| A-600 Incorrect/inaccurate equation used | 35.2 | 13.6 | 0 | 0 |
| A-800 Missing computation | 10.8 | 18.2 | 0 | 0 |
| B-000 LOGIC ERRORS | 2.1 | 8.3 | 0 | 4.3 |
| B-100 Incorrect operand in logical expression | 21.3 | 6.2 | 7.1 | 4.3 |
| B-200 Logic activities out of sequence | 17.0 | 29.2 | 10.7 | 10.6 |
| B-300 Wrong variable being checked | 4.3 | 8.3 | 14.3 | 2.1 |
| B-400 Missing logic or condition test | 46.8 | 39.6 | 60.7 | 76.6 |
| C-000 DATA INPUT ERRORS | 16.7 | 38.5 | 0 | 0 |
| C-100 Invalid input read from correct data file | 16.7 | 38.5 | 33.3 | 50.0 |
| C-300 Incorrect input format | 66.6 | 7.7 | 66.7 | 50.0 |

Table 4-6. Project 5 Detailed Error Category Breakdown (Continued)

| Detailed Error Categories | Percent of Major Category | | | |
| --- | --- | --- | --- | --- |
| | Applications S/W | Simulator S/W | Operating System S/W | PA Tools |
| D-000 DATA HANDLING ERRORS | 10.0 | 21.1 | 11.8 | 70.0 |
| D-100 Data initialization not done | 6.7 | 10.5 | 17.6 | 0 |
| D-200 Data initialization done improperly | 20.0 | 10.5 | 41.2 | 10.0 |
| D-300 Variable used as a flag or index not set properly | 20.0 | 5.3 | 23.5 | 10.0 |
| D-400 Variable referred to by wrong name | 6.7 | 21.1 | 0 | 0 |
| D-500 Bit manipulation done incorrectly | 10.0 | 0 | 0 | 0 |
| D-600 Incorrect variable type | 3.3 | 10.5 | 0 | 0 |
| D-700 Data packing/unpacking error | 10.0 | 5.3 | 0 | 10.0 |
| D-900 Subscripting error | 13.3 | 15.7 | 5.9 | 0 |
| E-000 DATA OUTPUT ERRORS | 0 | 33.3 | 25.0 | 0 |
| E-200 Data written according to wrong format statement | 14.3 | 0 | 0 | 100.0 |
| E-300 Data written in wrong format | 0 | 22.3 | 25.0 | 0 |
| E-500 Incomplete or missing output | 85.7 | 11.1 | 25.0 | 0 |
| E-600 Output field size too small | 0 | 33.3 | 0 | 0 |

Table 4-6. Project 5 Detailed Error Category Breakdown (Continued)

| Detailed Error Categories | | Percent of Major Category | | | |
|---|---|---|---|---|---|
| | | Applications S/W | Simulator S/W | Operating System S/W | PA Tools |
| F-000 | INTERFACE ERRORS | 25.9 | 68.8 | 33.3 | 0 |
| F-300 | Subroutine arguments not consistent | 11.1 | 0 | 50.0 | 0 |
| F-500 | Software/data base interface error | 25.9 | 6.2 | 16.7 | 0 |
| F-600 | Software/user interface error | 11.1 | 12.5 | 0 | 0 |
| F-700 | Software/software interface error | 18.6 | 6.2 | 0 | 0 |
| G-000 | DATA DEFINITION ERRORS | 21.1 | 41.9 | 33.3 | 0 |
| G-100 | Data not properly defined/ dimensioned | 47.4 | 41.9 | 66.7 | 50.0 |
| G-300 | Data referenced at wrong location | 10.4 | 3.2 | 0 | 0 |
| G-400 | Data pointers not incremented properly | 15.8 | 13.0 | 0 | 50.0 |
| H-000 | DATA BASE ERRORS | 4.4 | 59.5 | 25.0 | 33.3 |
| H-100 | Data should have been initialized but wasn't | 29.4 | 5.4 | 0 | 66.7 |
| H-200 | Data initialized to wrong value | 64.7 | 35.1 | 50.0 | 0 |

Table 4-6. Project 5 Detailed Error Category Breakdown (Continued)

| Detailed Error Categories | | Percent of Major Category | | | |
| --- | --- | --- | --- | --- | --- |
| | | Applications S/W | Simulator S/W | Operating System S/W | PA Tools |
| J-000 | OTHER | 0 | 0 | 0 | 0 |
| J-100 | Time limit exceeded | 4.0 | 18.2 | 0 | 0 |
| J-200 | Core limit exceeded | 8.0 | 0 | 0 | 0 |
| J-500 | Code or design inefficient/not necessary | 8.0 | 27.2 | 18.2 | 10.5 |
| J-600 | User/programmer requested enhancement | 22.0 | 18.2 | 54.6 | 57.9 |
| J-700 | Design nonresponsive to requirements | 2.0 | 27.2 | 27.2 | 31.6 |
| J-900 | Software not compatible with standards | 8.0 | 9.2 | 0 | 0 |

## 4.2.2  When Were Specific Errors Found?

All error data analyzed in this study were the result of formal testing or, in the case of Projects 3 and 4, operational use. By formal testing we mean that testing performed after the programmer finishes his debug and checkout. Formal testing is documented through plans and procedures and is designed to demonstrate some predefined test objectives, e.g., interface integrity, requirement satisfaction, or use in the operational environment.

Software test personnel put forth the contention that they find certain types of errors first (e.g., aborts, endless loops, major interface errors, etc.), and once the software is cycling properly, attention is turned to detailed examination of such things as output accuracy, demonstration of requirements and timing performance.

As part of the analysis of Project 3 data, an attempt was made to determine if 1) specific types of errors are found at certain times within each test phase and 2) if these types could be traced to a particular type of test case or test strategy.

First of all, the contention that certain types of errors are found first was not borne out by the data. Error categories appeared to be distributed in time across each test phase in such a way that no trends were noted. This was also true for the one test phase represented in the Project 5 data.

A close examination of the text of Project 3 SPR's indicated numerous instances where individual test analysts (by name) documented problems of similar error type over a period of a day or two. That is, having detected a certain type of error, e.g., an entry computation error based on a misunderstanding of whether the first entry was the 0th or 1st entry, there was a tendency for that analyst to go looking for the same type of error elsewhere in the code. No attempt was made to quantify the extent to which this phenomenon occurred; however, it is believed that this could have some very positive effects on the rate and completeness of error discovery, in spite of a diversion of the test analyst's attention away from a broader search for all types of errors and especially if the test analyst is intimately familiar with all the code produced by an individual programmer.

To get a picture of the relative magnitude of documented errors as a function of time, Figures 4-4 through 4-8 are presented. These histograms are from Projects 2 and 3 and depict the buildup of problem reports partly due to a "learning curve" on the part of the test personnel and partly due to the serial nature of the software and test cases. That is, not all of the software can be tested at once due to the need to develop data bases in early test cases for input to subsequent test cases. The typical tailoff of problem reports as the backlog of errors detectable by a specific test strategy are found and corrected is also visible. Note that successive test phases, each representing a different set of principal test objectives, produce a new buildup, peak, and tailoff of problem reports over time. Hopefully, each peak is lower than its predecessor, but as may be seen, this was not always the case.

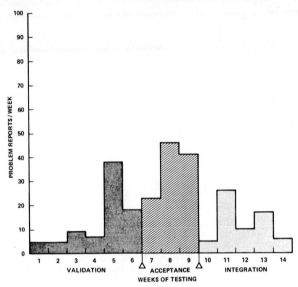

Figure 4-4. Software Problems Encountered During Testing

PROJECT 2
MOD1A

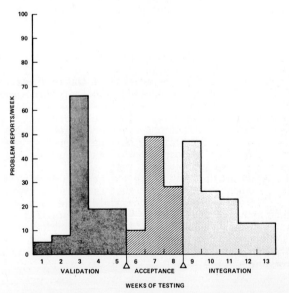

Figure 4-5. Software Problems Encountered During Testing

PROJECT 2
MOD1B

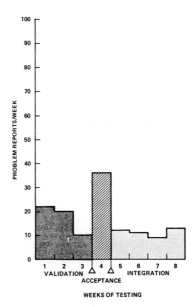

Figure 4-6. Software Problems Encountered During Testing

PROJECT 2
MOD1BR

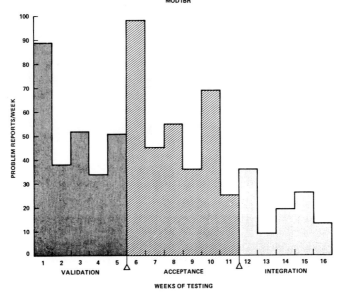

Figure 4-7. Software Problems Encountered During Testing

PROJECT 2
MOD2

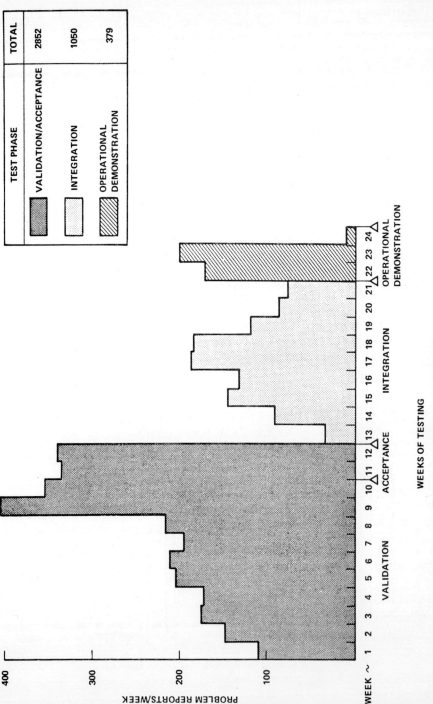

| TEST PHASE | | TOTAL |
|---|---|---|
| ▨ | VALIDATION/ACCEPTANCE | 2852 |
| ☐ | INTEGRATION | 1050 |
| ▨ | OPERATIONAL DEMONSTRATION | 379 |

Figure 4-8.   Software Problems Encountered During Testing

Although principal test objectives varied from phase to phase, there was considerable overlap and, admittedly, duplication. As will be pointed out in Section 4.7, test cases in each phase were extended purposely to broaden the scope of the error detection process. For example, the principal objectives of validation testing were to verify that major software capabilities documented in the approved design, including those necessitated by software requirements, were present and operating correctly. Yet, test case designers also addressed selected interface tests and operational scenarios using operational-like data. Tests executed during acceptance or requirements testing; system integration testing, where a concerted effort was made to exercise interfaces and test anomalous conditions to "break" the software; and operational demonstrations, where tests followed an operational timeline, were all quite similar. Each phase detected errors from every major error category. And more importantly, each phase caught errors which should have been detected earlier. This expansion of test objectives, coupled with the changes in personnel performing and analyzing tests (thereby bringing in a "fresh" viewpoint), is believed to have been very beneficial to the overall quality of the delivered product.

### 4.2.3  When Were Errors Introduced?

Although all errors being considered in this study were found in the code during test or operational usage of the software, not all are necessarily coding errors. Some may be traced to other sources. Four development activities have been identified as sources of error.

- requirements specification

- design

- coding

- maintenance (correction of other errors)

In trying to determine where each error was introduced, the temptation was great to go down the detailed error category list and judiciously assign a source, i.e., assign a probable source. For Project 3 this was done, since no attempt was made to determine error source as each SPR was written. Results, summarized by major error category, are presented in Table 4-7 for the 2019 errors which produced a change in the Project 3 code. Note that only design and coding sources are assigned. This is because the list of four sources given above actually breaks down to either design or coding sources for Projects 2 and 3. That is, no good data exist on the number of errors introduced as a result of correcting previously documented errors, and errors attributed to a source in software requirements were probably recorded as design errors in this investigation, although no problem report specifically cited requirements in either project's data. This is partly due to the fact that requirements were formally reviewed, approved, and baselined prior to the beginning of design and held unchanging for the remainder of the development cycle. However, the assumption should not be made that the requirements were flawless, even in this type of controlled development environment where requirements were formally specified and well understood by both customer and development contractor as well. This is because, in the collection of

Table 4-7. Project 3 Error Sources

| MAJOR ERROR CATEGORIES | | % OF TOTAL CODE CHANGE ERRORS | PROBABLE SOURCES | |
|---|---|---|---|---|
| | | | PERCENT DESIGN | PERCENT CODE |
| Computational | (AA) | 9.0 | 90 | 10 |
| Logic | (BB) | 26.0 | 88 | 12 |
| I/O | (CC) | 16.4 | 24 | 76 |
| Data Handling | (DD) | 18.2 | 25 | 75 |
| Operating System/System Support Software | (EE) | 0.1 | (1) | |
| Configuration | (FF) | 3.1 | 24 | 76 |
| Routine/Routine Interface | (GG) | 8.2 | 93 | 7 |
| Routine/System Software Interface | (HH) | 1.1 | 73 | 27 |
| Tape Processing Interface | (II) | 0.3 | 90 | 10 |
| User Interface | (JJ) | 6.6 | 83 | 17 |
| Data Base Interface | (KK) | 0.8 | 10 | 90 |
| User Requested Change | (LL) | 0 | (2) | |
| Preset Data Base | (MM) | 4.1 | 79 | 21 |
| Global Variable/Compool Definition | (NN) | 0.8 | 62 | 38 |
| Recurrent | (PP) | 1.3 | (1) | |
| Documentation | (QQ) | 0.8 | (1) | |
| Requirements Compliance | (RR) | 0.4 | 89 | 11 |
| Unidentified | (SS) | 1.0 | (1) | |
| Operator | (TT) | 0.7 | (1) | |
| Questions | (UU) | 1.1 | (1) | |
| | | Averages | 62% | 38% |

NOTES: (1) Although errors in these categories required changes to the code, their source breakdown of design versus code is not attempted here. Those categories considered in all other categories encompass 95 percent of all code change errors.

(2) For Project 3 product enhancements or changes to the design baseline were considered "out-of-scope" and, therefore are not present here.

supporting data to explain software error histories, poorly stated requirements or changing interpretation of requirements were offered as reasons
for difficulty in developing several error-prone routines.

A quantitative breakdown between the design and coding sources can
be derived from Project 2 data by virtue of the fact that design documentation for this project was very detailed, to the extent that flow charts
contained detail at the source code level. This detailed design documentation went through a formal review and customer approval cycle prior to
coding of each Project 2 update. For the most part, the coding task
involved transferral, rather than translation, of the approved design
into source code. Since Project 2 is continually being updated, rigorous
controls are used to maintain the design documentation in a current
state. One of these is the Documentation Update Transmittal or DUT.
For Project 2 every software problem which necessitates a change to
the design documentation requires a DUT. Therefore, to get a feel for
the percentage of errors that are attributable to design, the Project 2
problem report history can be used if two assumptions are made.

1) The detailed design specification is the approved
design.

2) Any errors which require a change to the code and
necessitate a change to the detailed design specification are to be considered design errors. Those
requiring only a code change are coding errors.

Data from seven updates to the Project 2 software are presented in
Table 4-8.

The approaches taken above support the contention that errors in
one category might be traced back to a source in some previous development phase, e.g., that not all errors in index computation are coding
errors. However, since analysis was done retrospectively, we've had to
work with what data are available, and accuracy has suffered. Project 5,
on the other hand, has allowed us an opportunity to tailor data collection
requirements to both increase the scope of the error sources and the accuracy of the source assignments. That is, by getting analysis help from
project performers, a further breakdown of error source, including requirements specification and maintenance, has been possible. Since it is not
always possible to determine where the error was introduced, a fifth "not
known" category was introduced to cover this situation.[*]

Project 5 data provides a unique opportunity to examine the variation
of error source as a result of the top down, multiple increment approach to
development. It is also a unique opportunity from the standpoint of software requirements, since unlike Projects 2 and 3, the Project 5 software
requirements were not as well understood at project outset and have been
the subject of continual controlled restatement and refinement. Project 5
can be considered a state of the art realtime software system with highly
complex and detailed requirements.[**] In this respect, it is typical of

---

[*] A fact of life in real world data collection.

[**] In sheer numbers alone Project 5 has 1165 software requirements as
opposed to 188 for Project 3. Both projects employ baseline management techniques with requirements reviews and maintenance of traceability.

Table 4-8.  Project 2 Error Sources

| MODIFICATION | NO. OF SOURCE STATEMENTS IN MODIFICATION | TOTAL ERRORS ENCOUNTERED | PERCENT DESIGN ERRORS | PERCENT CODING ERRORS |
|---|---|---|---|---|
| MOD1A | 1253 | 152 | 73.6 | 26.4 |
| MOD1B | 9880 | 156 | 73.7 | 26.3 |
| MOD1BR* | 779 | 73 | 35.6 | 64.4 |
| MOD2 | 9631 | 419 | 51.6 | 48.4 |
| MOD3 | 4575 | 199 | 58.8 | 41.2 |
| MOD3.1 | ** | 113 | 61.9 | 38.1 |
| MOD3.2 | ** | 120 | 65.8 | 34.2 |

*MOD1BR was a small "retrofit" update to Project 2, which may have had something to do with the low design error percentage.
**Size data not accurate.

the current trend for rigorous requirements specification becoming more common in the industry.

The data examined were from 689 Project 5 code change problem reports written during integration testing.  Four portions of the Project 5 code are represented in the following tables:

● real-time applications software (Table 4-9)

● real-time simulator software (Table 4-10)

● batch mode Product Assurance Tools (Table 4-11)

● realtime operating system software*** (Table 4-11)

***These values are presented only as a sample of operating system software data.  Data must not be considered complete because Project 5 is not complete and development schedules have not provided a good breaking point for analysis.

Table 4-9.  Project 5 Error Sources by Increment
(Applications Program Software)

| ERROR SOURCE / TOP DOWN ITERATION | PERCENT CODE OR DATA BASE CHANGE ERRORS FOR EACH INCREMENT | | | |
|---|---|---|---|---|
| | INCREMENT 0 | INCREMENT 1 | INCREMENT 2 | INCREMENT 3 |
| Requirements | 0 | 3.5 | 10.3 | 12.4 |
| Design | 95.7 | 60.0 | 41.0 | 10.1 |
| Code | 4.3 | 27.1 | 35.9 | 56.2 |
| Maintenance* | 0 | 4.7 | 5.1 | 9.0 |
| Not Known | 0 | 4.7 | 7.7 | 12.3 |

|  |  |  |  |  | TOTALS |
|---|---|---|---|---|---|
| Code or Data Base Change Errors | 23 | 85 | 78 | 89 | 275 |
| Total Errors Reported** | 44 | 114 | 101 | 118 | 377 |

*This refers to errors introduced as a result of fixing previously documented errors.

**These include non-code or data base change errors such as operator errors, documentation errors, and "no problem" reports.

Table 4-10.  Project 5 Error Sources by Increment
(Simulator Software)

| ERROR SOURCE ╲ TOP DOWN ITERA- TION | PERCENT CODE OR DATA BASE CHANGE ERRORS FOR EACH INCREMENT | | | |
|---|---|---|---|---|
| | INCREMENT 0 | INCREMENT 1 | INCREMENT 2 | INCREMENT 3 |
| Requirements | 0 | 0 | 1.1 | 18.5 |
| Design | 39.3 | 44.8 | 63.3 | 43.2 |
| Code | 60.7 | 51.8 | 32.2 | 30.9 |
| Maintenance* | 0 | 0 | 1.1 | 2.5 |
| Not Known | 0 | 3.4 | 2.3 | 4.9 |

|  | | | | | TOTALS |
|---|---|---|---|---|---|
| Code or Data Base Change Errors | 28 | 29 | 87 | 81 | 225 |
| Total Errors Reported** | 29 | 32 | 98 | 128 | 287 |

*This refers to errors introduced as a result of fixing previously documented errors.
**These include non-code or data base change errors such as operator errors, documentation errors, and "no problem" reports.

Results for the various portions of the Project 5 system are not con-sistent, as may be seen in the following tables.  Several trends do appear in the data, however.

   1)  For each of the software packages being developed in a top-down, multiple increment approach (Tables 4-9 and 4-10) the percentage of errors attributable to requirements is increasing, although the total num-ber of errors found per increment is remaining fairly constant.  A closer look at these errors shows that they fall principally in the logical, computational, interface, and data structure categories.  However, the text of these problem reports doesn't necessarily point to an error.  Project 5 is so complex that in some areas, such as performance (timing and accuracy)

Table 4-11.  Project 5 Error Sources (Batch Mode PA Tools and Real-Time Operating System Software)

| ERROR SOURCE | PERCENT CODE OR DATA BASE CHANGE ERRORS | |
| --- | --- | --- |
| | BATCH MODE PA TOOLS | REAL-TIME OPERATING SYSTEM SOFTWARE* |
| Requirements | 0.9 | 7.4 |
| Design | 32.4 | 43.3 |
| Code | 61.1 | 40.7 |
| Maintenance** | 2.8 | 0 |
| Not Known | 2.8 | 8.6 |
| Code or Data Base Change Errors | 108 | 81 |
| Total Errors Reported | 131 | 99 |

*Values in this column cannot be considered final.
**This refers to errors introduced as a result of fixing previously documented errors.

requirements, it is necessary to build a portion of the system and play it off against a real-time simulator to verify that requirements are valid. The percentage of these "errors" goes up because the number of requirements implemented increases with each successive increment. The multiple increment approach has allowed continual validation of requirements along with validation of the software.

2) The breakdown of design and coding errors is not the same as that seen for Projects 2 and 3, partly due to the larger number of categories being evaluated and partly due to the nature of Project 5. Note in Table 4-9 that the percentage of design errors has gone down to 10.1 percent in Increment 3 (from a high of 95.7 percent in the predominantly stub structure of Increment 0). This may be a desirable feature of the

multiple increment approach since coding errors have been shown by Shooman and Bolsky [4] to be less costly to diagnose and correct than design errors.* Their results showed that design errors required an average of 3.1 manhours to diagnose and 4.0 manhours to correct. Coding errors required an average of 2.2 manhours to diagnose and 0.8 manhours to correct. This result is not surprising since early increments effectively establish the major design features.

3) Maintenance errors, i.e., those errors resulting from the correction of previously documented errors, reached a maximum of 9.0 percent of all code change errors in one case. A practical norm for this error source, however, is probably in the range of from 2 to 5 percent.

---

*Unfortunately, we were unable to collect this type of information during the S.R.S.

## 4.2.4  Preoperational vs Operational Problems

One of the popular beliefs held by test personnel in the Project 3 environment is that the routines which are error prone during preoperational testing are also the routines which are error prone once the software is operational.  Project 3 operational data collected during this study made it possible to investigate the accuracy of this belief.

Figure 4-9 shows a plot of operational problems versus preoperational problems for the 249 Project 3 routines.  From this we$_*$see that the correlation isn't very strong at the routine level, r = 0.406 .  Figure 4-10, which presents the same data at the function level shows a stronger correlation with r = 0.920.  Results at the routine level probably would have been much improved had an assessment of problem criticality been available for use in the investigation.

One interesting fact was revealed in the course of trying to identify reasons why routines were statistical outliers, i.e., falling outside the 90 percent confidence limits in Figure 4-9.  Turning to the routine difficulty information collected early in the S.R.S., an attempt was made to determine why routines were outliers above the regression line[**], i.e., had a higher number of operational problems compared to other routines.  First, the average "difficulty to develop" of the nine high outliers is 12.1 while the average for all of TRW's 174 routines was 9.2, where the difficulty range is from a minimum of 5 to a maximum of 15.  A summary of difficulty data for the nine outliers is given in Table 4-12 below.

Table 4-12.  Difficulty Ratings for Operational Outliers

| Routine Name | Difficulty | | | | | |
|---|---|---|---|---|---|---|
| | Design | Code | Implement | Checkout | Document | Totals |
| A313 | 1 | 2 | 3 | 2 | 2 | 10 |
| A504 | 3 | 3 | 3 | 3 | 3 | 15 |
| B107 | 2 | 2 | 2 | 2 | 2 | 10 |
| C104 | 3 | 2 | 3 | 3 | 3 | 14 |
| C107 | 3 | 2 | 2 | 2 | 2 | 11 |
| C108 | 2 | 2 | 2 | 1 | 2 | 9 |
| C302 | 3 | 2 | 3 | 2 | 3 | 13 |
| D203 | 3 | 3 | 3 | 3 | 2 | 14 |
| G108 | 3 | 2 | 3 | 3 | 2 | 13 |
| Averages | 2.6 | 2.2 | 2.7 | 2.3 | 2.3 | 12.1 |

*Note:  Deleting routines with zero problems didn't improve the correlation.

**Note:  Only one routine was an outlier below the regression line.  This was judged to be a difficult routine to develop (difficulty = 14) but "thoroughly" tested.  The chief reason given was that it was an easily modularized, primarily computational routine.  See also Section 4.3.5.8.

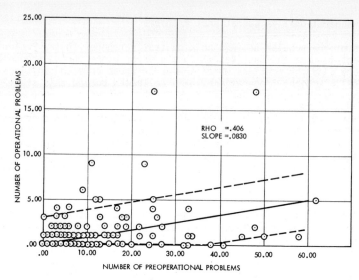

Figure 4-9.
Project 3 Operational Problems versus Preoperational Problems At Routine Level

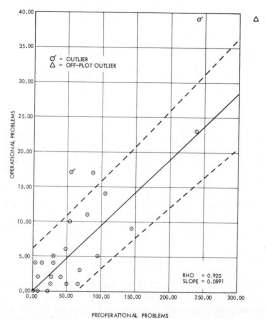

Figure 4-10.
Project 3 Function Level Operational Problems versus Preoperational Problems

Most interesting were the reasons given for the generally high difficulty ratings. Complex logic, core loading problems, and data interfaces were given as reasons, but these reasons were also applied to routines that were not outliers. A fourth reason was given for three of the nine outlier routines which was not given for any other routines, and that reason was "changing requirements." However, statements of requirements were not changed after the software requirement specification was approved and baselined, so this points to changes in interpretation of poorly stated requirements. In fact, requirements for one of these outlier routines continued to be a point of contention well into the operational phase of the Project 3 life cycle.

## 4.2.5  Software Problems as a Function of Routine Size*

One of our beliefs at the beginning of the Software Reliability Study was that the number of problems encountered in a routine would correlate well with the routine's size measured in total source statements. This was a finding in an earlier study done by TRW for the CCIP-85 Study Group [5], which stated that "there is a strong correlation between the number of problems encountered during testing and the size/complexity of the programs being tested." The subject project in that study was the initial version of Project 2.

An attempt to plot actual problems for all Project 3 routines, Figure 4-11, generally indicated that larger routines did experience more problems, bearing out the earlier findings. However, in an attempt to discover if certain types of routines were more error prone than others, routines were grouped functionally into subsystems according to their position in the Project 3 software architecture, and correlation improved considerably.** Figures 4-12 through 4-21 present results of this investigation. Figure 4-22 presents a summary of linear regression lines translated through the origin for the sake of comparison. Results may be summarized by the following:

1) The correlation coefficient, r, for the linear best fit ranged from a low of 0.5408 to a maximum of 0.9449.

2) The linear best fit for all subsystems fell roughly between 10 and 20 problems per 1000 total JOVIAL source statements***with the exception of two routine groupings.

The two routine groupings which did not fall in the 10 to 20 problems per 1000 statements range were Subsystem D, Figure 4-17, and Subsystem F and Function G2, Figure 4-19, both falling below 10 problems per 1000 statements. The reason for this is most likely thoroughness of development testing.**** Subsystem D, although it contained the largest routine in the Project 3 system (in excess of 2300 total statements), was highly proceduralized (modularized) computational code that was testable in small segments. Also, since this subsystem executed at the end of the serial processing order, system level tests of Subsystem D were not possible until predecessor tests

---

*Section 4.3.3.2 *et seq.* presents a generalized statistical regression analysis which also considers some of the data presented in this Section; in particular see Section 4.3.4.1 and Tables 4-16 and 4-17 in regard to parameter $Z_1$.

**Groupings by routine purpose (e.g., computational, input, output, etc.) are addressed in Section 4.3.5.1.

***These include executable and non-executable statements, but not comments.

****That testing done by the developers prior to delivery of the software to the independent test team.

were successfully completed, allowing testing at the routine level to be completed. Subsystem F and Function G2 were functionally similar because they contained utility routines. These routines also received more thorough testing because their relatively smaller size made them easier to test, dependencies of other routines on these utilities forced testing to be completed earlier, and additional testing was performed by users of these utilities.

Explanation of error rates experienced in the other Project 3 subsystems is not so easy, although such things as complexity and difficulty, as well as thoroughness of testing*, are believed to be factors. Examination of the relationship of software problems to other attributes is presented in Section 4.3.

A look at problems documented during Project 3 operations brings out an interesting fact related to size, however. By calculating an average of errors encountered for routines in size groupings it was noted that the large routines, say greater than 1000 total source statements, were the routines which tended to experience more errors** after preoperational testing, Figure 4-23. Preoperational data showed a linear relationship of errors to routine size, i.e., a large routine was no more error prone than a small one. Although data are limited and further investigation with other sources of data is recommended, Project 3 results suggest that the best fit may not be a straight line when operational errors are included, Figure 4-24. In this figure light shaded bars are preoperational data and dark shaded bars are operational data. This would support the contention that it is the small routines which are easiest to test thoroughly in preoperational testing and the larger routines that go into the operational environment containing residual, undetected errors.

Investigations of size on the other source projects was not fruitful, although Project 2 showed similar results, but not so well correlated, as those for Project 3. Project 4, which is written in a macro language and with only operational error data, showed no correlation at all between errors and size.

Project 5 has a limit on routine size, 100 executable statements, so investigations of errors and size were performed by combining routines to form larger modules called tasks. Even so, there was very poor correlation. Correlations may improve after completion of all Project 5 testing.

---

*
We have no quantitative measure of test thoroughness for Project 3.
**
To a user it is often a simple count of errors per routine, rather than any other measure, that shapes his opinion of reliability.

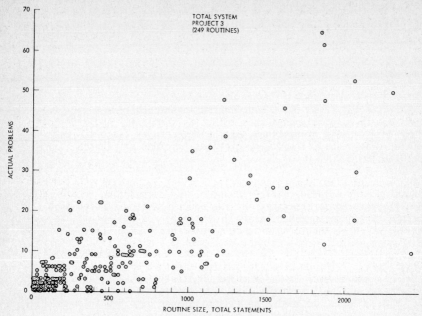

Figure 4-11.  Actual Problems vs. Routine Size
(Project 3, Total System)

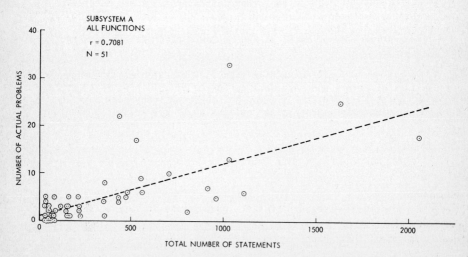

Figure 4-12.  Actual Problems vs. Routine Size
(Project 3, Subsystem A)

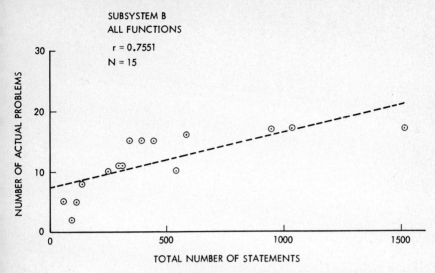

Figure 4-13. Actual Problems vs. Routine Size
(Project 3, Subsystem B)

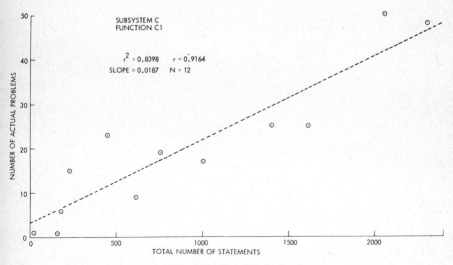

Figure 4-14. Actual Problems vs. Routine Size
(Project 3, Subsystem C, Function C1)

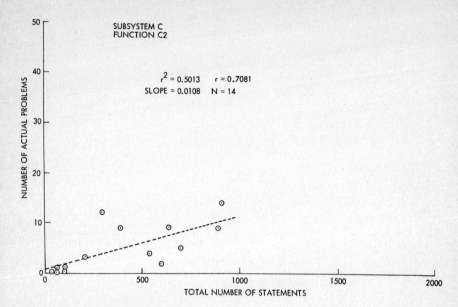

Figure 4-15.  Actual Problems vs. Routine Size
(Project 3, Subsystem C, Function C2)

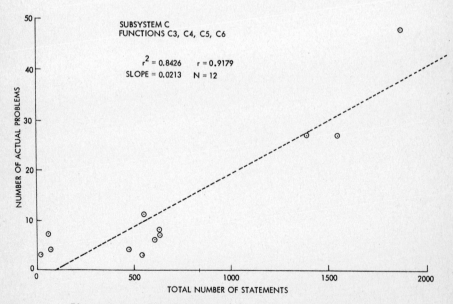

Figure 4-16.  Actual Problems vs. Routine Size (Project 3,
Subsystem C, Functions C3, C4, C5, C6)

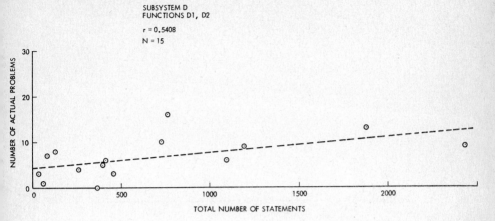

Figure **4-17.**   Actual Problems vs. Routine Size
(Project 3, Subsystem D)

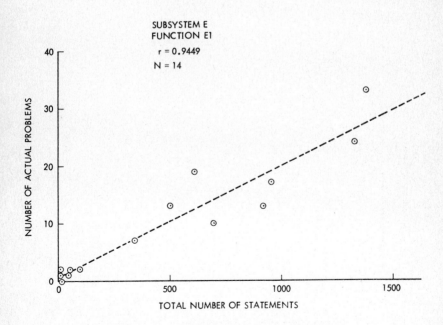

Figure **4-18.**   Actual Problems vs Routine Size
(Project 3, Subsystem E)

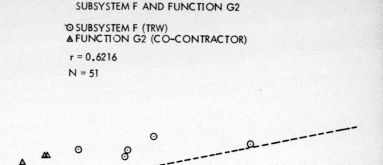

Figure 4-19. Actual Problems vs. Routine Size (Project 3, Subsystems F and G (Function G2))

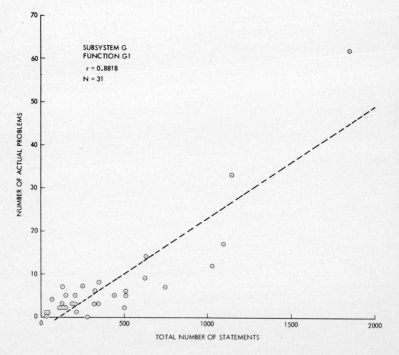

Figure 4-20. Actual Problems vs. Routine Size (Project 3, Subsystem G, Function G1)

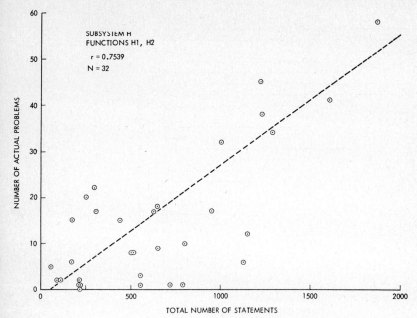

Figure 4-21.  Actual Problems vs Routine Size
(Project 3, Subsystem H)

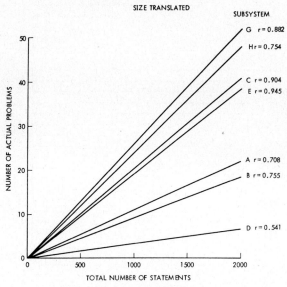

Figure 4-22.  Actual Problems vs. Routine Size, Regression Lines
Translated Through Origin

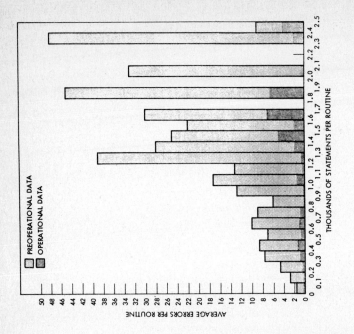

Figure 4-24.

Preoperational and Operational Errors per Routine
Grouped by Size (Project 3)

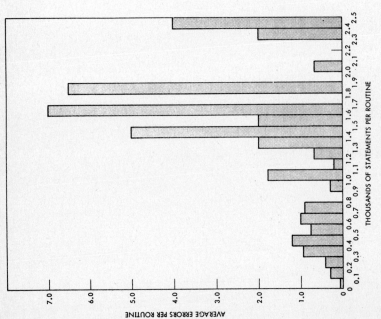

Figure 4-23.

Average Operational Errors per Routine
Grouped by Size (Project 3)

## 4.3   The Phenomenological Approach to Software Reliability

Some of the concepts discussed in this section were first proposed
to be applied to software by Rubey and Hartwick [6]. The authors of [6]
may have chosen the word "Quality" in part because of the empiricism of
the concepts, but clearly the intent is to measure and/or deal with Reliability, as defined earlier.

The Reference [6] method was to define attributes and their metrics;
the former being a prose expression of the particular quality desired of
the software; the latter a mathematical function of parameters thought to
relate to or define the attribute. The major attributes, such as, for
example: "$A_1$ - mathematical calculations are correctly performed"; or:
"$A_5$ - The program is intelligible"; or: "$A_6$ - The program is easy to
modify," were each further categorized in [6] to describe less abstract;
i.e., more concrete, attributes capable of being measured as to whether
the attribute is present to some degree (on a scale of 0 to 100). Only a
few metrics were defined in [6], although a detailed breakdown of each
major attribute was given; and no particular application was mentioned in
the reference.

TRW Systems reported in [7] on a study which included the formulation of metrics and their application in a controlled experiment to two
computer programs independently prepared to the same specification. In the
study only a limited number of attributes were considered, primarily those
corresponding to attributes $A_5$ and $A_6$ of [6], mentioned previously. It is
considered that the application in [7] was successful as far as it went,
in that the number of problems encountered, as well as the reliabilities
of each program (determined by the methods described in Section 5.2.4)
appeared to correlate well with the metrics' values.

In [1], a more basic approach to software reliability in terms of
attributes, or characteristics, and their metrics was attempted. This
study focused primarily upon that which could be termed as good (or bad)
practices and standards applying to FORTRAN coding. The use of the
good practice or adherence to the specified standard was defined as the
value of the metric, (i.e., 1 or 0), although in many cases a graduation
of values between 0 and 1 could be defined. The study related the type
of practice or standard to more abstract characteristics such as "understandability," "testability," "maintainability," etc. Reference [1]
expresses in great detail the rationale for and relationships between the
primitive characteristics, more concrete characteristics, and the metrics,
together with a subjective analysis of their suitability or correlation
with quality, i.e., high reliability software.

### 4.3.1   Current Approach

Early in the current study it was decided to make the phenomenological
approach to software reliability via a route more closely related to that
taken in Reference [7] rather than [1]. The primary reasons for this
choice were the availability of 'TMETRIC, a software tool developed to
analyze characteristics of programs written in JOVIAL J4 language, and the
unavailability of both tools and manpower to accomplish the analysis set
forth in [1] on Projects 2 or 3 programs.

Consequently the approach for this study has been to use 'TMETRIC to collect data on characteristics connoting complexity, and by implication error-proneness and/or difficulty of error detection and correction. The capabilities of 'TMETRIC are described in Section 2 of this report.

### 4.3.2 The Relationship of Reliability With 'TMETRIC Information

The basic assumption is that certain measurable characteristics can be selected to provide a sufficiently accurate and precise indicator of reliability. To utilize the numbers of problems encountered during the test program as an indicator of reliability, it must first be recognized that it would be the reliability as of the beginning of the test program, since during the course of testing the detected errors are corrected (with high probability). However, it would also have to be assumed that new errors introduced by correcting a problem, if detected during the course of the test program, are recognized as newly created. These would not be counted in the total number of problems measuring reliability. Furthermore, it needs to be assumed that the same number of originally present errors would occur whether or not other originally present errors are detected and corrected. A final major assumption which would support the hypothesis that numbers of problems are an indicator of reliability is that the test program uses a set of test cases representative of the operational profile.

Note that the word "indicator" was used instead of "estimator." By this is meant that numbers of problems under the above assumptions would be proportional to unreliability, so that if a similar test program followed the first test program, in which number of errors occurring were less by a factor of (say) two, then it could be inferred that the unreliability was also reduced by a factor of two.

Hence, with no further assumptions, such as those of the Shooman or Jelinski — Moranda models (Section 5.2) needed to predict future reliability, the numbers of problems occurring during testing would only reflect the previous reliability of the software. Furthermore, as observed in [7], the complexity parameters of the software (as collected and analyzed by 'TMETRIC) will remain essentially constant even though coding changes are made to correct errors. This means that if the values of the complexity parameters have any meaning, they also can only reflect the reliability of the software prior to the test program, i.e., that of the basic design.

As a consequence of the preceding assumptions, two basic models, similar in several respects, were considered for predicting numbers of software problems as a function of 'TMETRIC data. The first model represents a preliminary attempt to construct a set of metrics which both separately and together measure the attribute "complexity". The model was tested using standard linear regression analysis in order to determine, primarily by the value of the multiple correlation coefficients, how well the chosen complexity metrics explained or predicted the number of software problems. The results of this analysis, given in Section 4.3.3.1, showed that fair-to-good correlations were obtained.

On the other hand, in constructing a complexity model to predict
numbers of software problems, subjective judgements were made as to the
relative influence of each of the (sub)metrics (obtained from 'TMETRIC data)
comprising the several complexity metrics by directly assigning numerical
"weights" or influence coefficients.  Secondly, the functional forms chosen
for the set of metrics were considered somewhat complex for their purpose.

The second model, which was the main subject of investigation in this
study, was formulated based upon the philosophy that it should be simple
in form, and that the relative influence of the various (sub)metrics should
be estimated from the data.  As a consequence the primary model chosen to
relate software problems to 'TMETRIC data was the well-known linear regression model

$$N_p = \sum a_i f_i(T_i)$$

where $N_p$ is the number of actual problems* for the software module under
analysis, and $f(T_i)$ is some specified function of the ith 'TMETRIC parameter value $T_i$.  For every $T_i$, $f(T_i)$ is defined to be nondecreasing in $T_i$
so that increasing the value of $T_i$ should result in greater or at least
equal complexity.  Consequently, it is worthwhile to constrain the coefficients $a_i$ to be nonnegative; that is, number of problems should either
increase, or at least not decrease with increasing value of any one complexity parameter.  One of the objectives will then be to determine if one
or more of the coefficients are small with respect to the remaining coefficients.  These would then be assigned the value zero, reflecting the information that the corresponding parameters are not influential in predicting
$N_p$.  The main objective is to find a "best-fitting" set of coefficients $a_i$,
(some of which will be zero) and then evaluate the statistical consequences
in terms of confidence limits on $N_p$.  The choice of functions f (in most
cases $f(x) = x$) and the manner in which this general constrained regression
problem is solved and applied to the Project 3 data is the major topic of
Section 4.3.3.

## 4.3.3  Analysis of Software Problem Data Models

### 4.3.3.1  Complexity Model

Initially it was hypothesized that numbers of software problems could
be explained or predicted from certain measures of complexity.  In order to
investigate this hypothesis several factors which are believed to contribute
to complexity were considered and metrics were defined in order to provide
a numerical measure of these complexity factors.

These categories of complexity were considered:

1.  Logic Complexity — related to source-code statements of logical
    relationships, primarily branching decisions, but including loop
    and IF-nesting level measures.

---

*"Actual" problems are problems (errors) which required a change to the
code or data base to effect corrective action.

2. Interface complexity — measured by number of application program interfaces (number of other routines called), and number of system interfaces (number of system routines called).

3. Computational complexity — measured by assignment statements containing arithmetic operators.

4. Input/output complexity — measured by number of I/O statements.

5. Readability — measured by number of comments statements.

<u>Definitions of Complexity Metrics</u>

1. The Logic Complexity metric, referred to as Total Logic Complexity, $L_{TOT}$, can be numerically evaluated for each routine by calculating:

$$L_{TOT} = LS/EX + L_{LOOP} + L_{IF} + L_{BR}$$

where

$LS$   = number of logic statements

$EX$   = number of executable statements

$L_{LOOP}$ = a measure of loop complexity defined in Table 4-14

$L_{IF}$  = a measure of IF- condition statement complexity, also defined in Table 4-14.

$L_{BR}$  = number of branches BR*, times 0.001 (the factor 0.001 was chosen to assign what was believed to be the relative importance of number of branches within the expression for total logic complexity).

2. The Interface Complexity Metric $C_{INF}$ is defined as follows:

$$C_{INF} = AP + 0.5 (SYS)$$

where

$AP$   = number of application program interfaces

$SYS$  = number of system program interfaces

$0.5$  = a factor chosen to assign what was believed to be the relative importance of system program interfaces to application program interfaces

---

*The number of branches parameter as used in the complexity model of this section was redefined in subsequent analyses to include all branch-producing statements.

3.  The Computational Complexity metric CC is defined as follows:

$$CC = (CS/EX) \times (L_{SYS}/\sum CS) \times CS$$

where

$CS$ = number of computational statements

$L_{SYS}$ = $\sum L_{TOT}$, the sum over all routines of $L_{TOT}$, the Total Logic Complexity for each routine (defined previously)

$\sum CS$ = the sum over all routines of the values of CS for each routine

4.  The Input/Output Complexity metric is defined for each routine as follows:

$$C_{I/O} = (S_{I/O}/EX) \times (L_{SYS}/\sum S_{I/O}) \times S_{I/O}$$

where

$S_{I/O}$ = number of Input/Output statements

$\sum S_{I/O}$ = the sum over all routines of the values of $S_{I/O}$ for each routine

5.  Readability, an uncomplexity metric, is defined for each routine as follows:

$$U_{READ} = COM/(TS+COM)$$

where

$TS$ = total number of statements (executable plus non-executable, exclusive of comments statements)

$COM$ = number of comments statements

The Total Complexity Metric, $C_{TOT}$, is defined for each routine by

$$C_{TOT} = L_{TOT} + 0.1C_{INF} + 0.2CC + 0.4C_{I/O} + (-0.1)U_{READ}$$

The factors 0.1, 0.2, 0.4, and -0.1 applied to Interface Complexity ($C_{INF}$), Computational Complexity (CC), Input/Output Complexity ($C_{I/O}$) and Readability ($U_{READ}$), respectively, represent what are believed to be the relative weights of these metrics in an additive model for total complexity.

Although five complexity metrics were defined as predictors for numbers of problems, it was decided at first to place emphasis upon the analysis of Total Logic Complexity ($L_{TOT}$), as a single predictor, and to group the remaining four metrics into a single complexity metric, labeled Total-Logic. Subsequently, in the more general regression analysis described in Section 4.3.3.2 *et seq.*, the parameters making up the remaining metrics were considered individually as predictors although not directly in the above form.

Figures 4-25 presents selected results of regression analyses of number of actual problems versus Total Complexity Metric $C_{TOT}$, for Subsystems A, B, C, D, E, and Function G1. The data for Subsystems F and H were plotted and found to be extremely "noisy", as had been expected to a certain extent, since Subsystem F consists of utility routines and Subsystem H of data management routines with a varied history, some routines being well established and unmodified, others modified for Project 3, and the remainder newly developed.

Consequently, plots of number of problems versus $C_{TOT}$ for subsystems F and H are not presented. Routines exhibiting anomalous values of number of problems were removed from the data before computing the regression line, as indicated on the plots. Values of r (actually $r^2$) indicate the fraction of the variance of numbers of problems accounted for by the particular regression function.

Table 4-13 compares correlation coefficients r of number of problems with each of the metrics $C_{TOT}$, $L_{TOT}$ and $C_{TOT} - L_{TOT}$ for subsystems A, B, C, D, E and function G1. The values of r range from "fair" to "good," in that $100r^2$ (%) usually exceeds 50%, and for function G1 exceeds 80%.

### 4.3.3.2 Generalized Regression Model

A "nonclassical" method for predicting numbers of software problems as a function of measurable parameters of the source code was applied to Project 3 data. The basic technique is to determine the coefficients of a linear function of the defined parameters by minimizing the sum of squares of deviations of the observed number of software problems from the assumed linear function; i.e., by "least squares," or "linear regression." However, the distinguishing feature of the method applied for this study is that those coefficients corresponding to parameters adjudged to have a positive (increasing) effect on number of software problems were constrained to be nonnegative. Conversely the coefficients of those parameters which would cause a decrease in number of software problems were constrained to be nonpositive. These added judgement factors applied to the least-squares (or

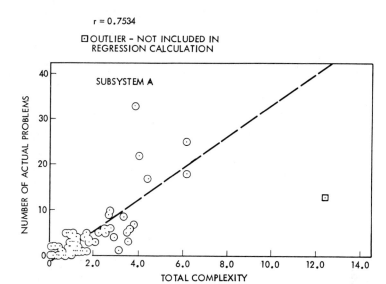

r = 0.7534

⊡ OUTLIER – NOT INCLUDED IN
REGRESSION CALCULATION

SUBSYSTEM A

Figure 4-25.   Total Complexity Metric Subsystem A
(Sheet 1 of 6)

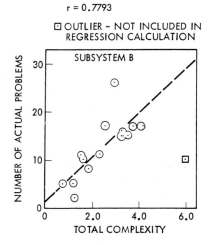

r = 0.7793

⊡ OUTLIER – NOT INCLUDED IN
REGRESSION CALCULATION

SUBSYSTEM B

Figure 4-25.   Total Complexity Metric Subsystem B
(Sheet 2 of 6)

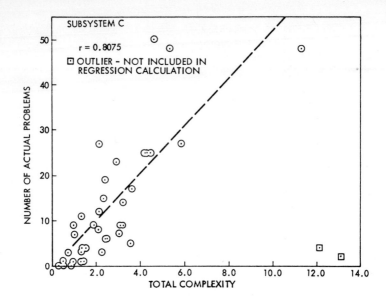

Figure 4-25. Total Complexity Metric Subsystem C
(Sheet 3 of 6)

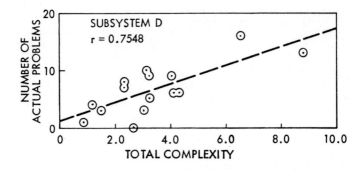

Figure 4-25. Total Complexity Metric Subsystem D
(Sheet 4 of 6)

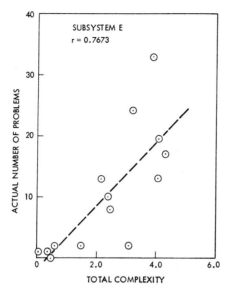

Figure 4-25. Total Complexity Metric Subsystem E
(Sheet 5 of 6)

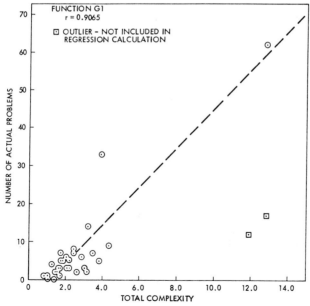

Figure 4-25. Total Complexity Metric Function G1
(Sheet 6 of 6)

Table 4-13.  Correlation Coefficients for Number of Software
Problems versus Complexity Metrics

CORRELATION COEFFICIENTS

| COMPLEXITY METRIC | SUBSYSTEM | | | | | FUNCTION |
| | A | B | C | D | E | G1 |
|---|---|---|---|---|---|---|
| TOTAL COMPLEXITY, $C_{TOT}$ | 0.7534 | 0.7793 | 0.8075 | 0.7548 | 0.7673 | 0.9065 |
| TOTAL LOGIC COMPLEXITY, $L_{TOT}$ | 0.6335 | 0.8453 | 0.7142 | 0.6804 | 0.9058 | 0.9138 |
| TOTAL COMPLEXITY – LOGIC COMPLEXITY, $C_{TOT} - L_{TOT}$ | 0.7081 | 0.6088 | 0.7686 | 0.5730 | 0.5231 | 0.4343 |

linear regression) problem converts it from a relatively simple technique to a nonlinear programming problem with a quadratic objective function (function to be minimized) and linear inequality constraints.

Statistical analysis of the estimators of the coefficients for nonlinear programming problems (e.g., evaluation of correlations, and also confidence limits on the coefficients) appears to be essentially untouched in the literature, even in the relatively simple cases of a quadratic objective function (as opposed to some arbitrary convex nonlinear function) and the simple nonnegative (or nonpositive) linear inequality constraints*. Nevertheless, the estimated variance of the observed number of problems about the best-fitting linear function of a given set of parameters supplies a good measure, although not strictly valid, for judging the goodness of fit relative to alternate choices of parameter sets, and is used in this analysis for this purpose.

Following the constrained least squares analysis, subsequent linear regression analyses without the previously described inequality constraints were applied considering only certain subsets of the originally selected parameters. Since the parameters not considered were eliminated because their influence coefficients were estimated as zeroes in the constrained least squares analysis, it would not be strictly valid to make the usual inferences obtained from standard regression analysis methods. However, if the reduced sets of parameters were the only ones to then be considered in future predictions, then subsequent inferences based upon the standard regression analysis could claim more validity. On the other hand, should it be found in future unconstrained regression analyses that one or more of the important influence coefficients are found to be negative when it had been "firmly established" that the corresponding parameter(s) had a positive effect on producing software problems, then the analysis would need to be re-started at some point, or else the theory improved.

It is also possible that with an improvement in the theoretical development of a model for prediction of software problems, the regression might be, more appropriately, nonlinear. In that circumstance, the tools described by Reference [8] could be used, in general.

Reference [9] discusses the constrained least-squares technique and provides a set of FORTRAN programs** in its Appendix C for solving the problem described in this report. Since we did not happen to have these programs, a set of programs already available to us, which handle general nonlinear programming problems based on Reference [8], were used for the analysis.

---

*Private communication by Professor A. Madansky, University of Chicago.

**To purchase code and data in machine-readable form, inquiries should be directed to International Mathematical and Statistical Libraries, Inc., Suite 510, 6200 Hillcroft, Houston, Texas 77036.

The basic data element consists of a single (sub)routine, identified by a label indicating the portion of a given function it performs, and the subsystem grouping of the required functions of the software. The data obtained for each routine consist of the total number of actual problems together with measured values of sixteen parameters. Table 4-14 defines the parameters used in the analysis, and Table 4-15 presents the parameter values for each routine, primarily obtained by use of 'TMETRIC, a JOVIAL source code static tool. In Table 4-15, two of the parameters, LLOOP and LIF, were developed from the 'TMETRIC data by accounting for nesting level of the Loop and IF statements used.* Also two parameters, RAT and WK-LD (programmer rating and work-load respectively), were developed from data obtained from interviews with management personnel connected with Project 3. Data for these two parameters were unobtainable for subsystems G and H, however. All parameters except COM (number of comments) and RAT were considered as having a positive effect on number of software problems. For simplicity in the computation,** the latter two parameters were given minus signs, and in this way all coefficients could be constrained to be nonnegative.

### 4.3.3.3 Analysis of the Generalized Regression Model

Assume there are N parameters $Z_j$, j = 1, 2, ... , N and K routines in a specified grouping. $Y_i$ is the (theoretically) expected number of software problems in the ith routine, i = 1, 2, ..., K.

The expected number of software problems is assumed to be expressible as a linear function of the parameters:

$$Y_j = \sum_{J=1}^{N} a_j Z_{ji} \qquad (1)***$$

---

*Calculated values of $L_{LOOP}$ AND $L_{IF}$ are shown multiplied by 1000, in order to avoid convergence problems in the estimation process.

**It is an automatic feature of the nonlinear programming problem computational software that all solutions are constrained to be nonnegative, unless explicitly programmed otherwise.

***Note that in this model a constant term ($Z_{0i}$ = 1.0) is not used; i.e., it is postulated that zero problems would occur if the parameters were all zero. In other words, the regression plane is being forced to go through the origin.

Table 4-14.    Parameter Definitions

ROUT                            Coded routine identifier.  Each routine has
                                an identifier which replaces its real name.
                                This identifier indicates the routine's
                                parent subsystem and function as well.

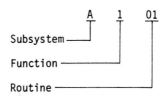

PROBS                           Number of actual problems encountered in the
                                routine.  Actual problems are those that
                                required an update to the routine's code.

$Z_1 = TS$                      Total routine statements [TS = NEX + EX]

$Z_2 = L_{LOOP} = LL\ E3$       Computed loop complexity* for the routine
                                according to the following equation.

$$L_{LOOP} = \Sigma m_i W_i$$

where:

$$W_i = 4^{i-1}\left(\frac{3}{4^Q - 1}\right) \quad \text{so that} \quad \sum_{i=1}^{Q} W_i = 1$$

and:

$m_i$ = number of loops in routine at
indenture or nesting level i.

$W_i$ = weighting factor

$Q$ = maximum level of indentures in the
system

4 = shaping value

---
*Values were multiplied by 1000 as a scaling factor.

Table 4-14.   Parameter Definitions (Continued)

| | |
|---|---|
| $Z_3 = L_{IF} = IF\ E3$ | Computed IF complexity* for the routine according to the following equation |

$$L_{IF} = \sum n_i W_i$$

where:

$n_i$ = number of IFs in routine at indenture or nesting level i

$W_i$ = weighting factor (the same as for $L_{LOOP}$)

| | |
|---|---|
| $Z_4 = BR$ | Total routine branches |
| $Z_5 = LS$ | Routine logical statements (IF, ORIF, IFEITH) |
| $Z_6 = AP$ | Direct routine interfaces with other applications routines (not a count of calls to other routines) |
| $Z_7 = SYS$ | Direct routine interfaces with operating system or system support routines (not a count of calls to system routines) |
| $Z_8 = I/O$ | Routine input/output statements |
| $Z_9 = COMP$ | Routine computational statements |
| $Z_{10} = DATA$ | Routine data handling statements |
| $Z_{11} = NEX$ | Routine nonexecutable statements |
| $Z_{12} = EX$ | Routine executable statements |
| $Z_{13} = TI$ | Total routine interfaces with other routines TI = AP + SYS |
| $Z_{14} = COM$ | Total routine comments.  Comments are not included in the count of nonexecutable statements, NEX. |
| $Z_{15} = RAT$ | Average programmer rating.  This parameter is an average based on the ratings of each programmer who worked on the routine. |
| $Z_{16} = WK\text{-}LD$ | Average workload of programmers who worked on the routine. |

---
*Values were multiplied by 1000 as a scaling factor.

## Table 4-15. Project 3 Routine Parameters by Subsystem

ROUTINE PARAMETERS FOR SUBSYSTEM A

| RGUT | PROBS | TS | LL E3 | IF E3 | BR | LS | AP | SYS | I/O | COMP | DATA | NEX | EX | TI | COM | BAT | WK-LD |
|---|---|---|---|---|---|---|---|---|---|---|---|---|---|---|---|---|---|
| A101 | 0 | 54 | 0.0 | 20.3 | 23 | 7 | 4 | 1 | 0 | 0 | 0 | 23 | 31 | 5 | -125 | -8.0 | 1.0 |
| A102 | 4 | 355 | 23.3 | 134.0 | 114 | 34 | 4 | 8 | 23 | 22 | 116 | 90 | 265 | 12 | -293 | -8.0 | 1.0 |
| A103 | 4 | 34 | 0.0 | 11.6 | 21 | 4 | 14 | 1 | 0 | 0 | 0 | 9 | 25 | 15 | -25 | -19.0 | 1.5 |
| A104 | 18 | 2065 | 34.9 | 2682.2 | 734 | 330 | 9 | 11 | 0 | 91 | 570 | 675 | 1390 | 20 | -1131 | -19.0 | 1.5 |
| A201 | 1 | 30 | 2.9 | 23.3 | 12 | 6 | 2 | 3 | 1 | 2 | 0 | 7 | 23 | 5 | -46 | -8.0 | 1.0 |
| A202 | 1 | 69 | 2.9 | 40.8 | 43 | 10 | 9 | 1 | 0 | 0 | 6 | 22 | 47 | 10 | -112 | -8.0 | 1.0 |
| A203 | 5 | 211 | 20.3 | 178.0 | 76 | 35 | 3 | 5 | 3 | 3 | 54 | 68 | 143 | 8 | -158 | -6.0 | 1.0 |
| A204 | 3 | 112 | 8.7 | 149.2 | 39 | 15 | 2 | 1 | 1 | 1 | 31 | 36 | 76 | 3 | -69 | -6.0 | 1.4 |
| A205 | 9 | 561 | 357.6 | 640.3 | 165 | 71 | 9 | 8 | 26 | 20 | 146 | 196 | 365 | 17 | -344 | -16.0 | 1.4 |
| A206 | 33 | 1027 | 128.3 | 643.7 | 352 | 163 | 11 | 8 | 87 | 34 | 282 | 287 | 740 | 19 | -726 | -13.3 | 1.2 |
| A207 | 0 | 51 | 75.7 | 52.5 | 28 | 9 | 7 | 1 | 0 | 0 | 5 | 18 | 33 | 8 | -72 | -8.0 | 1.0 |
| A208 | 5 | 473 | 0.0 | 323.7 | 137 | 74 | 3 | 10 | 22 | 20 | 132 | 145 | 328 | 13 | -405 | -7.0 | 1.0 |
| A209 | 3 | 26 | 69.8 | 17.5 | 9 | 3 | 2 | 0 | 0 | 2 | 7 | 8 | 18 | 2 | -8 | -19.0 | 1.5 |
| A210 | 7 | 913 | 17.5 | 1366.4 | 233 | 124 | 6 | 10 | 23 | 35 | 249 | 359 | 554 | 16 | -754 | -19.0 | 1.5 |
| A301 | 2 | 50 | 29.1 | 11.6 | 12 | 7 | 1 | 3 | 2 | 2 | 11 | 20 | 30 | 4 | -35 | -18.0 | 1.4 |
| A302 | 5 | 159 | 0.0 | 207.6 | 42 | 27 | 0 | 5 | 11 | 17 | 31 | 51 | 108 | 5 | -2 | -18.0 | 1.4 |
| A303 | 0 | 27 | 2.9 | 17.5 | 7 | 3 | 0 | 0 | 0 | 3 | 0 | 12 | 15 | 0 | -21 | -13.5 | 1.4 |
| A304 | 2 | 50 | 17.4 | 17.4 | 80 | 7 | 1 | 0 | 0 | 10 | 10 | 14 | 36 | 5 | -65 | -20.0 | 1.4 |
| A305 | 2 | 215 | 2.9 | 116.5 | 49 | 31 | 2 | 4 | 14 | 17 | 56 | 73 | 142 | 6 | -168 | -18.5 | 1.4 |
| A306 | 1 | 76 | 2.9 | 40.7 | 26 | 12 | 2 | 0 | 2 | 0 | 12 | 30 | 46 | 9 | -76 | -18.0 | 1.5 |
| A307 | 1 | 154 | 134.0 | 195.5 | 66 | 33 | 1 | 7 | 0 | 0 | 31 | 66 | 88 | 6 | -64 | -18.0 | 1.4 |
| A308 | 25 | 1632 | 34.6 | 3049.4 | 489 | 242 | 2 | 5 | 13 | 103 | 405 | 594 | 1038 | 11 | -135 | -11.0 | 1.0 |
| A309 | 0 | 707 | 11.6 | 407.0 | 231 | 124 | 1 | 8 | 3 | 49 | 149 | 282 | 425 | 6 | -243 | -17.0 | 1.0 |
| A310 | 3 | 146 | 0.0 | 55.1 | 57 | 23 | 3 | 2 | 2 | 0 | 42 | 36 | 110 | 2 | -73 | -17.0 | 1.5 |
| A311 | 0 | 79 | 5.8 | 20.3 | 12 | 7 | 0 | 0 | 0 | 19 | 19 | 29 | 50 | 0 | -45 | -13.0 | 1.2 |
| A312 | 0 | 57 | 0.0 | 14.5 | 10 | 7 | 0 | 1 | 0 | 10 | 19 | 29 | 28 | 12 | -20 | -13.0 | 1.2 |
| A313 | 3 | 216 | 0.0 | 145.5 | 62 | 35 | 1 | 0 | 5 | 16 | 63 | 76 | 140 | 0 | -162 | -17.0 | 1.5 |
| A314 | 0 | 51 | 0.0 | 20.7 | 8 | 4 | 0 | 11 | 0 | 11 | 6 | 21 | 30 | 1 | -23 | -13.0 | 1.2 |
| A315 | 0 | 44 | 0.0 | 8.7 | 10 | 3 | 0 | 0 | 0 | 11 | 5 | 18 | 26 | 21 | -25 | -13.0 | 1.0 |
| A401 | 2 | 803 | 826.2 | 261.3 | 205 | 111 | 4 | 17 | 19 | 55 | 197 | 297 | 506 | 23 | -440 | -20.0 | 1.0 |
| A402 | 6 | 567 | 55.4 | 470.0 | 154 | 78 | 8 | 15 | 23 | 55 | 122 | 203 | 364 | 26 | -294 | -20.0 | 1.0 |
| A403 | 8 | 766 | 31.9 | 624.4 | 237 | 111 | 5 | 21 | 43 | 59 | 141 | 275 | 491 | 36 | -370 | -20.0 | 1.0 |
| A404 | 22 | 438 | 69.8 | 247.8 | 127 | 65 | 22 | 14 | 15 | 32 | 108 | 141 | 297 | 17 | -107 | -17.0 | 1.0 |
| A405 | 2 | 156 | 20.4 | 63.9 | 65 | 24 | 10 | 7 | 7 | 3 | 25 | 54 | 102 | 9 | -106 | -17.0 | 1.5 |
| A406 | 1 | 56 | 17.5 | 14.5 | 19 | 9 | 3 | 6 | 0 | 0 | 0 | 27 | 29 | 15 | -35 | -15.5 | 1.0 |
| A501 | 2 | 162 | 0.0 | 770.9 | 44 | 20 | 6 | 9 | 9 | 3 | 40 | 63 | 99 | 8 | -258 | -15.5 | 1.3 |
| A502 | 5 | 37 | 17.5 | 17.4 | 22 | 6 | 5 | 9 | 0 | 0 | 3 | 8 | 29 | 12 | -60 | -17.0 | 1.5 |
| A503 | 4 | 431 | 630.0 | 396.7 | 139 | 76 | 6 | 6 | 1 | 17 | 93 | 165 | 266 | 22 | -421 | -17.0 | 1.3 |
| A504 | 13 | 1031 | 7418.9 | 2931.7 | 293 | 170 | 11 | 8 | 8 | 37 | 243 | 397 | 634 | 27 | -1023 | -19.5 | 1.3 |
| A505 | 5 | 1116 | 269.1 | 889.1 | 331 | 191 | 8 | 11 | 28 | 111 | 237 | 394 | 722 | 9 | -524 | -19.0 | 1.3 |
| A506 | 1 | 163 | 2521.1 | 49.3 | 105 | 22 | 2 | 19 | 28 | 19 | 32 | 32 | 95 | 12 | -152 | -19.0 | 1.3 |
| A507 | 6 | 363 | 1013.7 | 314.6 | 139 | 76 | 2 | 7 | 8 | 52 | 63 | 113 | 250 | 18 | -147 | -17.0 | 1.3 |
| A508 | 1 | 483 | 386.5 | 212.3 | 63 | 39 | 11 | 6 | 20 | 61 | 100 | 154 | 329 | 8 | -143 | -19.0 | 1.3 |
| A509 | 5 | 224 | 5.8 | 432.9 | 290 | 167 | 2 | 6 | 0 | 61 | 31 | 80 | 144 | 21 | -93 | -17.0 | 1.3 |
| A510 | 5 | 964 | 87.6 | 1074.3 | 135 | 58 | 10 | 10 | 17 | 94 | 256 | 268 | 696 | 16 | -269 | -12.0 | 1.3 |
| A511 | 2 | 403 | 8.7 | 309.1 | 18 | 13 | 11 | 5 | 44 | 10 | 94 | 110 | 293 | 5 | -94 | -12.0 | 1.0 |
| A512 | 2 | 82 | 4.6 | 298.8 | 34 | 25 | 1 | 4 | 51 | 9 | 16 | 37 | 45 | 8 | -35 | -12.0 | 1.0 |
| A513 | 17 | 142 | 2.9 | 594.7 | 166 | 93 | 1 | 4 | 1 | 18 | 30 | 55 | 87 | 22 | -60 | -12.0 | 1.3 |
| A514 | 5 | 527 | 2.9 | 1050.0 | 28 | 23 | 9 | 9 | 36 | 22 | 158 | 144 | 383 | 7 | -172 | -12.0 | 1.0 |
| A515 | 5 | 92 | 2.9 | 160.6 | 69 | 17 | 3 | 4 | 3 | 6 | 31 | 23 | 69 | 3 | -22 | -12.0 | 1.0 |
| A516 | 3 | 56 | 2.9 | 64.0 | 22 | 17 | 2 | 1 | 12 | 1 | 8 | 12 | 44 | 3 | -11 | -12.0 | 1.0 |

Table 4-15. Project 3 Routine Parameters by Subsystem (Continued)

ROUTINE PARAMETERS FOR SUBSYSTEM B

| ROUT | PROBS | TS | LL E3 | IF E3 | BR | LS | AP | SYS | I/O | COMP | DATA | NEX | EX | TI | COM | RAT | WK-LD |
|---|---|---|---|---|---|---|---|---|---|---|---|---|---|---|---|---|---|
| B101 | 17 | 1027 | 101.9 | 523.6 | 387 | 157 | 22 | 17 | 35 | 29 | 215 | 346 | 681 | 39 | -608 | -17.0 | 1.3 |
| B102 | 26 | 748 | 222.1 | 566.0 | 220 | 117 | 11 | 11 | 33 | 35 | 189 | 246 | 502 | 22 | -154 | -16.5 | 1.2 |
| B103 | 5 | 112 | 5.8 | 20.3 | 26 | 9 | 8 | 5 | 8 | 6 | 37 | 33 | 79 | 13 | -60 | -17.0 | 1.3 |
| B104 | 15 | 387 | 304.7 | 145.4 | 70 | 49 | 12 | 17 | 44 | 40 | 103 | 119 | 268 | 29 | -261 | -14.0 | 1.3 |
| B105 | 16 | 583 | 40.7 | 417.0 | 158 | 85 | 11 | 11 | 17 | 51 | 151 | 195 | 388 | 22 | -391 | -13.0 | 1.1 |
| B106 | 15 | 444 | 79.0 | 151.0 | 114 | 52 | 13 | 14 | 72 | 25 | 110 | 117 | 327 | 27 | -466 | -15.0 | 1.2 |
| B107 | 11 | 304 | 43.8 | 145.4 | 98 | 45 | 9 | 8 | 10 | 13 | 67 | 111 | 193 | 17 | -220 | -16.3 | 1.2 |
| B201 | 11 | 287 | 2.9 | 145.3 | 117 | 42 | 18 | 10 | 14 | 14 | 55 | 86 | 201 | 28 | -243 | -17.0 | 1.3 |
| B202 | 17 | 947 | 99.2 | 770.3 | 281 | 141 | 14 | 18 | 49 | 29 | 240 | 332 | 615 | 32 | -419 | -15.3 | 1.1 |
| B203 | 10 | 247 | 32.1 | 43.5 | 63 | 20 | 8 | 9 | 23 | 17 | 81 | 58 | 189 | 17 | -261 | -15.0 | 1.3 |
| B204 | 15 | 336 | 29.0 | 131.1 | 71 | 37 | 12 | 13 | 18 | 21 | 140 | 76 | 260 | 25 | -195 | -15.5 | 1.2 |
| B205 | 5 | 55 | 8.7 | 0.0 | 10 | 3 | 2 | 8 | 0 | 19 | 15 | 8 | 47 | 10 | -34 | -15.5 | 1.2 |
| B206 | 2 | 98 | 17.4 | 11.6 | 10 | 10 | 4 | 1 | 2 | 9 | 45 | 30 | 68 | 5 | -71 | -15.5 | 1.0 |
| B207 | 17 | 1507 | 78.5 | 596.6 | 473 | 169 | 7 | 9 | 71 | 81 | 383 | 488 | 1019 | 16 | -753 | -20.0 | 1.0 |
| B208 | 8 | 135 | 4.6 | 66.9 | 38 | 19 | 3 | 6 | 19 | 10 | 26 | 40 | 95 | 9 | -110 | -17.0 | 1.3 |
| B209 | 10 | 541 | 11.6 | 3365.8 | 194 | 65 | 14 | 17 | 26 | 12 | 123 | 196 | 345 | 31 | -404 | -14.0 | 1.1 |

Table 4-15. Project 3 Routine Parameters by Subsystem (Continued)

ROUTINE PARAMETERS FOR SUBSYSTEM C

| ROUT | PROBS | TS | LL E3 | IF E3 | BR | LS | AP | SYS | I/O | COMP | DATA | NEX | EX | TI | CCM | RAT | WK-LC |
|------|-------|------|-------|---------|-----|-----|-----|-----|-----|------|------|-----|------|-----|-------|-------|-------|
| C101 | 15 | 227 | 64.4 | 60.9 | 92 | 25 | 10 | 10 | 16 | 10 | 62 | 43 | 184 | 20 | -205 | -17.5 | 1.4 |
| C102 | 48 | 2309 | 403.3 | 6262.1 | 612 | 336 | 20 | 16 | 39 | 201 | 592 | 832 | 1477 | 36 | -1639 | -19.6 | 1.5 |
| C103 | 9 | 615 | 201.4 | 232.4 | 177 | 101 | 5 | 7 | 12 | 82 | 90 | 236 | 379 | 12 | -172 | -18.5 | 1.5 |
| C104 | 25 | 1406 | 69.8 | 1190.4 | 391 | 210 | 9 | 9 | 17 | 149 | 346 | 485 | 921 | 18 | -817 | -20.0 | 1.5 |
| C105 | 50 | 2064 | 180.7 | 1442.7 | 604 | 314 | 14 | 13 | 11 | 221 | 564 | 629 | 1435 | 27 | -1401 | -18.0 | 1.3 |
| C106 | 19 | 665 | 330.8 | 316.8 | 233 | 108 | 1 | 7 | 32 | 50 | 103 | 227 | 438 | 8 | -364 | -16.3 | 1.3 |
| C107 | 25 | 1619 | 233.0 | 957.1 | 585 | 294 | 19 | 15 | 33 | 85 | 423 | 465 | 1154 | 34 | -536 | -15.5 | 1.2 |
| C108 | 23 | 450 | 251.8 | 221.2 | 109 | 66 | 9 | 11 | 20 | 37 | 156 | 114 | 336 | 20 | -145 | -15.5 | 1.2 |
| C109 | 6 | 177 | 61.5 | 242.6 | 53 | 35 | 2 | 3 | 6 | 16 | 37 | 62 | 115 | 6 | -148 | -18.0 | 1.3 |
| C110 | 1 | 161 | 5.8 | 93.0 | 52 | 28 | 18 | 4 | 5 | 7 | 27 | 68 | 93 | 3 | -231 | -18.0 | 1.3 |
| C111 | 17 | 1002 | 72.8 | 570.4 | 300 | 152 | 6 | 12 | 33 | 90 | 241 | 322 | 680 | 30 | -591 | -18.0 | 1.3 |
| C112 | 1 | 24 | 14.6 | 8.7 | 9 | 15 | 6 | 1 | 1 | 0 | 9 | 15 | 15 | 3 | -21 | -18.0 | 1.3 |
| C201 | 12 | 296 | 29.2 | 186.7 | 96 | 35 | 10 | 12 | 25 | 5 | 96 | 70 | 226 | 22 | -400 | -20.0 | 1.2 |
| C202 | 5 | 695 | 55.2 | 478.3 | 232 | 99 | 19 | 17 | 13 | 42 | 182 | 210 | 485 | 36 | -793 | -17.0 | 1.1 |
| C203 | 1 | 105 | 0.0 | 49.3 | 34 | 17 | 5 | 7 | 2 | 19 | 11 | 39 | 66 | 12 | -184 | -17.0 | 1.1 |
| C204 | 0 | 102 | 8.7 | 26.1 | 21 | 12 | 0 | 0 | 1 | 13 | 23 | 42 | 60 | 7 | -136 | -20.0 | 1.2 |
| C205 | 0 | 65 | 26.3 | 5.8 | 9 | 5 | 2 | 10 | 1 | 17 | 11 | 24 | 41 | 12 | -129 | -19.0 | 1.3 |
| C206 | 4 | 534 | 17.5 | 10986.3 | 137 | 80 | 5 | 4 | 15 | 62 | 157 | 160 | 374 | 9 | -474 | -19.0 | 1.3 |
| C207 | 2 | 595 | 465.0 | 11619.3 | 147 | 101 | 5 | 11 | 16 | 45 | 168 | 206 | 389 | 16 | -511 | -18.5 | 1.4 |
| C208 | 0 | 33 | 0.0 | 2.9 | 2 | 1 | 0 | 4 | 0 | 12 | 2 | 17 | 16 | 4 | -82 | -18.5 | 1.4 |
| C209 | 0 | 64 | 0.0 | 2.9 | 10 | 1 | 2 | 2 | 0 | 23 | 3 | 27 | 37 | 4 | -60 | -18.7 | 1.0 |
| C210 | 3 | 211 | 11.6 | 26.1 | 29 | 13 | 8 | 11 | 13 | 50 | 45 | 70 | 141 | 19 | -166 | -18.5 | 1.0 |
| C211 | 9 | 380 | 11.6 | 162.4 | 119 | 60 | 3 | 5 | 8 | 7 | 119 | 123 | 257 | 8 | -224 | -12.5 | 1.1 |
| C212 | 9 | 637 | 37.9 | 914.6 | 240 | 113 | 12 | 10 | 18 | 54 | 147 | 171 | 466 | 22 | -506 | -17.0 | 1.1 |
| C213 | 14 | 906 | 69.8 | 909.1 | 218 | 113 | 8 | 14 | 59 | 57 | 229 | 325 | 581 | 22 | -642 | -12.5 | 1.1 |
| C214 | 9 | 886 | 78.4 | 482.6 | 250 | 154 | 8 | 14 | 35 | 78 | 178 | 321 | 565 | 22 | -700 | -11.0 | 1.0 |
| C301 | 7 | 62 | 0.0 | 20.3 | 24 |  | 6 | 5 | 11 | 0 | 15 | 21 | 41 | 11 | -14 | -17.0 | 1.5 |
| C302 | 48 | 1873 | 209.9 | 918.6 | 549 | 289 | 14 | 25 | 119 | 124 | 452 | 590 | 1293 | 39 | -1071 | -15.0 | .9 |
| C401 | 27 | 1389 | 533.0 | 2273.7 | 164 | 164 | 11 | 19 | 60 | 154 | 315 | 541 | 848 | 30 | -768 | -14.2 | .9 |
| C501 | 4 | 71 | 2.9 | 14.5 | 17 |  | 8 | 9 | 1 | 0 | 12 | 40 | 31 | 12 | -47 | -15.0 | 1.0 |
| C502 | 8 | 632 | 274.4 | 238.5 | 189 | 102 | 7 | 4 | 11 | 28 | 134 | 237 | 395 | 18 | -406 | -15.0 | 1.0 |
| C503 | 25 | 2074 | 432.0 | 1468.0 | 664 | 293 | 11 | 15 | 64 | 130 | 497 | 682 | 1392 | 20 | -1489 | -15.0 | 1.1 |
| C504 | 7 | 631 | 573.8 | 818.9 | 177 | 107 | 8 | 12 | 9 | 34 | 134 | 243 | 388 | 19 | -600 | -17.0 | 1.1 |
| C505 | 6 | 607 | 140.0 | 352.4 | 151 | 100 | 5 | 11 | 42 | 23 | 132 | 235 | 372 | 19 | -433 | -17.0 | 1.1 |
| C601 | 3 | 16 | 0.0 | 5.8 | 9 | 2 | 2 | 1 | 1 | 0 | 1 | 5 | 11 | 7 | -13 | -11.5 | .6 |
| C602 | 27 | 1542 | 99.1 | 827.8 | 490 | 177 | 5 | 2 | 39 | 61 | 395 | 538 | 1004 | 13 | -217 | -18.0 | .6 |
| C603 | 3 | 541 | 46.6 | 288.4 | 191 | 73 | 4 | 1 | 6 | 41 | 96 | 216 | 325 | 9 | -493 | -13.5 | .6 |
| C604 | 1 | 476 | 251.5 | 180.2 | 131 | 74 | 3 | 5 | 22 | 45 | 91 | 169 | 307 | 10 | -349 | -13.0 | .6 |
| C605 | 11 | 556 | 151.9 | 191.8 | 177 | 76 | 4 | 5 | 17 | 24 | 108 | 230 | 326 | 9 | -413 | -12.3 | .6 |

Table 4-15.  Project 3 Routine Parameters by Subsystem (Continued)

ROUTINE PARAMETERS FOR SUBSYSTEM D

| ROUT | PROBS | TS | LL E3 | IF E3 | BR | LS | AP | SYS | I/O | COMP | DATA | NEX | EX | TI | CCM | RAT | WK-LD |
|------|-------|------|--------|--------|-----|-----|-----|-----|-----|------|------|-----|------|-----|-------|-------|-------|
| D101 | 7  | 80   | 2.9    | 69.9   | 41  | 16  | 10 | 9  | 3  | 2   | 5   | 28  | 52   | 19 | -39   | -20.0 | 1.5 |
| D102 | 10 | 725  | 116.6  | 267.4  | 239 | 96  | 5  | 11 | 37 | 62  | 162 | 203 | 522  | 16 | -170  | -12.0 | 1.0 |
| D103 | 1  | 64   | 61.5   | 34.9   | 52  | 12  | 4  | 1  | 2  | 0   | 6   | 29  | 35   | 5  | -28   | -17.0 | 1.3 |
| D104 | 9  | 2428 | 134.1  | 466.9  | 649 | 186 | 14 | 6  | 29 | 249 | 739 | 737 | 1691 | 20 | -1368 | -17.0 | 1.4 |
| D105 | 3  | 454  | 37.9   | 151.1  | 115 | 50  | 11 | 11 | 19 | 40  | 91  | 182 | 272  | 22 | -172  | -17.0 | 1.3 |
| D106 | 6  | 412  | 791.4  | 142.3  | 105 | 61  | 7  | 19 | 54 | 24  | 100 | 111 | 301  | 26 | -237  | -13.0 | 1.2 |
| D107 | 0  | 368  | 40.7   | 189.5  | 89  | 47  | 1  | 3  | 35 | 24  | 74  | 137 | 231  | 4  | -199  | -13.0 | 1.2 |
| D108 | 13 | 1875 | 3934.0 | 859.1  | 535 | 243 | 8  | 20 | 87 | 120 | 511 | 566 | 1309 | 28 | -408  | -12.0 | 1.0 |
| D109 | 9  | 1188 | 130.8  | 398.5  | 293 | 138 | 13 | 9  | 4  | 118 | 305 | 441 | 747  | 17 | -267  | -17.0 | 1.3 |
| D110 | 8  | 125  | 26.3   | 49.4   | 65  | 17  | 16 | 9  | 4  | 1   | 9   | 43  | 82   | 25 | -43   | -20.0 | 1.5 |
| D111 | 5  | 392  | 295.9  | 379.8  | 116 | 57  | 8  | 8  | 29 | 19  | 80  | 137 | 255  | 17 | -193  | -13.0 | 1.2 |
| D112 | 16 | 762  | 336.5  | 3115.6 | 234 | 135 | 6  | 10 | 11 | 42  | 193 | 257 | 505  | 14 | -325  | -15.0 | 1.3 |
| D201 | 3  | 34   | 0.0    | 38.0   | 17  | 4   | 8  | 5  | 8  | 1   | 1   | 11  | 23   | 18 | -58   | -19.0 | 1.0 |
| D202 | 4  | 260  | 58.4   | 236.5  | 72  | 41  | 3  | 5  | 8  | 14  | 61  | 97  | 163  | 8  | -476  | -19.0 | 1.0 |
| D203 | 6  | 1092 | 1851.2 | 969.3  | 305 | 190 | 3  | 13 | 29 | 73  | 196 | 436 | 656  | 16 | -2095 | -19.0 | 1.0 |

Table 4-15. Project 3 Routine Parameters by Subsystem (Continued)

| ROUT | PROBS | TS | LL E3 | IF E3 | BR | LS | AP | SYS | I/O | COMP | DATA | NEX | EX | TI | CCM | RAT | WK-LD |
|------|-------|------|-------|-------|-----|-----|----|-----|-----|------|------|-----|-----|----|------|-------|-------|
|      |       |      |       |       |     |     |    | ROUTINE PARAMETERS FOR SUBSYSTEM E ||||||||||
| E101 | 2  | 60   | 17.5  | 11.6  | 19  | 7   | 4  | 7  | 4  | 0  | 9   | 25  | 35  | 11 | -44  | -19.0 | 1.5 |
| E102 | 10 | 699  | 142.7 | 390.5 | 222 | 109 | 6  | 13 | 41 | 42 | 128 | 244 | 455 | 19 | -890 | -12.0 | 1.0 |
| E103 | 2  | 96   | 2.9   | 72.9  | 96  | 15  | 26 | 3  | 2  | 0  | 14  | 28  | 68  | 29 | -53  | -19.0 | 1.5 |
| E104 | 9  | 610  | 120.0 | 305.4 | 225 | 91  | 13 | 6  | 26 | 6  | 138 | 227 | 383 | 15 | -210 | -12.0 | 1.0 |
| E105 | 13 | 921  | 433.1 | 667.8 | 310 | 153 | 6  | 9  | 50 | 40 | 201 | 314 | 607 | 15 | -231 | -15.0 | 1.2 |
| E106 | 24 | 1327 | 321.4 | 693.7 | 533 | 266 | 6  | 5  | 36 | 34 | 330 | 395 | 932 | 11 | -312 | -12.0 | 1.1 |
| E107 | 13 | 502  | 152.0 | 223.4 | 190 | 91  | 5  | 5  | 17 | 10 | 114 | 156 | 346 | 10 | -638 | -12.0 | 1.1 |
| E108 | 2  | 10   | 0.0   | 0.0   | 7   | 0   | 4  | 4  | 2  | 0  | 0   | 1   | 9   | 8  | -12  | -17.0 | 1.3 |
| E109 | 17 | 963  | 134.3 | 387.2 | 296 | 108 | 11 | 22 | 69 | 40 | 211 | 332 | 631 | 3  | -742 | -17.0 | 1.3 |
| E110 | 33 | 1378 | 462.9 | 987.8 | 587 | 221 | 9  | 17 | 36 | 28 | 358 | 480 | 898 | 26 | -326 | -12.0 | 1.0 |
| E111 | 0  | 15   | 2.9   | 5.8   | 7   | 3   | 1  |    | 0  | 0  | 1   | 6   | 9   | 2  | -10  | -19.0 | 1.5 |
| E112 | 7  | 345  | 75.8  | 131.0 | 114 | 45  | 8  | 1  | 36 | 6  | 85  | 96  | 249 | 16 | -235 | -17.0 | 1.5 |
| E113 | 1  | 4    | 0.0   | 0.0   | 3   | 0   | 1  | 1  | 0  | 0  | 0   | 1   | 3   | 2  | -23  | -17.0 | 1.3 |
| E114 | 1  | 40   | 0.0   | 5.8   | 9   | 2   | 1  | 4  | 1  | 0  | 11  | 19  | 21  | 5  | -40  | -17.0 | 1.3 |

Table 4-15. Project 3 Routine Parameters by Subsystem (Continued)

ROUTINE PARAMETERS FOR SUBSYSTEM F

| ROUT | PROBS | TS | LL E3 | IF E3 | BR | LS | AP | SYS | I/O | COMP | DATA | NEX | EX | TI | CCM | RAT | WK-LD |
|------|-------|------|-------|--------|-----|-----|----|-----|-----|------|------|-----|-----|----|-------|-------|-------|
| F101 | 0 | 294 | 17.5 | 127.7 | 95 | 44 | 1 | 12 | 26 | 13 | 76 | 81 | 213 | 13 | -260 | -13.0 | 1.0 |
| F102 | 4 | 153 | 5.8 | 66.9 | 58 | 21 | 1 | 6 | 2 | 0 | 28 | 67 | 86 | 7 | -163 | -13.8 | 1.0 |
| F103 | 0 | 231 | 12.5 | 81.8 | 83 | 30 | 1 | 13 | 23 | 2 | 34 | 90 | 141 | 14 | -130 | -11.0 | .9 |
| F201 | 0 | 454 | 512.5 | 555.9 | 108 | 68 | 0 | 12 | 15 | 19 | 61 | 226 | 228 | 12 | -140 | -10.0 | .7 |
| F202 | 0 | 558 | 72.7 | 443.9 | 151 | 78 | 0 | 8 | 8 | 64 | 113 | 206 | 352 | 9 | -239 | -10.0 | .7 |
| F203 | 8 | 53 | 5.8 | 11.6 | 15 | 6 | 0 | 0 | 0 | 5 | 9 | 22 | 31 | 0 | -24 | -10.0 | .8 |
| F204 | 0 | 597 | 397.9 | 158.4 | 174 | 85 | 2 | 0 | 46 | 11 | 114 | 229 | 358 | 22 | -398 | -12.8 | 1.0 |
| F205 | 8 | 40 | 11.6 | 5.8 | 15 | 6 | 0 | 0 | 0 | 7 | 6 | 17 | 23 | 0 | -90 | -10.0 | .7 |
| F301 | 3 | 723 | 90.2 | 250.1 | 211 | 87 | 5 | 19 | 20 | 21 | 155 | 294 | 429 | 24 | -422 | -6.0 | .8 |
| F302 | 0 | 19 | 5.8 | 0.0 | 5 | 2 | 1 | 8 | 1 | 3 | 4 | 4 | 15 | 8 | -21 | -6.0 | .8 |
| F303 | 1 | 121 | 14.5 | 31.9 | 36 | 16 | 0 | 11 | 0 | 29 | 15 | 36 | 85 | 12 | -63 | -13.5 | 1.0 |
| F304 | 0 | 64 | 2.9 | 14.6 | 12 | 3 | 0 | 7 | 0 | 15 | 14 | 22 | 42 | 7 | -15 | -14.0 | 1.2 |
| F305 | 0 | 140 | 5.8 | 32.0 | 43 | 10 | 2 | 6 | 0 | 44 | 12 | 39 | 101 | 6 | -33 | -12.0 | .9 |
| F306 | 1 | 378 | 0.0 | 209.8 | 111 | 42 | 2 | 11 | 0 | 54 | 74 | 139 | 239 | 13 | -145 | -16.0 | .8 |
| F307 | 0 | 96 | 17.5 | 20.3 | 33 | 10 | 1 | 3 | 0 | 26 | 13 | 21 | 75 | 5 | -24 | -10.0 | 1.0 |
| F308 | 3 | 152 | 2.9 | 152.0 | 48 | 17 | 5 | 8 | 2 | 17 | 20 | 64 | 88 | 9 | -73 | -10.0 | .9 |
| F309 | 10 | 84 | 5.8 | 90.5 | 28 | 15 | 3 | 1 | 0 | 1 | 27 | 26 | 58 | 6 | -49 | -15.0 | 1.0 |
| F401 | 1 | 703 | 20.3 | 270.3 | 190 | 83 | 3 | 7 | 4 | 112 | 110 | 292 | 421 | 10 | -258 | -15.0 | 1.1 |
| F402 | 4 | 138 | 14.5 | 5.8 | 23 | 7 | 2 | 12 | 0 | 21 | 31 | 58 | 90 | 14 | -33 | -13.2 | 1.1 |
| F403 | 4 | 92 | 8.7 | 17.4 | 24 | 9 | 4 | 10 | 0 | 8 | 16 | 41 | 51 | 14 | -25 | -13.7 | .9 |
| F404 | 1 | 90 | 0.0 | 43.7 | 18 | 9 | 3 | 3 | 0 | 16 | 22 | 34 | 56 | 6 | -88 | -13.6 | 1.0 |
| F405 | 3 | 79 | 0.0 | 23.2 | 31 | 9 | 0 | 0 | 0 | 6 | 10 | 31 | 48 | 0 | -5 | -6.0 | .8 |
| F406 | 0 | 63 | 2.9 | 14.5 | 10 | 5 | 0 | 5 | 2 | 11 | 17 | 23 | 40 | 5 | -2 | -18.5 | 1.5 |
| F407 | 3 | 301 | 143.3 | 78.4 | 64 | 37 | 4 | 13 | 1 | 44 | 45 | 133 | 168 | 17 | -131 | -13.4 | .8 |
| F408 | 0 | 89 | 2.9 | 26.1 | 27 | 10 | 3 | 8 | 0 | 15 | 11 | 34 | 55 | 11 | -22 | -6.0 | .9 |
| F409 | 1 | 129 | 5.8 | 43.5 | 58 | 17 | 0 | 2 | 6 | 12 | 13 | 54 | 75 | 2 | -134 | -13.0 | .9 |
| F410 | 0 | 98 | 5.8 | 40.8 | 15 | 10 | 1 | 6 | 0 | 8 | 13 | 44 | 44 | 3 | -56 | -6.0 | .9 |
| F411 | 2 | 71 | 11.6 | 98.9 | 15 | 3 | 1 | 2 | 0 | 18 | 1 | 37 | 34 | 7 | -9 | -12.0 | .9 |
| F412 | 1 | 189 | 11.6 | 52.2 | 63 | 29 | 0 | 6 | 9 | 16 | 33 | 73 | 116 | 2 | -164 | -13.0 | .9 |
| F413 | 2 | 135 | 17.4 | 78.9 | 36 | 19 | 2 | 6 | 0 | 13 | 20 | 56 | 79 | 8 | -207 | -13.0 | 1.3 |
| F501 | 1 | 128 | 0.0 | 43.7 | 25 | 15 | 2 | 2 | 7 | 7 | 35 | 48 | 30 | 4 | -102 | -15.0 | 1.1 |
| F502 | 2 | 406 | 79.0 | 43.7 | 27 | 9 | 0 | 5 | 23 | 5 | 15 | 58 | 70 | 5 | -4 | -8.0 | 1.1 |
| F503 | 8 | 406 | 79.0 | 1189.3 | 118 | 56 | 8 | 7 | 8 | 33 | 93 | 148 | 258 | 15 | -371 | -12.5 | 1.0 |
| F504 | 9 | 1077 | 93.1 | 1166.7 | 449 | 224 | 4 | 9 | 39 | 58 | 172 | 342 | 735 | 13 | -1192 | -13.5 | .9 |
| F505 | 3 | 900 | 84.7 | 1066.0 | 429 | 152 | 2 | 7 | 0 | 33 | 126 | 237 | 563 | 25 | -421 | -13.0 | .9 |
| F506 | 7 | 586 | 20.3 | 595.3 | 205 | 100 | 9 | 16 | 35 | 34 | 142 | 163 | 473 | 25 | -396 | -15.7 | 1.2 |
| F507 | 0 | 36 | 2.9 | 5.8 | 10 | 3 | 1 | 1 | 4 | 0 | 7 | 14 | 22 | 2 | -37 | -12.5 | 1.0 |

## Table 4-15. Project 3 Routine Parameters by Subsystem (Continued)

RCUTINE PARAMETERS FOR SUBSYSTEM 5

| PCUT | PROBS | TS | LL E3 | IF E3 | BR | LS | AP | SYS | I/O | COMP | DATA | NEX | EX | TI | CCM | RAT | WK-LC |
|------|-------|------|-------|---------|-----|-----|-----|-----|-----|------|------|-----|------|-----|-------|-----|-------|
| G101 | 2  | 500  | 87.5  | 89.9    | 150 | 69  | 18 | 5 | 13 | 24  | 117 | 191 | 319  | 23 | -450  | | |
| G102 | 5  | 513  | 23.2  | 1035.4  | 150 | 98  | 12 | 5 | 12 | 19  | 99  | 189 | 324  | 17 | -656  | | |
| G103 | 17 | 1098 | 212.9 | 10186.0 | 358 | 217 | 12 | 5 | 11 | 38  | 189 | 461 | 634  | 17 | -1050 | | |
| G104 | 1  | 31   | 5.8   | 11.6    | 10  | 6   | 0  | 0 | 0  | 2   | 9   | 8   | 23   | 0  | -49   | | |
| G105 | 2  | 133  | 17.4  | 72.8    | 45  | 22  | 11 | 1 | 0  | 5   | 23  | 54  | 79   | 12 | -186  | | |
| G106 | 7  | 746  | 587.4 | 1117.5  | 212 | 124 | 6  | 3 | 0  | 36  | 157 | 305 | 441  | 9  | -660  | | |
| G107 | 9  | 624  | 43.5  | 1850.6  | 152 | 113 | 8  | 5 | 3  | 18  | 153 | 255 | 359  | 13 | -578  | | |
| G108 | 12 | 1033 | 104.6 | 9219.0  | 290 | 180 | 16 | 5 | 21 | 50  | 216 | 441 | 552  | 21 | -1115 | | |
| G109 | 14 | 629  | 52.3  | 1501.9  | 207 | 102 | 12 | 2 | 6  | 15  | 186 | 206 | 423  | 14 | -552  | | |
| G110 | 33 | 1141 | 142.6 | 1298.0  | 372 | 166 | 15 | 7 | 0  | 47  | 219 | 462 | 679  | 22 | -1346 | | |
| G111 | 1  | 32   | 2.9   | 2.9     | 13  | 7   | 10 | 0 | 7  | 1   | 6   | 11  | 21   | 10 | -47   | | |
| G112 | 4  | 72   | 2.9   | 43.8    | 16  | 2   | 3  | 3 | 4  | 1   | 27  | 23  | 49   | 6  | -102  | | |
| G113 | 62 | 1849 | 383.2 | 9198.5  | 704 | 343 | 15 | 9 | 5  | 130 | 290 | 688 | 1161 | 24 | -2067 | | |
| G114 | 5  | 150  | 34.8  | 325.0   | 69  | 20  | 12 | 3 | 0  | 5   | 23  | 51  | 99   | 15 | -169  | | |
| G115 | 8  | 351  | 11.6  | 198.2   | 98  | 50  | 13 | 4 | 0  | 17  | 78  | 145 | 206  | 17 | -399  | | |
| G116 | 3  | 206  | 29.1  | 96.2    | 61  | 22  | 11 | 5 | 2  | 14  | 40  | 83  | 123  | 16 | -272  | | |
| G117 | 6  | 344  | 61.1  | 643.6   | 126 | 59  | 14 | 3 | 0  | 19  | 62  | 130 | 214  | 17 | -413  | | |
| G118 | 2  | 327  | 18.8  | 183.6   | 34  | 51  | 12 | 7 | 1  | 19  | 61  | 198 | 198  | 19 | -460  | | |
| G119 | 7  | 163  | 5.8   | 64.1    | 41  | 15  | 14 | 4 | 0  | 28  | 30  | 62  | 101  | 18 | -223  | | |
| G120 | 3  | 130  | 17.4  | 59.3    | 34  | 17  | 12 | 1 | 1  | 12  | 39  | 39  | 91   | 13 | -156  | | |
| G121 | 1  | 138  | 2.9   | 571.3   | 41  | 22  | 4  | 2 | 0  | 2   | 27  | 46  | 92   | 6  | -151  | | |
| G122 | 6  | 515  | 26.1  | 417.4   | 153 | 71  | 13 | 1 | 21 | 18  | 111 | 208 | 307  | 20 | -572  | | |
| G123 | 1  | 45   | 8.7   | 14.5    | 9   | 8   | 6  | 0 | 15 | 0   | 14  | 9   | 9    | 7  | -67   | | |
| G124 | 2  | 112  | 2.9   | 1014.3  | 24  | 20  | 2  | 7 | 0  | 13  | 23  | 50  | 36   | 2  | -146  | | |
| G125 | 1  | 216  | 20.3  | 40.6    | 58  | 21  | 12 | 0 | 7  | 4   | 60  | 80  | 62   | 19 | -234  | | |
| G126 | 7  | 250  | 108.2 | 535.8   | 74  | 37  | 9  | 4 | 6  | 12  | 47  | 104 | 136  | 13 | -295  | | |
| G127 | 3  | 188  | 34.9  | 69.8    | 58  | 23  | 11 | 4 | 11 | 5   | 53  | 56  | 132  | 15 | -182  | | |
| G128 | 5  | 440  | 34.9  | 409.4   | 119 | 47  | 8  | 6 | 5  | 21  | 108 | 178 | 262  | 14 | -439  | | |
| G129 | 5  | 209  | 8.7   | 213.3   | 60  | 28  | 6  | 5 | 5  | 11  | 54  | 76  | 133  | 11 | -176  | | |
| G130 | 0  | 276  | 8.7   | 433.0   | 68  | 37  | 5  | 4 | 4  | 18  | 64  | 119 | 157  | 9  | -327  | | |
| G131 | 3  | 323  | 52.4  | 183.5   | 110 | 50  | 4  | 3 | 2  | 13  | 55  | 131 | 192  | 7  | -285  | | |
| G201 | 0  | 140  | 213.9 | 770.7   | 81  | 30  | 5  | 3 | 1  | 0   | 36  | 47  | 93   | 8  | -93   | | |
| G202 | 0  | 79   | 2.9   | 40.8    | 21  | 10  | 0  | 1 | 0  | 1   | 22  | 33  | 46   | 8  | -66   | | |
| G203 | 0  | 66   | 0.0   | 0.0     | 10  | 0   | 0  | 0 | 0  | 0   | 7   | 49  | 17   | 1  | -127  | | |
| G204 | 1  | 147  | 0.0   | 105.3   | 23  | 9   | 0  | 8 | 11 | 3   | 50  | 60  | 87   | 8  | -159  | | |
| G205 | 0  | 131  | 5.8   | 90.4    | 47  | 18  | 6  | 7 | 1  | 0   | 36  | 42  | 89   | 7  | -136  | | |
| G206 | 7  | 268  | 5.8   | 790.9   | 99  | 36  | 3  | 6 | 1  | 24  | 59  | 89  | 179  | 12 | -166  | | |
| G207 | 6  | 178  | 5.8   | 154.6   | 76  | 29  | 1  | 4 | 9  | 5   | 33  | 59  | 119  | 7  | -105  | | |
| G208 | 0  | 136  | 20.4  | 61.1    | 37  | 19  | 0  | 0 | 0  | 7   | 27  | 66  | 70   | 1  | -200  | | |
| G209 | 0  | 67   | 0.0   | 46.7    | 16  | 5   | 3  | 1 | 0  | 2   | 5   | 39  | 28   | 1  | -135  | | |
| G210 | 0  | 47   | 0.0   | 23.3    | 17  | 10  | 0  | 0 | 0  | 7   | 3   | 25  | 22   | 2  | -80   | | |
| G211 | 7  | 273  | 11.6  | 764.4   | 77  | 40  | 3  | 2 | 0  | 23  | 41  | 128 | 145  | 9  | -251  | | |
| G212 | 0  | 217  | 0.0   | 230.3   | 82  | 43  | 0  | 6 | 0  | 1   | 46  | 97  | 130  | 16 | -233  | | |
| G213 | 1  | 221  | 5.8   | 298.1   | 59  | 36  | 0  | 9 | 5  | 1   | 56  | 92  | 129  | 9  | -172  | | |
| G214 | 0  | 30   | 0.0   | 2.9     | 9   | 1   | 1  | 0 | 0  | 2   | 4   | 15  | 15   | 1  | -48   | | |

Table 4-15. Project 3 Routine Parameters by Subsystem (Continued)

ROUTINE PARAMETERS FOR SUBSYSTEM H

| ROUT | PROBS | TS | LL E3 | IF E3 | BR | LS | AP | SYS | I/O | COMP | DATA | NEX | EX | TI | CCM | RAT | WK-LC |
|---|---|---|---|---|---|---|---|---|---|---|---|---|---|---|---|---|---|
| H1C1 | 1 | 553 | 140.4 | 6834.1 | 177 | 77 | 7 | 11 | 23 | 53 | 75 | 218 | 340 | 19 | -148 | | |
| H2O1 | 3 | 554 | 26.2 | 23959.1 | 184 | 107 | 18 | 6 | 5 | 6 | 108 | 235 | 309 | 24 | -515 | | |
| H2CO | 1 | 251 | 29.1 | 7492.2 | 49 | 32 | 4 | 0 | 0 | 13 | 57 | 95 | 125 | 4 | -203 | | |
| H2C3 | 0 | 723 | 32.3 | 38940.2 | 160 | 119 | 5 | 2 | 1 | 62 | 181 | 287 | 436 | 7 | -591 | | |
| H2O4 | 1 | 220 | 0.0 | 16225.6 | 74 | 36 | 7 | 6 | 0 | 1 | 63 | 81 | 139 | 13 | -204 | | |
| H2O5 | 1 | 791 | 102.3 | 13119.5 | 253 | 132 | 11 | 13 | 40 | 9 | 187 | 291 | 500 | 24 | -751 | | |
| H2O6 | 17 | 318 | 46.6 | 800.2 | 222 | 52 | 14 | 2 | 0 | 3 | 54 | 138 | 160 | 18 | -224 | | |
| H2O7 | 9 | 657 | 95.9 | 824.7 | 404 | 103 | 16 | 3 | 5 | 25 | 126 | 255 | 402 | 17 | -550 | | |
| H2O8 | 38 | 1236 | 46.4 | 503.5 | 474 | 196 | 16 | 3 | 0 | 93 | 251 | 472 | 704 | 19 | -979 | | |
| H2O9 | 2 | 218 | 5.8 | 148.8 | 379 | 25 | 6 | 3 | 5 | 10 | 46 | 75 | 143 | 19 | -107 | | |
| H210 | 34 | 1294 | 72.6 | 25841.7 | 319 | 229 | 8 | 13 | 15 | 87 | 268 | 516 | 778 | 21 | -1181 | | |
| H211 | 10 | 805 | 11.6 | 18249.3 | 222 | 130 | 10 | 6 | 22 | 29 | 162 | 291 | 514 | 16 | -377 | | |
| H212 | 18 | 651 | 37.9 | 2460.4 | 18 | 88 | 16 | 14 | 0 | 22 | 184 | 205 | 446 | 30 | -458 | | |
| H213 | 5 | 59 | 2.9 | 49.4 | 641 | 15 | 2 | 7 | 11 | 1 | 15 | 13 | 46 | 9 | -57 | | |
| H214 | 41 | 1612 | 37.8 | 25600.7 | 437 | 251 | 22 | 2 | 15 | 62 | 329 | 555 | 1057 | 4 | -1071 | | |
| H215 | 32 | 1005 | 20.3 | 2650.6 | 147 | 129 | 22 | 4 | 2 | 21 | 247 | 291 | 724 | 26 | -521 | | |
| H217 | 2 | 504 | 181.4 | 2800.9 | 36 | 88 | 7 | 5 | 5 | 14 | 92 | 232 | 272 | 15 | -318 | | |
| H218 | 2 | 115 | 2.9 | 31.9 | 91 | 12 | 6 | 5 | 4 | 4 | 27 | 43 | 72 | 11 | -131 | | |
| H219 | 15 | 446 | 128.1 | 2715.9 | 273 | 67 | 11 | 6 | 1 | 42 | 103 | 187 | 239 | 17 | -288 | | |
| H2.O | 17 | 953 | 131.1 | 16218.0 | 79 | 189 | 5 | 11 | 0 | 35 | 205 | 413 | 540 | 16 | -926 | | |
| H221 | 20 | 256 | 17.4 | 1186.7 | 273 | 45 | 5 | 2 | 27 | 25 | 49 | 97 | 159 | 7 | -231 | | |
| H222 | 17 | 633 | 23.2 | 600.8 | 216 | 112 | 3 | 18 | 0 | 15 | 139 | 228 | 405 | 21 | -543 | | |
| H224 | 6 | 174 | 0.0 | 1612.4 | 72 | 28 | 4 | 2 | 0 | 16 | 22 | 64 | 110 | 6 | -129 | | |
| H225 | 45 | 1226 | 26.1 | 8872.6 | 381 | 187 | 20 | 2 | 0 | 52 | 315 | 469 | 757 | 22 | -988 | | |
| H224 | 2 | 90 | 2.9 | 34.9 | 22 | 10 | 0 | 0 | 0 | 5 | 21 | 41 | 49 | 0 | -76 | | |
| H225 | 8 | 513 | 2.9 | 715.5 | 193 | 96 | 6 | 4 | 1 | 25 | 116 | 177 | 336 | 10 | -501 | | |
| H226 | 15 | 175 | 5.8 | 204.5 | 49 | 27 | 3 | 0 | 0 | 5 | 47 | 72 | 103 | 17 | -167 | | |
| H227 | 1 | 221 | 5.8 | 218.8 | 67 | 38 | 9 | 14 | 5 | 14 | 49 | 84 | 137 | 6 | -187 | | |
| H229 | 6 | 1127 | 55.2 | 11834.5 | 236 | 143 | 9 | 3 | 12 | 54 | 341 | 468 | 659 | 16 | -1029 | | |
| H2.O | 22 | 300 | 26.2 | 2244.7 | 129 | 46 | 23 | 3 | 0 | 6 | 51 | 108 | 192 | 26 | -231 | | |
| H230 | 58 | 1872 | 93.0 | 44476.0 | 736 | 344 | 16 | 4 | 0 | 112 | 299 | 699 | 1173 | 20 | -1583 | | |
| H231 | 12 | 1159 | 130.7 | 1253.5 | 402 | 187 | 9 | 13 | 15 | 46 | 265 | 395 | 764 | 22 | -939 | | |

where $Z_{ji}$ is the value of $Z_j$ for the ith routine and $a_j$ is the "influence coefficient" for the jth parameter. The observed number of software problems for the ith routine is denoted by $Y_i$ and the methodology for estimating the $a_j$ is to minimize the sum of squares of the deviations of the observed $\hat{Y}_i$ from their expected values, $Y_i$, i.e., minimize

$$Q = \sum_{i=1}^{K} (\hat{Y}_i - Y_i)^2 \qquad (2)$$

$$= \sum_{i=1}^{K} (\hat{Y}_i - \sum_{j=1}^{N} a_j Z_{ji})^2 \qquad (3)$$

The "influence coefficients" $a_j$ are constrained to be nonnegative:

$$a_j \geq 0 \qquad j = 1, 2, \ldots, N \qquad (4)$$

consequently the problem of evaluating the $a_j$ becomes a nonlinear programming problem with quadratic objective function Q given by (3) and inequality constraints (4).

Although, as pointed out in Section 4.3.3.2, the well-established statistical methods of regression analysis do not apply when inequality constraints are applied to the estimators,* the usual standard error may still be calculated and used as a measure of the closeness of fit of Y to a linear function of the specified parameters.

The standard error of Y estimates the square root of the residual variance of Y, which is a measure of the greatest closeness of fit that may be obtained when representing Y as a linear function of the parameters $Z_1, \ldots, Z_N$. Its formula is

$$\hat{\sigma} = [Q_{min}/(K-N')]^{\frac{1}{2}} \qquad (5)$$

where $Q_{min}$ is the value of Q in (3) obtained by substituting in the values $a_j$ which minimize Q, and N' is the number of nonzero $a_j$.

When $Y_i$ is assumed to be a linear function of only one parameter (say) $Z_k$, the solution is particularly simple, and we have

$$\hat{a}_k = \sum_{i=1}^{K} Y_i Z_{ki} / \sum_{i=1}^{K} Z_{ki}^2 \qquad (6)$$

---

*The basic reason is that the joint distribution of the estimators have positive probability over regions which have (potentially) irregular boundaries, and consequently the analysis would become much more intricate.

and
$$\hat{\sigma}_k = \left[ \sum_{i=1}^{K} (\hat{Y}_i - \hat{a}_k Z_{ki})^2 / (K-1) \right]^{\frac{1}{2}} \tag{7}$$

In the single parameter case, the estimator $\hat{a}_k$ is guaranteed to be positive (negative) since each $Y_i$ is nonnegative and all $Z_{ki}$ are positive (negative)*, so that ordinary regression methods apply.

The correlation coefficient $\hat{r}_k$ will be used as a measure of association of Y and the single parameter $Z_k$. The value of $\hat{r}_k^2$, sometimes called the "coefficient of determination," measures the fraction of the total variance of number of problems Y accounted for by the particular regression function shown. The correct formula for $\hat{r}_k$ when the regression line is forced through the origin is

$$\hat{r}_k = \hat{a}_k \left\{ \sum Z_{ki}^2 / \sum Y_i^2 \right\}^{\frac{1}{2}} \tag{8**}$$

(where all summations are from i = 1 to K). One must be careful in using other formulas for the correlation coefficient, as, for example

$$\hat{r}_k = \hat{a}_k \left\{ \frac{\sum Z_{ki}^2 - K(\sum Z_{ki})^2}{\sum Y_i^2 - K(\sum Y_i)^2} \right\}^{\frac{1}{2}} \tag{9}$$

which is not valid when the regression line is forced through the origin.***

During the course of the analysis the parameter subsets for the linear regression function were changed, as discussed below.

Initially all sixteen parameters were considered, even though some were expressible as linear combinations of, or were strongly related to, other parameters. For example, total number of statements equals the sum of the numbers of executable statements plus nonexecutable statements (TS = EX + NEX). Also, total number of interfaces equals the sum of the numbers of application program interfaces plus system program interfaces (TI = AP + SYS). Subsequently, a subset of ten parameters considered to be essentially unrelated were selected for re-analysis. These were $L_{LOOP}$ $L_{IF}$, BR, AP, SYS, I/O, COMP, DATA, NEX and COM. Although also independent the programmer-related parameters RAT and WK-LD were deleted from consideration at this point, since values for these parameters were not available for all routines. Thus, following the analyses using the full set of

---

*The parameters COM and RAT are given minus signs as noted previously.

**Searle, S.R., *Linear Models*, John Wiley and Sons, Inc., New York, 1971, pp. 95-98.

***Bowker, A. H. and Lieberman, G.J., Engineering Statistics, Prentice-Hall, Inc., 1959, p. 274.

parameters (Phase I) in which the influence coefficients were constrained
to be nonnegative (nonpositive for COM and RAT), a standard linear regression
analysis (Phase II) was performed on the independent parameters with no
constraints on the influence coefficients; however the regression plane
was forced through the origin.

Subsidiary analyses were also performed. These included a linear
regression analysis of number of problems as a function of any single
parameter, in order to compare the benefits of using several parameters
versus one parameter for predicting number of problems. Secondly, for those
of the ten independent parameters which appeared to be significant (in
having nonzero influence coefficients) the residuals, or differences between
the observed number of problems and the number calculated from the regression function, were plotted in order to evaluate the chosen model or determine, if possible, changes to the model (e.g., quadratic instead of linear).
Third, a scheme of smoothing out the single parameter linear regression by
systematically eliminating "outlier points", or routines that showed excessive
statistical deviations from the predicted number of problems, was applied.
In nearly all cases an explanation for the anomalous behavior could be
found based upon independent data, including an intimate knowledge of the
routine and circumstances surrounding its development and test. Fourth,
an analysis was performed of several types of software problems, each type
being considered as a function of the parameter considered to be the best
metric for the corresponding attribute (as labeled by type of problem).
Thus, for example, numbers of interface problems were considered to be
a linear function of total number of interfaces ($Z_{13}$); etc.

The subsequent sections present the data, analysis and discussion of
the results, as well as suggested hypotheses to be tested with new data.

### 4.3.4  Description of Regression Analyses Results (Phase I)

#### 4.3.4.1  Data Grouped by Subsystem

Table 4-16 shows the computed influence coefficients and the standard
error $\hat{\sigma}$, using the full set of parameters when the data are grouped by subsystem. As noted before all sixteen (16) parameters (the independent
variables) were used for evaluation of subsystems A, B, ..., F, but only
fourteen (14) were available for subsystems G and H. Table 4-17 shows the
influence coefficients and standard errors, $\hat{\sigma}$, for the cases when number
of software problems $Y_i$ is proportional to only one parameter, for each
parameter. Correlation coefficients (Eq. (8)) are shown only for those
parameters whose influence coefficients are non-zero in Table 4-16.

In all cases, except for subsystem E, it can be noted that the
standard error $\hat{\sigma}$ when the full set of parameters is considered (Table 4-16)
is less than every standard error when one parameter alone is assumed to
be the determiner of the number of software problems (Table 4-17). In other
words, except for subsystem E data, in no case does a single parameter allow
prediction of number of problems with more precision than does the combination of parameters for each software subsystem as given in Table 4-16.

Table **4-16.** Influence Coefficients for Software Reliability Parameters

| Subsystem | TS $z_1$ $a_1$ | LL $z_2$ $a_2$ | L-IF* $z_3$ $a_3$ | BR $z_4$ $a_4$ | LS $z_5$ $a_5$ | AP-CL $z_6$ $a_6$ | SYS-CL $z_7$ $a_7$ | I/O $z_8$ $a_8$ | COMP $z_9$ $a_9$ | DATA $z_{10}$ $a_{10}$ | NEX $z_{11}$ $a_{11}$ | EX $z_{12}$ $a_{12}$ | TI $z_{13}$ $a_{13}$ | COM $z_{14}$ $a_{14}$ | RAT $z_{15}$ $a_{15}$ | WK-LD $z_{16}$ $a_{16}$ | $Q_{min}$ | K | N' | $\theta$ |
|---|---|---|---|---|---|---|---|---|---|---|---|---|---|---|---|---|---|---|---|---|
| A | 0 | 0 | 1.481 | 0.0168 | 0 | 0.333 | 0 | 0.1259 | 0 | 0.02094 | 0 | 0 | 0.1235 | -0.0090 | -0.412 | 4.78 | 652.13 | 51 | 9 | 3.94 |
| B | 0 | 0 | 0.426 | 0 | 0.0642 | 0.470 | 0 | 0.1184 | 0.1506 | 0.01338 | 0 | 0 | 0 | -0.0283 | -0.472 | 8.46 | 80.428 | 16 | 9 | 3.39 |
| C | 0 | 0 | 0 | 0 | 0 | 0.239 | 0 | 0.0971 | 0.0840 | 0.06047 | 0 | 0 | 0 | -0.0118 | -0.201 | 2.69 | 984.26 | 39 | 7 | 5.55 |
| D | 0 | 0 | 0.338 | 0.0047 | 0.0151 | 0.227 | 0.0906 | 0 | 0 | 0 | 0 | 0 | 0.0648 | -0.0022 | 0 | 0 | 41.822 | 15 | 7 | 2.29 |
| E | 0 | 0 | 0 | 0.0203 | 0 | 0.0159 | 0.1194 | 0 | 0 | 0.01285 | 0.0257 | 0 | 0.0140 | -0.0042 | -1.569 | 19.9 | 82.070 | 14 | 9 | 4.05 |
| F | 0 | 0 | 0.677 | 0 | 0.0085 | 0.627 | 0 | 0 | 0.0301 | 0 | 0 | 0 | 0 | 0 | -0.0158 | 0 | 78.706 | 37 | 5 | 1.57 |
| G | 0 | 0 | 0 | 0.0580 | 0 | 0 | 0 | 0 | 0.2153 | 0 | 0 | 0 | 0 | -0.0072 | N/A | N/A | 655.190 | 45 | 3 | 3.95 |
| H | 0 | 0 | 0 | 0.00031 | 0.1958 | 0.441 | 0 | 0 | 0.2168 | 0 | 0 | 0.01715 | 0 | -0.0446 | N/A | N/A | 2003.42 | 32 | 6 | 8.78 |

*These coefficients multiply the actual values of L-IF, not L-IF x $10^3$, for a given routine.

Table 4-17. Single Variable Predictor Coefficients, Standard Errors, and Correlation Coefficients

| Subsystem | * | TS z₁ | LL** z₂ | L-1F** z₃ | BR z₄ | LS z₅ | AP-CL z₆ | SYS-CL z₇ | I/O z₈ | COMP z₉ | DATA z₁₀ | NEX z₁₁ | EX z₁₂ | TI z₁₃ | COM z₁₄ | RAT z₁₅ | WK-LD z₁₆ |
|---|---|---|---|---|---|---|---|---|---|---|---|---|---|---|---|---|---|
| A | a | 0.01237 | 0.00211 | 0.00777 | 0.03937 | 0.07812 | 0.9546 | 0.7188 | 0.3058 | 0.1591 | 0.04921 | 0.03506 | 0.01893 | 0.4704 | -0.01796 | -0.3303 | 4.154 |
|  | σ | 4.88 | 8.29 | 5.76 | 4.83 | 4.94 | 5.88 | 6.36 | 5.74 | 6.25 | 4.80 | 5.15 | 4.77 | 5.71 | 6.12 | 6.87 | 6.80 |
|  | ρ |  |  | 0.742 | 0.827 |  | **0.730** |  | 0.744 |  | 0.829 |  | 0.831 |  |  |  |  |
| B | a | 0.01982 | 0.1021 | 0.00744 | 0.05992 | 0.1503 | 1.0740 | 1.0860 | 0.3463 | 0.3850 | 0.08006 | 0.05908 | 0.02969 | 0.5530 | -0.03426 | -0.7831 | 10.21 |
|  | σ | 6.42 | 8.75 | 12.40 | 7.41 | 6.12 | 5.86 | 5.04 | 6.86 | 6.61 | 6.15 | 6.89 | 6.22 | 5.07 | 6.92 | 6.02 | 6.30 |
|  | ρ |  |  |  | 0.854 |  | 0.911 | 0.935 | 0.876 | 0.886 | 0.902 |  | 0.899 |  |  |  |  |
| C | a | 0.01845 | 0.05938 | 0.00234 | 0.06140 | 0.1226 | 1.624 | 1.407 | 0.4720 | 0.2187 | 0.07491 | 0.05397 | 0.02783 | 0.7963 | -0.02598 | -0.7364 | 10.49 |
|  | σ | 6.15 | 13.37 | 17.22 | 6.85 | 6.64 | 10.98 | 10.23 | 10.70 | 7.37 | 5.83 | 6.81 | 5.97 | 9.96 | 8.93 | 13.58 | 13.65 |
|  | ρ | 0.943 |  |  |  |  | 0.804 |  | 0.815 | 0.917 | 0.949 |  | 0.946 |  |  |  |  |
| D | a | 0.00659 | 0.00394 | 0.00680 | 0.02472 | 0.06081 | 0.7328 | 0.6267 | 0.1711 | 0.06725 | 0.02273 | 0.02040 | 0.00965 | 0.3782 | -0.00642 | -0.3893 | 5.413 |
|  | σ | 4.85 | 6.68 | 5.15 | 4.52 | 4.04 | 4.62 | 4.45 | 5.72 | 5.73 | 5.32 | 4.84 | 4.89 | 3.88 | 6.77 | 4.76 | 4.41 |
|  | ρ |  |  | 0.776 | 0.833 | 0.869 |  | 0.838 |  |  |  |  | 0.800 | 0.880 |  |  | 0.842 |
| E | a | 0.01999 | 0.06329 | 0.03298 | 0.05277 | 0.1179 | 0.9414 | 1.241 | 0.3813 | 0.5153 | 0.08457 | 0.06017 | 0.02981 | 0.6530 | -0.02696 | -0.5647 | 7.199 |
|  | σ | 3.35 | 5.98 | 4.26 | 2.94 | 4.28 | 11.38 | 8.17 | 7.88 | 8.49 | 2.94 | 3.17 | 3.56 | 8.79 | 9.92 | 11.38 | 11.20 |
|  | ρ |  |  |  | 0.980 |  | 0.634 | 0.832 |  |  | 0.980 | 0.976 | 0.970 |  |  |  |  |
| F | a | 0.00781 | 0.01278 | 0.00670 | 0.01991 | 0.0461 | 0.8725 | 0.2620 | 0.1585 | 0.08045 | 0.04289 | 0.02141 | 0.01203 | 0.2354 | -0.01041 | -0.1967 | 2.354 |
|  | σ | 2.18 | 3.28 | 2.57 | 2.42 | 2.31 | 1.87 | 2.83 | 2.77 | 2.56 | 2.15 | 2.22 | 2.19 | 2.44 | 2.23 | 2.67 | 2.74 |
|  | ρ | 0.796 |  | 0.700 | 0.740 |  | 0.854 |  |  | 0.702 | 0.801 |  | 0.794 |  |  |  |  |
| G | a | 0.02190 | 0.06298 | 0.00341 | 0.06851 | 0.1281 | 0.8128 | 1.256 | 0.6843 | 0.4170 | 0.1046 | 0.05460 | 0.03637 | 0.5793 | -0.02050 | –– | –– |
|  | σ | 5.17 | 9.12 | 8.12 | 4.23 | 5.05 | 9.27 | 9.97 | 10.87 | 4.35 | 6.47 | 5.58 | 4.95 | 9.08 | 4.92 |  |  |
|  | ρ |  |  |  | 0.935 |  |  |  |  | 0.931 |  |  | 0.910 |  | -0.911 |  |  |
| H | a | 0.02306 | 0.1398 | 0.00090 | 0.05666 | 0.1405 | 1.430 | 1.349 | 0.5789 | 0.4227 | 0.1012 | 0.06061 | 0.03694 | 0.8794 | -0.02709 | –– | –– |
|  | σ | 9.87 | 18.07 | 16.40 | 12.83 | 9.85 | 13.57 | 18.01 | 19.90 | 11.30 | 11.35 | 10.35 | 9.71 | 14.35 | 11.18 |  |  |
|  | ρ | 0.884 |  |  | 0.794 | 0.884 | 0.592 |  |  | 0.844 |  | 0.871 | 0.888 |  |  |  |  |

\* - Predictor Coefficient
σ - Standard Error
ρ - Correlation Coefficient
\*\* - Multiply values of $a$ by $10^3$

In the case of subsystem E, the least squares solution is suspect since only 14 observations are available. For the same reason the solutions for subsystems D and B should also be regarded with caution. The values are given in Table 4-16, nevertheless, since the iteration procedure to solve the constrained least squares problem converged. Possibly the reason for convergence is that if only the parameters for which nonzero coefficients were obtained had been considered, the solutions for the coefficients would have been the same as given in Table 4-16. Thus nine coefficients would have been estimated from 14 observations, which is adequate. However the fact that for subsystem E alone, five of the 16 parameters showed single variable standard errors of prediction less than that of the best linear prediction considering all of the variables, is sufficient justification to discard the solution for subsystem E.

It is apparent by inspection of Table 4-16 that different sets of parameters combine to give best linear predictors of numbers of software problems for the eight subsystems of Project 3. For example the best combination of parameters for subsystem G are the three parameters $Z_4$, $Z_9$, and $-Z_{14}$ (number of branch statements, number of computational statements, and number of comments).

The number of errors for subsystems A, B and E are best predicted by linear functions with nine (9) parameters as shown in Table 4-16, generally different sets of parameters for each subsystem.

On the other hand, the parameters $Z_1$ (Total Statements) and $Z_2$ (weighted loop nesting level parameters) are not contained in any of the sets of best predictors. In the case of $Z_1$, an explanation would be simply that the components making up the total number of statements, when separately weighted and then added together constitute a better predictor than an unweighted sum of such components. This is not to say that the parameter $Z_1$ is a bad predictor, because, as shown in Table 4-17, the standard error of predicted versus observed errors when treating $Z_1$ as a single predictor is smaller than most of the standard errors associated with other variables.

A similar explanation for the parameter $Z_2$ not appearing in any set of best predictors in Table 4-16 is not available. Table 4-17 also indicates by its associated standard errors being relatively large, that $Z_2$ simply may not be a good predictor for number of errors.

The parameters $Z_{11}$ (nonexecutable statements) and $Z_{12}$ (executable statements) each appear in only one set of predictors, possibly for the same reason as given for $Z_1$, and also, since $Z_{11}$ appears in the set of predictors for the (anomalous) subsystem E, this fact should be ignored.

At the other end of the spectrum, parameters $Z_6$ (application program interfaces) and $Z_{14}$ (comments) appear in all but one of the best predictor parameter sets, indicating a relatively higher predictive capability than other parameters. As single parameter predictors, however, Table 4-17 does not indicate that $Z_6$ or $Z_{14}$ have outstanding capabilities, their associated standard errors varying over a wide range of their rank order for each subsystem as discussed in the next paragraph.

From Table 4-17, the standard errors associated with each parameter may be ordered from the smallest to the largest, as shown in Table 4-18. As a tentative means of evaluating relative merit of single parameter predictors, if the lowest to the fourth lowest standard deviations are assigned scores of 4, 3, 2, 1 points respective, then the three highest scoring parameters are $Z_{10}$, $Z_{12}$, and $Z_4$, with 13, 13, and 10 points, respectively. These scores are not significantly higher than those of some other parameters, however. On the other hand, if one had to choose a single predictor for number of errors, it would probably be $Z_{12}$ (executable statements) as being the simplest to evaluate. However, as discussed in the next-to-last paragraph, $Z_{12}$ appeared in only one set of predictors (Subsystem H, Table 4-16) possibly because of its being better represented by a weighted sum of other parameters.

Table 4-18

| Subsystem | Parameters in Order of Standard Deviation of Prediction |
|---|---|
| A | 12, 10, 4, 1, 5, 11, 13, 8, 3, 6, 14, 9, 7, 16, 15, 2 |
| B | 7, 13, 6, 15, 5, 10, 12, 16, 1, 9, 8, 11, 14, 4, 2, 3 |
| C | 10, 12, 1, 5, 11, 4, 9, 14, 13, 7, 8, 6, 2, 15, 16, 3 |
| D | 13, 5, 16, 7, 4, 6, 15, 11, 1, 12, 3, 10, 8, 9, 2, 14 |
| E | 4, 10, 11, 1, 12, 3, 5, 2, 8, 7, 9, 13, 14, 16, 6, 15 |
| F | 6, 10, 1, 12, 11, 14, 5, 4, 13, 9, 3, 15, 16, 8, 7, 2 |
| G | 4, 9, 14, 12, 5, 1, 11, 10, 3, 13, 2, 6, 7, 8 |
| H | 12, 5, 1, 11, 14, 9, 10, 4, 6, 13, 3, 7, 2, 8 |

## Basis for Subsequent Analysis

The preceding discussion was based upon (1): consideration of sixteen measurable software parameters, and (2): the parameter data being grouped by subsystems. Since some of the sixteen (16) parameters were known to be functionally related to others, it was decided to select a subset of ten (10) parameters considered as unrelated, and use these as the basic data. Secondly, some additional meaningful groups of routines were defined by classifying them by principal function performed. These were Control (group label CON), Input Processing (INP), Output Processing (OUT). Primarily Computational (PC), Set up or initialization (SET), Utilities (UTL), and Post-Processing (PP). The purpose of defining these groupings is based upon the assumption that the same functions could be defined generally for other software systems and for which the routines belonging to them would show similar software problem activity.

An additional set of routine groupings was defined in terms of the original subsystems. These groups are labeled $A_1$, $A_2$, ..., $H_2$, where for example $A_1$ denotes the collection of routines labeled $A_{101}$, $A_{102}$, $A_{103}$, and $A_{104}$, as defined in Table 4-15. The parameters for the group labeled $A_1$ were derived by summing the values of the corresponding parameters for each of $A_{101}$, ..., $A_{104}$, and similarly for $A_2$, ..., $H_2$. This grouping is given the label "U" consisting of twenty-five (25) (super) routines or functions.

## Table 4-19. Project 3 Routine Parameters by Function

SUBROUTINE PARAMETERS FOR SUBSYSTEM U

| ROUT | PROBS | TS | LL ES | IF ES | BR | LS | AP | SYS | I/O | COMP | DATA | NEX | EX | TI | COM | RAT | WK-LD |
|---|---|---|---|---|---|---|---|---|---|---|---|---|---|---|---|---|---|
| A1 | 26 | 2508 | 5862 | 2848.1 | 892 | 375 | 31 | 21 | 26 | 113 | 698 | 747 | 1711 | 52 | -1774 | | |
| A2 | 67 | 3473 | 3662 | 3435.4 | 1074 | 510 | 54 | 47 | 163 | 113 | 919 | 1146 | 2327 | 101 | -2686 | | |
| A3 | 54 | 3663 | 2589 | 4327.7 | 1161 | 565 | 11 | 50 | 52 | 271 | 851 | 1351 | 2312 | 61 | -1157 | | |
| A4 | 41 | 2780 | 1024.1 | 1681.9 | 907 | 393 | 52 | 80 | 107 | 213 | 596 | 997 | 1789 | 132 | -1352 | | |
| A5 | 79 | 6276 | 10106.5 | 9566.4 | 1862 | 1072 | 90 | 116 | 277 | 491 | 1438 | 2091 | 4185 | 206 | -3484 | | |
| B1 | 105 | 3505 | 7980.0 | 1968.7 | 1073 | 914 | 86 | 83 | 219 | 199 | 872 | 1167 | 2638 | 169 | -2160 | | |
| B2 | 95 | 4153 | 2840.0 | 2131.1 | 1257 | 506 | 62 | 91 | 222 | 208 | 1108 | 1314 | 2839 | 173 | -2490 | | |
| C1 | 239 | 10719 | 1389.9 | 11598.1 | 3217 | 1574 | 116 | 108 | 225 | 948 | 2644 | 3492 | 7227 | 224 | -6670 | | |
| C2 | 69 | 5509 | 311.2 | 25852.4 | 1544 | 804 | 87 | 130 | 206 | 484 | 1371 | 1805 | 3704 | 215 | -5007 | | |
| C3 | 55 | 1335 | 209.9 | 938.9 | 573 | 296 | 20 | 30 | 121 | 124 | 467 | 611 | 1324 | 50 | -1085 | | |
| C4 | 27 | 1389 | 533.0 | 2273.7 | 293 | 164 | 11 | 19 | 60 | 154 | 315 | 541 | 848 | 30 | -768 | | |
| C5 | 50 | 4015 | 1423.1 | 2892.3 | 1198 | 508 | 35 | 53 | 127 | 215 | 909 | 1437 | 2578 | 88 | -2975 | | |
| C6 | 48 | 3131 | 549.1 | 1454.0 | 998 | 402 | 18 | 30 | 85 | 171 | 691 | 1158 | 1973 | 48 | -1465 | | |
| D1 | 87 | 3873 | 5708.6 | 6124.4 | 2533 | 1058 | 103 | 110 | 314 | 701 | 2275 | 2671 | 6002 | 213 | -3449 | | |
| D2 | 13 | 1386 | 1209.6 | 1243.8 | 394 | 235 | 14 | 28 | 41 | 88 | 258 | 544 | 842 | 42 | -2629 | | |
| E1 | 144 | 6970 | 1435.5 | 3862.9 | 2618 | 1111 | 101 | 105 | 320 | 206 | 1600 | 2324 | 4646 | 206 | -3766 | | |
| F1 | 4 | 676 | 26.2 | 276.4 | 236 | 95 | 13 | 31 | 51 | 15 | 138 | 238 | 440 | 34 | -553 | | |
| F2 | 8 | 1702 | 1030.5 | 1185.6 | 454 | 243 | 13 | 30 | 69 | 106 | 303 | 700 | 1002 | 43 | -791 | | |
| F3 | 8 | 1777 | 145.4 | 801.2 | 527 | 202 | 16 | 74 | 23 | 210 | 334 | 645 | 1132 | 90 | -845 | | |
| F4 | 30 | 2167 | 215.8 | 723.5 | 574 | 247 | 23 | 76 | 24 | 230 | 342 | 900 | 1267 | 99 | -1164 | | |
| F5 | 30 | 3161 | 297.4 | 4145.7 | 1263 | 559 | 26 | 47 | 116 | 170 | 590 | 1010 | 2151 | 73 | -2525 | | |
| G1 | 238 | 12784 | 2125.9 | 41099.8 | 3936 | 2047 | 306 | 120 | 168 | 517 | 2640 | 4963 | 7801 | 426 | -13924 | | |
| G2 | 22 | 2303 | 272.0 | 3379.5 | 654 | 283 | 24 | 66 | 28 | 85 | 425 | 631 | 1169 | 90 | -1971 | | |
| H1 | 1 | 558 | 140.4 | 6834.1 | 177 | 77 | 11 | 11 | 23 | 53 | 75 | 218 | 340 | 18 | -648 | | |
| H2 | 466 | 20128 | 1500.4 | 276435.5 | 7258 | 3264 | 289 | 195 | 197 | 919 | 4419 | 7577 | 12541 | 484 | -16156 | | |

It was also decided to perform a standard (no constraints) linear regression analysis after having deleted from consideration those parameters whose influence coefficients were found to be zero, for each subsystem and each functional grouping mentioned previously. The primary reasons for doing this were (1): to check whether the standard (unconstrained) linear regression analysis would yield regression coefficients for the unscreened parameters identical with those obtained using the constrained analysis; (2): for convenience, in that the standard linear regression computer programs compute correlation coefficients, as well as the multiple correlation coefficient (of number of problems with the linear regression function); and (3): to statistically determine the closeness of fit of the regression function to the number of software problems by testing the observed multiple correlation coefficient for significance.

### 4.3.5  Description of Regression Analysis Results (Phase II)

### 4.3.5.1  Special Function Groupings

Table 4-19 lists the parameters for each of the function groupings, labeled $A_1$, $A_2$, ..., $H_2$. Programmer-related parameters $Z_{15}$, $Z_{16}$, are not included in any of the groupings, since these data were not available for groupings $G_1$, $G_2$, $H_1$, $H_2$. Table 4-20 gives the computed influence coefficients for the best linear predictor for numbers of errors and the standard error of prediction using the constrained least squares analysis.

Table 4-21 gives the labels for routines adjudged to belong to selected groupings CON, INP, OUT, PC, SET, UTL, and PP. The parameter data are as previously given in Table 4-15. Since the selected group PP contains only two routines, no further analysis was performed for this particular group.

Table 4-22 presents the computed influence coefficients and standard errors for the selected groupings CON, INP, OUT, PC, SET and UTL, using the constrained least squares analysis with all sixteen parameters present (note that the above groupings did not include routines from subsystems G nor H, for which only fourteen parameters were available). Group INP contains only eight (8) routines, which apparently did not lead to any difficulty in the constrained least squares prediction process, and resulted in six (6) nonzero coefficients*. Group SET contains only sixteen routines, and resulted in four (4) nonzero coefficients. Possibly the results for INP should be disregarded, but the remaining results in Table 4-22, including those for SET, appear satisfactory. However, no further analysis was performed subsequently for the grouping INP.

---

*Possibly as long as there are fewer nonzero coefficients than number of routines, a solution will be produced by the nonlinear programming program used.

Table 4-20. Influence Coefficients for Software Reliability Parameters Derived from Function Groupings "U"

| Parameter | TS | LL | L-IF | BR | LS | AP |
|---|---|---|---|---|---|---|
| Coefficient | $\hat{a}_1$ | $\hat{a}_2$ | $\hat{a}_3$ | $\hat{a}_4$ | $\hat{a}_5$ | $\hat{a}_6$ |
| Value | 0 | 0 | 0.4520 | 0 | 0.09818 | 0.30866 |

| Parameter | SYS | I/O | COMP | DATA | NEX | EX | TI | COM |
|---|---|---|---|---|---|---|---|---|
| Coefficient | $\hat{a}_7$ | $\hat{a}_8$ | $\hat{a}_9$ | $\hat{a}_{10}$ | $\hat{a}_{11}$ | $\hat{a}_{12}$ | $\hat{a}_{13}$ | $\hat{a}_{14}$ |
| Value | 0 | 0 | 0 | 0.00706 | 0 | 0 | 0 | -0.00639 |

Standard Error $\hat{\sigma} \approx 26.8$

Example: For all the routines which together perform a given function, the quantities $Z_3$ (L-IF), $Z_5$ (Logic Statements), $Z_6$ (Application Interfaces), $Z_{10}$ (Data Handling Statements), and $Z_{14}$ (comments) are evaluated as $Z_3 = 25.852$, $Z_5 = 804$, $Z_6 = 87$, $Z_{10} = 1371$, $Z_{14} = 5007$.

The predicted total number of errors for all routines in the function would then be:

$$PROBS = (0.4520)(25.852) + (0.09818)(804) + (0.30866)(87) + (0.00706)(1371) - (0.00639)(5007)$$
$$= 11.7 + 78.9 + 26.9 + 9.7 - 32.0 \approx 96.$$

Table 4-21. Selected Function Groupings by Routine Number (Project 3)

| CON (Control) | INP (Input Processing) | OUT (Output Processing) | PC (Primarily Computational) | | SET (Set-up) | UTL (Utilities) | PP (Post Processing) |
|---|---|---|---|---|---|---|---|
| A101 | A102 | A201 | A203 | C206 | A209 | A301 | C106 |
| A103 | A104 | A405 | A204 | C207 | A404 | A302 | C604 |
| A202 | A313 | A510 | A205 | C208 | A501 | A303 | |
| A207 | B101 | A512 | A206 | C209 | A503 | A304 | |
| A401 | C502 | A513 | A208 | C210 | C602 | A305 | |
| A502 | F504 | A514 | A210 | C211 | D102 | A306 | |
| A505 | F505 | A515 | A402 | C302 | D202 | A307 | |
| A511 | F506 | A516 | A403 | C401 | E102 | A308 | |
| B201 | | B202 | A406 | C503 | E104 | A309 | |
| B103 | | B203 | A504 | C504 | E105 | A310 | |
| C101 | | B207 | A506 | C603 | E106 | A311 | |
| C112 | | B208 | A507 | D103 | E107 | A312 | |
| C201 | | B209 | A508 | D104 | E109 | A314 | |
| C202 | | C108 | A509 | D105 | F204 | A315 | |
| C212 | | C213 | B102 | D109 | F302 | D107 | |
| C301 | | C214 | B104 | D110 | F407 | F102 | |
| C501 | | C505 | B105 | D111 | | F202 | |
| C601 | | C605 | B106 | D112 | | F203 | |
| D101 | | D106 | B107 | D203 | | F205 | |
| D201 | | D108 | B204 | F301 | | F405 | |
| E101 | | F101 | B205 | F303 | | F406 | |
| E103 | | F103 | B206 | F304 | | F409 | |
| E108 | | F201 | C102 | F305 | | F410 | |
| E110 | | F502 | C103 | F306 | | F412 | |
| E111 | | | C104 | F307 | | F501 | |
| E112 | | | C105 | F308 | | F503 | |
| E113 | | | C107 | F401 | | F507 | |
| E114 | | | C109 | F402 | | | |
| F309 | | | C110 | F403 | | | |
| F404 | | | C111 | F408 | | | |
| | | | C203 | F411 | | | |
| | | | C204 | F413 | | | |
| | | | C205 | | | | |

Table 4-22. Influence Coefficients for Software Reliability Parameters of Selected Functional Groups of Routines

| Routine Grouping | TS $z_1$ $\hat{a}_1$ | LL $z_2$ $\hat{a}_2$ | L-IF $z_3$ $\hat{a}_3$ | BR $z_4$ $\hat{a}_4$ | LS $z_5$ $\hat{a}_5$ | AP $z_6$ $\hat{a}_6$ | SYS $z_7$ $\hat{a}_7$ | I/O $z_8$ $\hat{a}_8$ | COMP $z_9$ $\hat{a}_9$ | DATA $z_{10}$ $\hat{a}_{10}$ | NEX $z_{11}$ $\hat{a}_{11}$ | EX $z_{12}$ $\hat{a}_{12}$ | TI $z_{13}$ $\hat{a}_{13}$ | COM $z_{14}$ $\hat{a}_{14}$ | RAT $z_{15}$ $\hat{a}_{15}$ | WK-LD $z_{16}$ $\hat{a}_{16}$ | $Q_{min}$ | K | N' | $\hat{\sigma}$ |
|---|---|---|---|---|---|---|---|---|---|---|---|---|---|---|---|---|---|---|---|---|
| CON | 0 | 0 | 0 | 0.03947 | 0 | 0.05174 | 0.41511 | 0.02980 | 0 | 0 | 0 | 0 | 0.04601 | -0.01758 | -0.2292 | 3.496 | 384.5 | 30 | 8 | 4.18 |
| INP | 0 | 1.6242 | 0 | 0 | 0 | 0.44597 | 0 | 0.01927 | 0 | 0.00705 | 0.01497 | 0 | 0 | 0 | -0.1390 | 1.410 | 6.578 | 8 | 7 | 2.56 |
| OUT | 0 | 0 | 0 | 0 | 0 | 0.70652 | 0 | 0 | 0 | 0.02150 | 0 | 0 | 0 | 0 | 0 | 0.611 | 464.8 | 24 | 3 | 4.70 |
| PC | 0 | 0 | 0 | 0 | 0.10010 | 0.47544 | 0 | 0.11757 | 0.01678 | 0 | 0 | 0 | 0 | -0.00643 | -0.1512 | 0.0305 | 1693.3 | 65 | 7 | 5.40 |
| SET | 0 | 0 | 0 | 0 | 0 | 0.64906 | 0 | 0 | 0 | 0.06663 | 0 | 0 | 0 | -0.00256 | -0.08735 | 0 | 104.21 | 16 | 4 | 2.95 |
| UTL | 0 | 0 | 2.1511 | 0.02150 | 0.03211 | 0.64944 | 0.02026 | 0 | 0 | 0 | 0 | 0 | 0.01965 | -0.01428 | 0 | 0.327 | 56.925 | 27 | 8 | 1.73 |

Example: For a routine in grouping OUT (Output Processing) whose values of $Z_6$ (Application Interfaces), $Z_{10}$ (Data Handling Statements) and $Z_{16}$ (Programmer Work Load) were 9, 158 and 1.0 respectively, the predicted number of errors would be

$$\text{PROBS} = (0.70652)(9) + (0.02150)(158) + (0.611)(1.0)$$
$$= 10.4 = 11$$

## 4.3.5.2 Reduction to Ten Unrelated Parameters

Some of the sixteen original parameters are functionally related, as mentioned previously. Consequently the ten parameters $L_{LOOP}$, $L_{IF}$, BR, AP, SYS, I/O, COMP, DATA, NEX, and COM were selected for further analysis. Another reason for selecting a nonfunctionally related subset of parameters at this point is that standard linear regression analyses (no constraints) will not work when two or more of the controllable or "independent" variables are linearly dependent.*

## 4.3.5.3 Analysis Using the Ten Parameters (Reduced Set)

At this point the analysis on the data Project 3 was restarted using the ten (hypothesized) independent parameters, referred to as the "reduced" set of parameters. Table 4-23 presents the computed influence coefficients and the standard error using the reduced set of parameters for subsystems A - H, Functions U, and special grouping CON, ..., UTL, defined previously, and using the constrained least squares method. The values of the influence coefficients and standard errors can be compared directly with those of Tables 4-16, 4-19 and 4-22, respectively (the latter tables give the results of the constrained least squares regression analysis for the full set of parameters).

As can be seen by comparison of the results for the reduced set of parameters with those for the full set of parameters, the coefficients showed a similar behavior, being either simultaneously zero in nearly all cases, or nearly of the same magnitude when nonzero. For example, subsystem B shows a nonzero coefficient for L-IF ($\hat{a}_3 = 0.426$) when the full set of parameters are considered, but $\hat{a}_3 = 0$ for the reduced set of parameters. Also for subsystem B and F, Functions U, and groupings C and SET, $\hat{a}_4$ shows the opposite behavior, being zero for the full set but positive for the reduced set. The latter is also true for $\hat{a}_{11}$ in subsystem H, and $\hat{a}_{10}$ in Group PC. These differences are generally not significant however, since when $\hat{a}_4$ is positive it is still fairly small and its contribution to the total number of problems (when multiplied by the number of branches) is not significant. For $\hat{a}_3$, the value of the parameter $Z_3$ is often very small, so again $\hat{a}_3 Z_3$ does not significantly contribute to the total number of problems. Since $\hat{a}_{10}$ for the reduced set of parameters for PC is relatively small, the same statement can be made in that case. For subsystem H, the discrepancy between $\hat{a}_{11}$ for the reduced set and for the full set appears more significant, however. When the standard regression analysis is discussed, the statistical significances of the influence coefficients are included, which further aids in screening out the less important parameters from the prediction.

---

*
The matrix of the controllable variables has a vanishing determinant and therefore cannot be inverted in attempting to solve for the coefficients.

### 4.3.5.4  Analysis of a Further Reduced Set of Parameters

A standard linear regression analysis was applied to a set of parameters
of each subsystem or grouping whose influence coefficients were not zero
from the previous analysis (these parameters can be directly read in
Table 4-23 as those with nonzero values of $\hat{a}_k$).  The analysis was nonstandard
in the following respect, however:  the regression plane was forced to go
through the origin.  The main reason for this choice of a linear regression
model without a constant term is to eliminate    nstructural, or undefined
parameters from the model.  This is based upon ρerhaps optimistic assumptions
that the linear regression model and the selected parameters are adequate
for predicting numbers of problems.  To some extent, as discussed in Section
4.3.5.6, this assumption has been examined by plotting residuals (observed
minus predicted numbers of problems) against the essential parameters.

Table 4-24 summarizes the results of the standard regression analysis.
Presented in the table is the standard error of the regression function for
the "further" reduced set of parameters for each grouping of routines A, ...,
H, U, and CON, ..., UTL, defined previously.  Since the standard errors have
the dimension "number of problems", they should not be compared for different
groupings of routines, but only for different choices of the set of parameters used as predictors for a given grouping.  The multiple correlation
coefficient, r, is then given and in all cases was found highly significant;
i.e., nonzero with high probability, based upon the usual normal distribution
assumptions.  The values of r range from slightly below 0.9 to 0.983, indicating that from about 80 to 96 percent ($100\ r^2$ %) of the variance of number
of problems is accounted for by the selected linear regression function.

### 4.3.5.5  Development of a Minimized Set of Parameters

The particular technique used for standard linear regression analysis
also attempts to find a minimized set of parameters such that the multiple
correlation coefficient (standard error) is not reduced (increased) significantly.  This minimization process results in the "minimized set of
parameters" whose subscripts are shown in Table 4-24, as well as the
regression coefficients $\hat{a}_k$ for each minimized set for each grouping of
routines, the new (slightly increased) standard error, and the new (slightly
reduced) multiple correlation coefficient.

In general, the analysis results showed that the alleged independent
parameters were essentially independent by their correlation coefficients
being ≈0.75 or less.  However, parameters $Z_4$ (number of branches) and $Z_{10}$
(number of data handling statements) when in the analyzed set, almost
consistently showed a high correlation coefficient (0.92 - 0.99).  This is
also reflected in the process to select a minimized set of parameters, in
that in no case do parameters $Z_4$, $Z_{10}$ occur together in a minimized set
(refer to Table 4-24).  Another way of interpreting these observations is
that if one of the parameters $Z_4$ or $Z_{10}$ is present in a set of predictors
for numbers of problems, then the other will add no new information, or in
other words will not reduce the standard error of regression, if included;
in fact, in some cases, the inclusion of both $Z_4$ and $Z_{10}$ could even lower
the prediction capability of the regression function, as compared to each
parameter being used separately.  Further, the high correlation will also
affect the appearance of residual plots, as noted in Section 4.3.5.6.

Table 4-23.  Influence Coefficients for Software Reliability Parameters (Reduced Set)

| Grouping | Coefficient | LL $z_2$ | L-IF $z_3$ | BR $z_4$ | AP $z_6$ | SYS $z_7$ | I/O $z_8$ | COMP $z_9$ | DATA $z_{10}$ | NEX $z_{11}$ | COM $z_{14}$ | C | K | N' | $\hat{\sigma}$ |
|---|---|---|---|---|---|---|---|---|---|---|---|---|---|---|---|
| A | $\hat{a}_k$ | 0 | 1.848 | 0.0082 | 0.356 | 0 | 0.111 | 0 | 0.0267 | 0 | -0.0088 | 722.4 | 51 | 6 | 4.01 |
| B | $\hat{a}_k$ | 0 | 0 | 0.0094 | 0.663 | 0.242 | 0.107 | 0.134 | 0.0230 | 0 | -0.0316 | 100.5 | 16 | 7 | 3.34 |
| C | $\hat{a}_k$ | 0 | 0 | 0 | 0.242 | 0 | 0.094 | 0.038 | 0.0588 | 0 | -0.0118 | 995.5 | 39 | 5 | 5.41 |
| D | $\hat{a}_k$ | 0 | 3.662 | 0.0094 | 0.265 | 0.194 | 0 | 0 | 0 | 0 | -0.0020 | 42.9 | 15 | 5 | 2.07 |
| E | $\hat{a}_k$ | 0 | 0 | 0.0096 | 0.093 | 0.030 | 0 | 0 | 0.0496 | 0.116 | -0.0006 | 96.6 | 14 | 6 | 3.48 |
| F | $\hat{a}_k$ | 0 | 1.140 | 0.0019 | 0.616 | 0 | 0 | 0.029 | 0 | 0 | 0 | 80.2 | 37 | 4 | 1.56 |
| G | $\hat{a}_k$ | 0 | 0 | 0.0580 | 0 | 0 | 0 | 0.215 | 0 | 0 | -0.0072 | 655.2 | 45 | 3 | 3.96 |
| H | $\hat{a}_k$ | 0 | 0 | 0.0099 | 0.396 | 0 | 0 | 0.187 | 0 | 0.095 | -0.0315 | 2594.1 | 32 | 5 | 9.80 |
| U | $\hat{a}_k$ | 0 | 0.387 | 0.0314 | 0.257 | 0 | 0 | 0 | 0.0179 | 0 | -0.00015 | 13633. | 25 | 5 | 26.1 |
| CON | $\hat{a}_k$ | 0 | 0 | 0.0405 | 0.171 | 0.430 | 0.036 | 0 | 0 | 0 | -0.0186 | 400.8 | 30 | 5 | 4.00 |
| OUT | $\hat{a}_k$ | 0 | 0 | 0 | 0.780 | 0 | 0 | 0 | 0.0213 | 0 | 0 | 467.6 | 24 | 2 | 4.56 |
| PC | $\hat{a}_k$ | 0 | 0 | 0.0240 | 0.412 | 0 | 0.146 | 0.016 | 0.0092 | 0 | -0.0026 | 2370.2 | 65 | 6 | 6.34 |
| SET | $\hat{a}_k$ | 0 | 0 | 0.0010 | 0.592 | 0 | 0 | 0 | 0.0625 | 0 | -0.0036 | 110.5 | 16 | 4 | 3.04 |
| UTL | $\hat{a}_k$ | 0 | 2.090 | 0.0374 | 0.628 | 0.102 | 0 | 0 | 0 | 0 | -0.0133 | 59.3 | 27 | 5 | 1.64 |

### Table 4-24. Summary of Standard Linear Regression Analysis (Regression Plane Forced Through Origin)

| Routine Grouping | Further Reduced Parameter Set Z( ) | Standard Error of Regression | Multiple Correlation Coefficient | Minimized Set of Parameters Z( ) | Statistics for Minimized Set of Parameters | | |
|---|---|---|---|---|---|---|---|
| | | | | | Regression Coefficients | Standard Error of Regression | Multiple Correlation Coefficient |
| A | 3,4,6,8,10,14 | 3.76 | 0.897 | 6,10 | $\hat{a}_6 = 0.438$<br>$\hat{a}_{10} = 0.0364$ | 4.23 | 0.868 |
| B | 4,6,7,8,9,10,14 | 2.51 | 0.983 | 6,9 | $\hat{a}_6 = 0.666$<br>$\hat{a}_9 = 0.202$ | 3.75 | 0.962 |
| C | 6,8,9,10,14 | 5.05 | 0.961 | 10 | $\hat{a}_{10} = 0.0749$ | 5.75 | 0.949 |
| D | 3,4,6,7,14 | 1.69 | 0.977 | 3,6 | $\hat{a}_3 = 0.00458$<br>$\hat{a}_6 = 0.538$ | 2.44 | 0.951 |
| E | 4,6,7,10,11,14 | 2.63 | 0.983 | 10 | $\hat{a}_{10} = 0.0846$ | 2.83 | 0.980 |
| F | 3,4,6,9 | 1.47 | 0.910 | 6,9 | $\hat{a}_6 = 0.685$<br>$\hat{a}_9 = 0.0389$ | 1.53 | 0.902 |
| G | 4,9,14 | 3.82 | 0.946 | 4,9 | $\hat{a}_4 = 0.0380$<br>$\hat{a}_9 = 0.196$ | 3.88 | 0.944 |
| H | 4,6,9,11,14 | 9.00 | 0.901 | 6,9 | $\hat{a}_6 = 0.669$<br>$\hat{a}_9 = 0.301$ | 9.68 | 0.885 |
| U | 3,4,6,10,14 | 23.35 | 0.983 | 4 | $\hat{a}_4 = 0.0598$ | 26.03 | 0.979 |
| CON | 4,6,7,8,14 | 3.66 | 0.896 | 4 | $\hat{a}_4 = 0.0460$ | 4.38 | 0.847 |
| OUT | 6,10 | 4.41 | 0.896 | 6,10 | $\hat{a}_6 = 0.780$<br>$\hat{a}_{10} = 0.0215$ | 4.41 | 0.896 |
| PC | 4,6,8,9,10,14 | 6.04 | 0.914 | 4,6,8 | $\hat{a}_4 = 0.0299$<br>$\hat{a}_6 = 0.458$<br>$\hat{a}_8 = 0.130$ | 6.10 | 0.912 |
| SET | 4,6,10,14 | 2.63 | 0.982 | 6,10 | $\hat{a}_6 = 0.531$<br>$\hat{a}_{10} = 0.0600$ | 2.80 | 0.980 |
| UTL | 3,4,6,7,14 | 1.48 | 0.965 | 4,6,14 | $\hat{a}_4 = 0.0506$<br>$\hat{a}_6 = 0.974$<br>$\hat{a}_{14} = -0.0169$ | 1.53 | 0.963 |

## 4.3.5.6  Residuals Analysis

The analysis used also tests the residuals (observed minus predicted number of problems) for normality, which if not rejected, justifies the significance tests on the correlations obtained in the analysis.  On the other hand, were the normality hypothesis to be rejected, it could indicate that the linear model was in some sense not suitable.  In all cases, except for subsystem A, the hypothesis of normality was not rejected.  Figures 4-26 through 4-29 show plots of residuals for subsystem A, versus $Z_4$ (number of branches), $Z_6$ (number of application program interfaces), $Z_8$ (number of I/O statements, and $Z_{10}$ (number of data handling statements), respectively. In general, the residuals appear to increase in absolute value as the parameter increases (fan out from the origin), implying that the variance of number of problems increases with the parameter, rather than remains constant (as is assumed in standard regression analysis).  On the other hand, as will be shown later, nearly all of the high positive residuals (observed minus predicted) represent "outliers", in that the corresponding routine exhibits anomalous statistical behavior for many of the parameters including these particular ones.  However, the large negative residuals, in general, are not outliers.  Consequently, if departure from a constant is assumed, the residuals may be showing a decrease to negative values for increasing values of the parameter, indicative of high correlation between two or more of the parameters.*

These conclusions are tentative however, and based upon a very limited examination of residual plots, and due to lack of time and resources, this part of the investigation could not be pursued further.

The results of the standard linear regression analysis can be summarized briefly by stating that a certain small number of parameters may be used to effectively predict numbers of software problems occurring in development. These parameters are $Z_4$ (number of branches); $Z_6$ (number of application program interfaces); $Z_9$ (number of computational statements); $Z_{10}$ (number of data handling statements; although since $Z_4$, $Z_{10}$ nearly always are highly correlated, only one should be used).

## 4.3.5.7  Evaluation of Internal and External Complexity Metrics

Since both $Z_4$ and $Z_6$ appear to be good predictors jointly, it was decided to determine their overall performance by constructing a linear regression analysis with just these two parameters, being evaluated for each subsystem A, ..., H.  Furthermore it is intriguing to hypothesize that total numbers of problems can best be predicted (or explained) by a combination of routine-internal complexity, as measured by number of branches, and routine-external complexity, as measured by number of application program (other routine) interfaces with the given routine.

Table 4-25 presents the numbers of problems for each subsystem, $\overline{Y}$, total number of branches, $\overline{Z}_4$, and total number of application program interfaces, $\overline{Z}_6$, each obtained by summing these quantities over all of the routines in the subsystem.  Table 4-26 summarizes the regression coefficients, their standard deviations, the multiple correlation coefficient and the standard error of regression.

---
*Private communication by N. R. Garner of TRW.

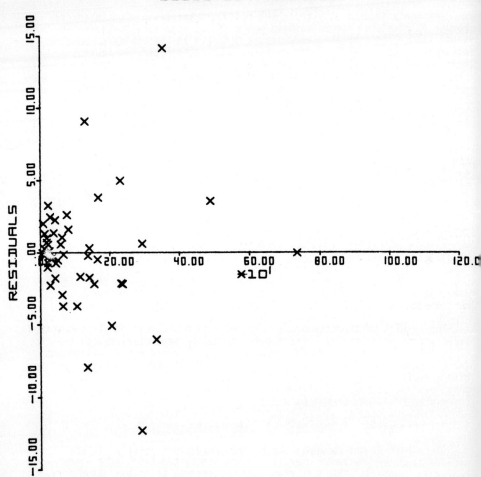

Figure 4-26. Residuals vs. Number of Branches (Subsystem A)

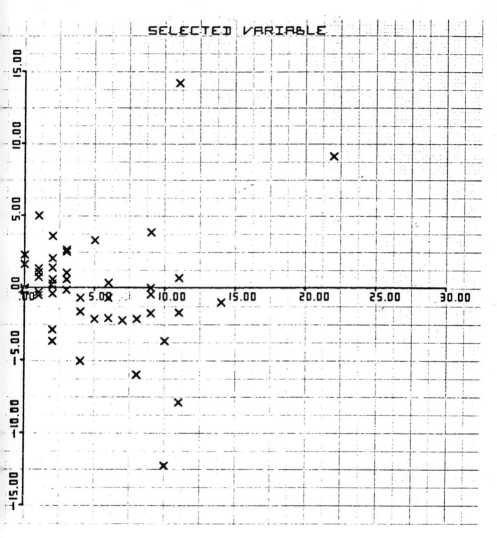

Figure 4-27.  Residuals vs. Number of Application Program
Interfaces (Subsystem A)

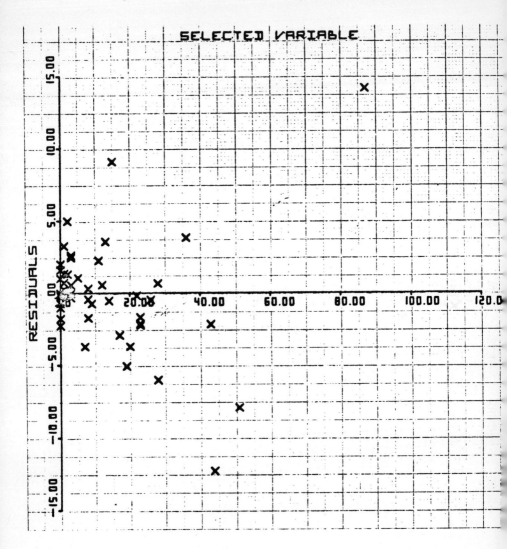

Figure 4-28. Residuals vs. Number of I/O Statements
(Subsystem A)

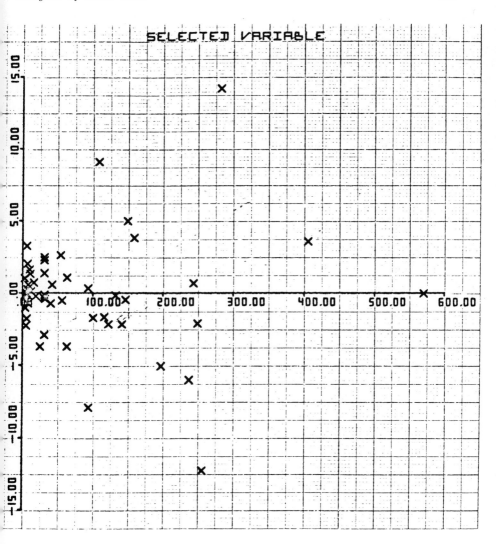

Figure 4-29. Residuals vs. Number of Data Handling Statements (Subsystem A)

Table 4-25. Summed Data for Project 3 Subsystems

| Subsystem | $\bar{Y}$ | $\bar{Z}_4$ | $\bar{Z}_6$ |
|-----------|-----------|-------------|-------------|
| A | 267 | 5814 | 238 |
| B | 200 | 2330 | 168 |
| C | 488 | 7823 | 287 |
| D | 100 | 2926 | 117 |
| E | 144 | 2618 | 101 |
| F | 80 | 3054 | 81 |
| G | 260 | 4590 | 330 |
| H | 467 | 7434 | 296 |

Table 4-26. Statistical Data Summary for Parameters $Z_4$ and $Z_6$

| Parameter | Regression Coefficient | Standard Deviation | Standard Error | Multiple Correlation Coefficient |
|-----------|------------------------|--------------------|----------------|----------------------------------|
| $\bar{Z}_4$ | $\hat{a}_4'' = 0.0454$ | $\hat{\sigma}_4'' = 0.0144$ | | |
| $\bar{Z}_6$ | $\hat{a}_6'' = 0.254$ | $\hat{\sigma}_6'' = 0.315$ | 54.4 | 0.982 |

It will be noted that the standard deviation $\hat{\sigma}_6'' = 0.315$ is large compared to $\hat{a}_6''$, and in fact the analysis indicates that $\hat{a}_6''$ is not significantly different from zero. Consequently, the results of the preceding analysis do not show that *both* internal and external interfaces are important in predicting or determining numbers of problems. Actually, the minimization feature of the regression analysis computer program used eliminates $Z_6$, resulting in a negligible increase in the standard error to 56.6 and decrease in r to 0.981. The overall "grand-average" regression or influence coefficient of $Z_4$ becomes $\hat{a}_4''' = 0.05665$.

Nevertheless if both $Z_4$ and $Z_6$ are *a priori* hypothesized important, their relative influence can be estimated by calculating the numbers of problems contributed by each in the two variable linear regression. Thus if $N_4$, $N_6$ are numbers of problems contributed by each parameter, respectively, then

$$\bar{\bar{N}}_4 = \hat{a}_4'' \bar{\bar{Z}}_4$$

$$= (0.0454) (4573.625) = 208$$

$$\bar{\bar{N}}_6 = \hat{a}_6'' \bar{\bar{Z}}_6$$

$$= (0.254) (202.25) = 51$$

| Routine ID | Parameter Group Where Outlier Appeared* | | | | | | | Difficulty Ratings | | | | | | | |
| | $Z_3$ Weighted IF | $Z_4$ No. of Branches | $Z_6$ Application I/F | $Z_7$ System I/F | $Z_8$ No. of I/O Stmts | $Z_9$ Comp. Stmts | $Z_{10}$ Data Hand Stmts | Design | Code | Implementation | Checkout | Documentation | Summed Routine Difficulty | Average Difficulty of Subsystem Outliers | Factors Contributing to Difficulty Ratings |
|---|---|---|---|---|---|---|---|---|---|---|---|---|---|---|---|
| A104 | | | A,PC | | A | PC | A | 3 | 3 | 3 | 3 | 3 | 15 | 12.0 | Complex logic |
| A206 | A | A | UTL | UTL | | | | 2 | 3 | 3 | 3 | 3 | 14 | | Interface with routine A308 |
| A302 | | | A,UTL | | A | | A | 1 | 1 | 2 | 2 | 1 | 7 | | Interface with routine A308 |
| A308 | UTL | | UTL | UTL | A | | | 3 | 3 | 3 | 3 | 3 | 15 | | Changing requirements, complex logic |
| A309 | UTL | | | | | | | 2 | 2 | 2 | 3 | 2 | 11 | | Late design reviews |
| A404 | A | A,SET | | | | | A | 2 | 1 | 2 | 3 | 2 | 10 | | Interfacing software not available (late) |
| A514 | A | A | | | | | A | 2 | 2 | 3 | 3 | 2 | 12 | | |
| B102 | | | PC | | | PC | | 3 | 2 | 3 | 3 | 2 | 13 | 13.0 | Poor requirements, core load problems |
| C102 | | | PC | | C,PC | | | 3 | 2 | 3 | 3 | 3 | 14 | 13.2 | Changing requirements, complex logic and interfaces, core load problems |
| C104 | | | PC | | PC | | | 3 | 2 | 3 | 3 | 3 | 14 | | Complex logic, core load problems |
| C105 | | | PC | | C,PC | | | 3 | 2 | 3 | 2 | 2 | 12 | | Changing requirements, complex interfaces |
| C302 | | | PC | | | PC | | 3 | 2 | 3 | 2 | 3 | 13 | | Complex interfaces |
| C401 | | | PC | | | | | 3 | 2 | 2 | 3 | 2 | 12 | | Complex logic |
| C503 | | | PC | | | | | 3 | 2 | 3 | 3 | 3 | 14 | | Changing requirements |
| D104 | PC | | PC | | | PC | PC | 3 | 3 | 3 | 3 | 2 | 14 | 13.5 | Easily modularized computational code |
| D112 | | | | | | | | 3 | 3 | 2 | 2 | 3 | 13 | | Complex logic, multiple designers |
| E110 | | | CON | CON | CON | | | 3 | 2 | 3 | 1 | 2 | 11 | 11.0 | Changing requirements, complex man/machine interface |
| F102 | | | F | | | | | 2 | 2 | 3 | 2 | 2 | 11 | 13.0 | Complex interfaces |
| F202 | F | UTL | | | | | | 2 | 3 | 2 | 3 | 2 | 12 | | Changing requirements, complex interfaces |
| F204 | | | | | | | | 3 | 2 | 3 | 2 | 2 | 12 | | Complex logic and interfaces |
| F401 | | | F | | | | | 3 | 3 | 3 | 3 | 3 | 15 | | Changing requirements, complex logic and interfaces |
| F504 | | | F | | | | | 3 | 3 | 3 | 3 | 3 | 15 | | Changing requirements, complex logic and interfaces |
| G110 | G | G | | | | G | | 3 | 2 | 3 | 3 | 2 | 13 | 13.5 | Complex logic and interfaces |
| G113 | G | G | | | | | | 3 | 3 | 3 | 3 | 2 | 14 | | Complex logic and interfaces |
| | | | | | | | Average Difficulty of All Outliers | | | | | | 12.8 | | |

*Each entry in this part of the table represents the routine group in which the outlier routine was found.

Table 4-27.

Analysis of Project 3 Outlier Routines

where $\bar{\bar{Z}}_4$, $\bar{\bar{Z}}_6$ are the respective means of the $\bar{Z}_4$, $\bar{Z}_6$ given in Table 4-25. These results would indicate that $Z_4$ (number of branches) contributes about a ratio of 4:1 of software problems as does $Z_6$ (number of applications program interfaces).

### 4.3.5.8 Single Variable Linear Regression Analysis

Although number of problems can nearly always be predicted with smaller standard error when two or more parameters are allowed in the regression function, as compared with using a single parameter, the single parameter regression analyses were repeated (forcing the regression line through the origin, with some exceptions) with additional purposes. The first was to attempt to remove "outliers" or routines in which the parameter data were anomalous statistically. Subsequently, having identified the outlier routines in this manner, the background data on each routine were reexamined, and in nearly all cases such observations as "complex logic", "changing requirements", "schedule problems", could be correlated with the outlier routine.

Secondly, assuming normality and constant variance (of number of problems over the full range of the parameter), 90 percent prediction limits for the number of software problems were calculated. The data points, regression line and 90 percent prediction limits are shown plotted in Figures 4-30 for a selected set of parameters. The plotted regression line and prediction limits are calculated from the smoothed data, obtained by eliminating the outliers, which are also shown on the plots. The criterion for rejection of outliers was chosen as ±3 times the standard error of regression for the original data, then the criterion was applied, repeatedly if necessary, to the data without the outliers, until no more outliers occurred.

Table 4-27 summarizes survey information obtained previously on relative "difficulties" of the outlier routines shown in the selected plots in addition to those routines identified as outliers for the remainder of the reduced set of parameters, as well as some additional parameters for which the smoothing analysis was accomplished. In a very few of these latter cases ±2 standard errors was used as an outlier rejection criterion. Section 2.0 describes the manner in which the "difficulty" data were obtained. As Table 4-27 shows, in comparison to all routines the outlier routines had been assessed as having a significantly higher average difficulty measure (Table 4-28). In only one case, an outlier routine was identified (D104), which had a significantly *lower* number of problems relative to its number of branches, all others having significantly high numbers of problems. Coincidentally, the comment by the developer on that particular routine was "...easily modularized computational code".

### 4.3.5.9 Analysis of Parameter Categories

Each parameter represents a metric which serves to measure a corresponding attribute, as indicated by the label. In order to correlate the metric with the attribute it purports to measure, software problems of Project 3 were grouped into "Interface," "Data Handling," "Computational" and "Logical

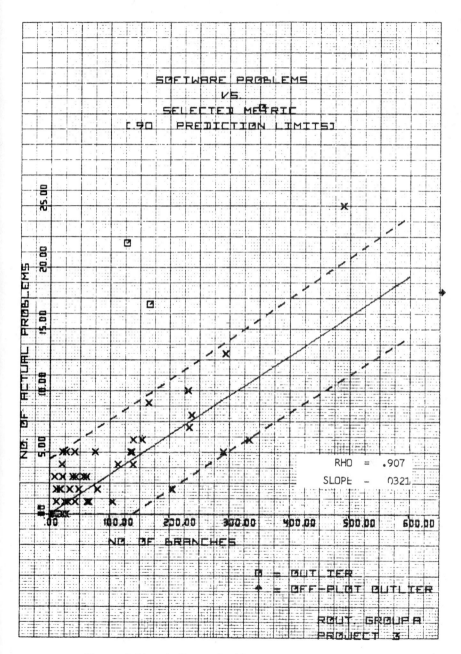

Figure 4-30.   Software Problems Vs. Number of Branches
(Sheet 1 of 10)

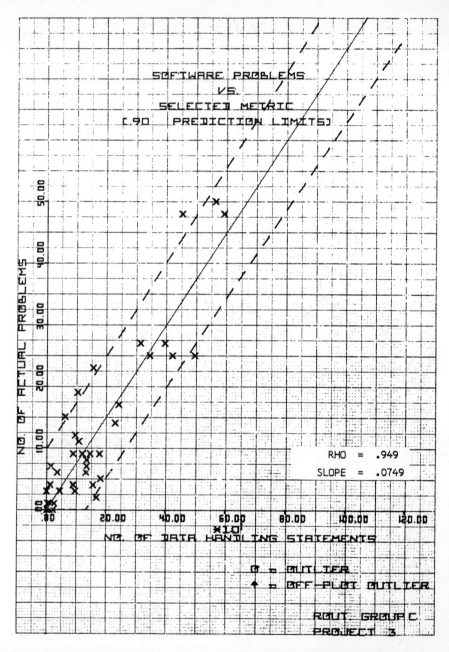

Figure 4-30.   Software Problems Vs. Number of Data Handling Statements
               (Sheet 2 of 10)

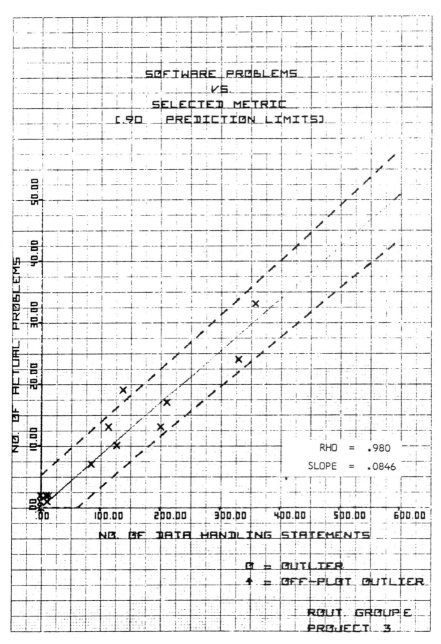

Figure 4-30.   Software Problems Vs. Number of Data Handling Statements
(Sheet 3 of 10)

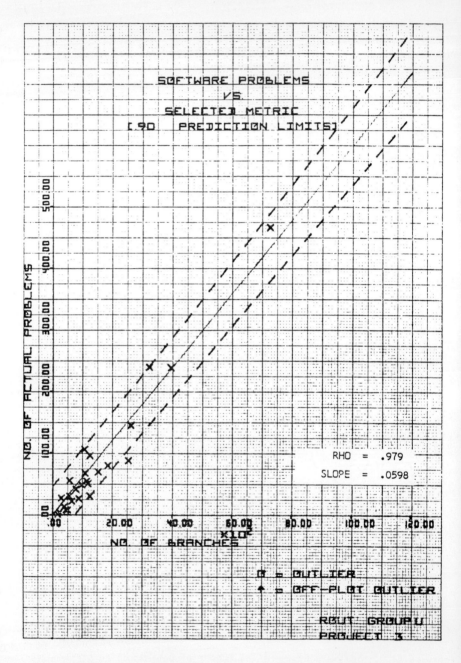

Figure 4-30.  Software Problems Vs. Number of Branches
(Sheet 4 of 10)

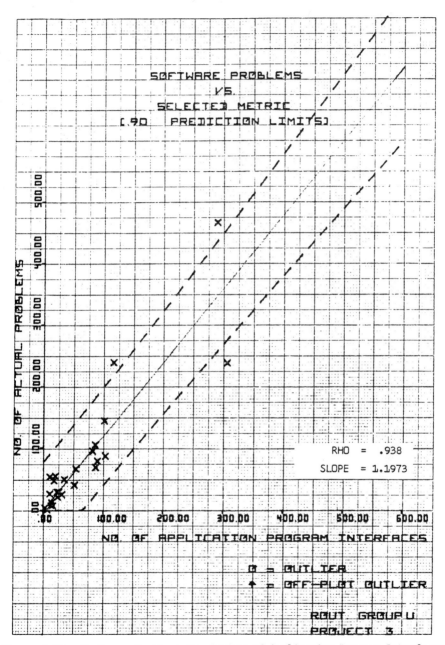

Figure 4-30. Software Problems Vs. Number of Application Program Interfaces
(Sheet 5 of 10)

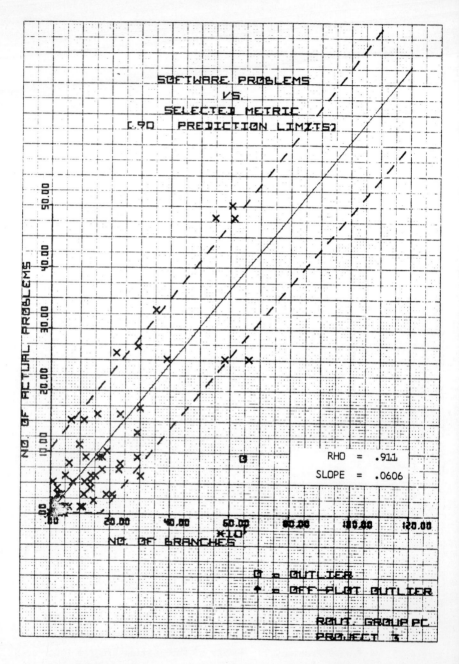

Figure 4-30. Software Problems Vs. Number of Branches
(Sheet 6 of 10)

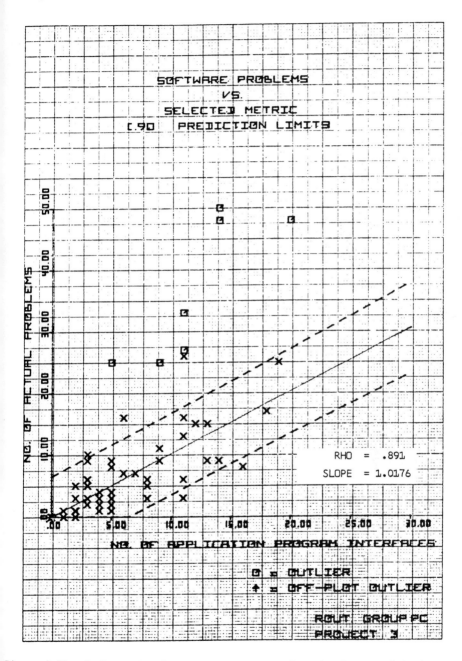

Figure 4-30.  Software Problems Vs. Number of Application Program Interfaces
(Sheet 7 of 10)

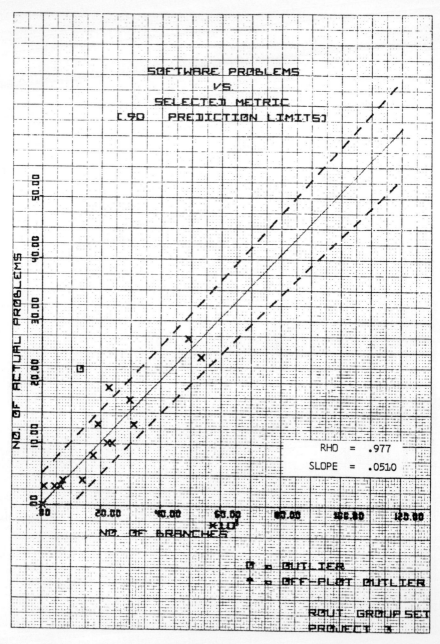

Figure 4-30.  Software Problems Vs. Number of Branches
(Sheet 8 of 10)

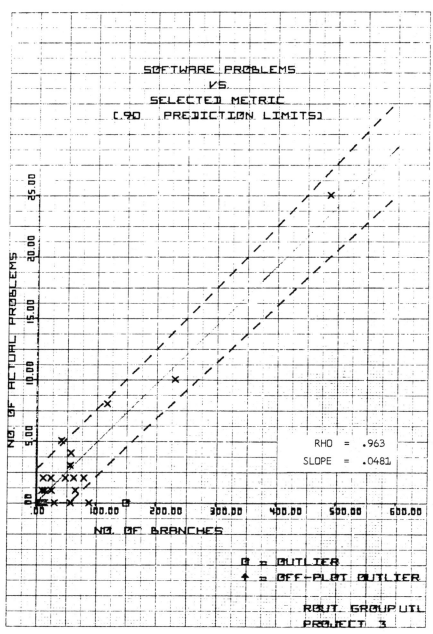

Figure 4-30.   Software Problems Vs. Number of Branches
(Sheet 9 of 10)

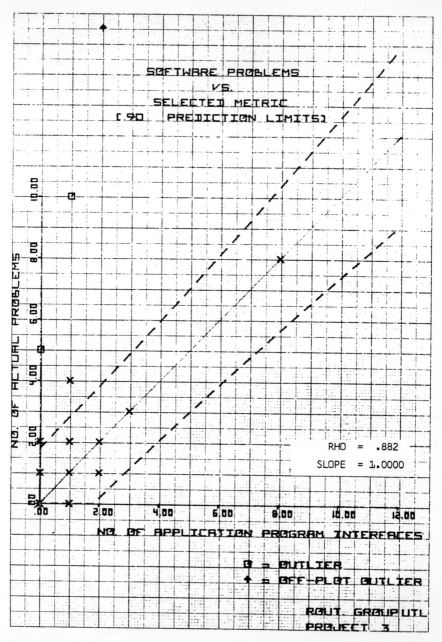

Figure 4-30. Software Problems Vs. Number of Application Program Interfaces (Sheet 10 of 10)

Table 4-28.  Project 3 Difficulty at the Function Level

| Function | Routines Contained | Function Difficulty Sum | Function Difficulty Average |
|----------|--------------------|-------------------------|------------------------------|
| A1 | 4  | 42  | 10.5 |
| A2 | 10 | 99  | 9.9  |
| A3 | 15 | 119 | 7.9  |
| A4 | 6  | 49  | 8.2  |
| A5 | 16 | 168 | 10.5 |
| B1 | 7  | 77  | 11.0 |
| B2 | 9  | 101 | 11.2 |
| C1 | 12 | 126 | 10.5 |
| C2 | 14 | 125 | 8.9  |
| C3 | 2  | 19  | 9.5  |
| C4 | 1  | 12  | 12.0 |
| C5 | 5  | 51  | 10.2 |
| C6 | 5  | 54  | 10.8 |
| D1 | 12 | 149 | 12.4 |
| D2 | 3  | 30  | 10.0 |
| E1 | 14 | 104 | 7.4  |
| F1 | 3  | 33  | 11.0 |
| F2 | 5  | 40  | 8.0  |
| F3 | 9  | 80  | 8.9  |
| F4 | 13 | 124 | 9.5  |
| F5 | 7  | 75  | 10.7 |
| Totals | 172* | 1677 | |
| Average Difficulty (All Routines) | | | 9.8 |

*TRW routines only

categories denoted by $Y_I$, $Y_D$, $Y_C$, and $Y_L$, respectively. The results of analysis in this section examine the relationship between number of interface problems, $Y_I$, versus number of interfaces, as measured by $Z_{13}$ (total number of system and application program interfaces); similarly the relationships $Y_D$ versus $Z_{10}$, $Y_C$ versus $Z_9$ and $Y_L$ versus $Z_5$, the numbers of problems of each category with the corresponding parameters.

To do this a standard, with intercept, regression analysis was performed in each case using the values of Y, Z for each of the 25 functions defined previously: $A_1$, $A_2$, ..., $H_2$.

Figures 4-31 show by the fairly high positive correlation coefficients for Data Handling problems ($Y_D$) and Logic Problems ($Y_L$) that the parameters $Z_{10}$ and $Z_5$ in fact provide good predictors of $Y_D$ and $Y_L$, respectively. The remaining two parameters $Z_{13}$ and $Z_9$ are only "fair" predictors for $Y_I$ and $Y_C$, respectively.

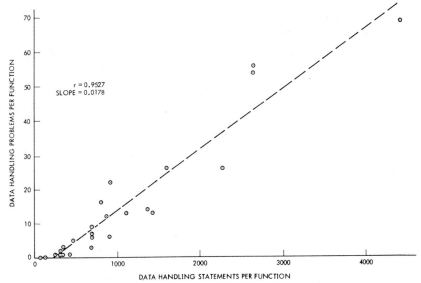

Figure 4-31.  Project 3 Data Handling Problems versus Data Handling Statements (Function Level) (Sheet 1 of 4)

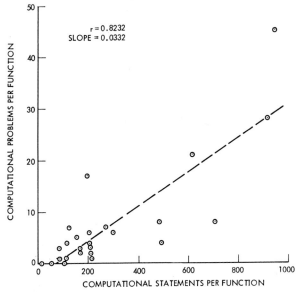

Figure 4-31.  Project 3 Computational Problems versus Computational Statements (Function Level)(Sheet 2 of 4)

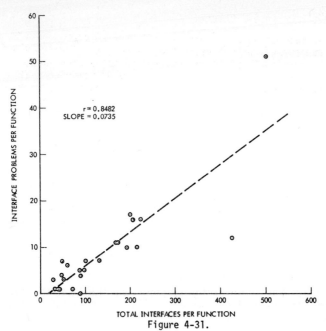

Figure 4-31.
Project 3 Interface Problems verus Interfaces (Function Level) (Sheet 3 of 4)

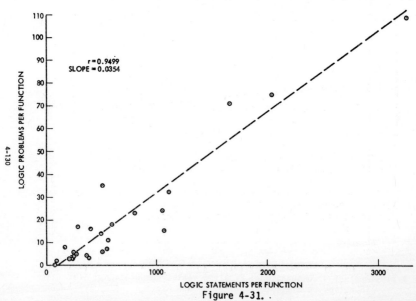

Figure 4-31. .
Project 3 Logic Problems versus Logical Statements (Function Level) (Sheet 4 of 4)

## 4.4  Analysis of Error Causes and Symptoms

An effort was made to develop a means of independently classifying both causes and symptoms of errors using Project 5 data.  Section 3.5 presents a discussion of the categories created in the attempt to define specific causes of software errors.  The list of symptomatic categories shown in Table 4-29 was created in order to provide a basis for deriving general relationships between software error causes and symptoms in other software projects.  The list of causative categories is contained in Table 3-2 (Section 3.5).

A total of 365 Project 5 problem reports were examined and their symptoms categorized.  A two-way table of frequencies for causes and symptoms was then produced for the 25 symptoms and 93 causes.  Owing to the relatively few entries in each of the 93 causes, or detailed error categories, it was decided to recast the frequencies into major causative error category groups, A, B, ..., K, X, by totalling all frequencies within a group.  Table 4-30 presents the reduced frequency data with the 25 symptom categories and 12 major causative categories.  Some quantitative relationships are apparent but in general very few meaningful inferences suggest themselves.  The following appear to be worthwhile observations:

(1)  The most frequently appearing symptoms are shown below, together with the percent of total problems (365) exhibiting the given symptoms.

| Symptom No. | No. of Problems | Percent of Total Frequency |
|:---:|:---:|:---:|
| 2 | 111 | 30.4 |
| 15 | 60 | 16.4 |
| 12 | 53 | 14.5 |
| 11 | 33 | 9.0 |
| 18 | 18 | 4.9 |
| 7 | 16 | 4.4 |
| | 291 | Total   79.6% |

Thus 291/365 = 79.6% or nearly 80% of the problems have the listed symptoms, with frequencies in the order given.

(2)  For each of the higher frequency symptoms given in the above table, the causes may also be tabulated in order of frequency, starting with the highest frequency cause.

| Symptom No. | Causes, in decreasing order of frequency for given symptom. |
|---|---|
| 2 | B (30%), A (26%), D (12%), H (9%) |
| 15 | J (65%), I (12%), X (12%) |
| 12 | H (53%), G (23%) |
| 11 | F (21%), C(15%), X (15%), H (12%), K (12%) |
| 18 | J (50%), B (33%) |
| 7 | F (31%), X (19%), B (12%), E (12%) |

Thus, given that Symptom 2 (e.g., answer out-of-tolerance) occurs, the probabilities that cause B or cause A are the source of the error would be estimated as 30% and 26%, respectively. In other words, the conditional probability that causes A or B (computational or logical errors, respectively) were operative is estimated as 56%.

The total frequencies for each cause do not show one or more predominant causes, but rather that causes J, H, B occurred most frequently, and nearly equally, and that the remainder of the causes taper slowly down in frequency, in the order A, X, D, F, I, G, C, E, K. Since causative category J is somewhat of a "catch-all," causes H (Data base errors) and B (Logic errors) represent the most frequent specific causes.

It can perhaps be concluded from the cursory examination of the Project 5 software problem data described above that little is to be gained by attempting to define and associate causes and symptoms of software errors, at least at present. This is only one aspect of the problem of diagnosing and correcting errors based upon the observed symptoms.

From the viewpoint of using this type of information as a diagnostic/maintenance aid to uncover software error causes, it appears that considerable refinement in both the cause and symptom categories are needed. To be useful in the detection of causative errors (i.e., debugging) the combinations of symptoms would need to include not only the symptom description, Table 4-29, but also certain auxiliary data such as a branch execution frequency table, a list of set/use discrepancies, and other dynamically obtained data. To obtain these additional data at the time of the software failure requires that the operational software be instrumented and that necessary software tools reside in core during execution.

Table 4-29.  Symptomatic Categories

| ID | DESCRIPTION |
|----|-------------|
| 0  | Void |
| 1  | Data Overflow |
| 2  | Incorrect Processing (i.e., wrong answer, answer or processing action not as expected) |
| 3  | Abort |
| 4  | Premature Program Exit |
| 5  | Loop |
| 6  | Too Much Output Produced |
| 7  | Routine - Routine Incompatability |
| 8  | Maximum Time Allotment Exceeded |
| 9  | Incorrect Initialization Processing |
| 10 | Incomplete Processing |
| 11 | Routine - Routine Data Incompatibility |
| 12 | Routine - Data Base Incompatibility |
| 13 | Run Time Too Long |
| 14 | Valid Data Destroyed |
| 15 | Change Control Activity |
| 16 | Standards Violation |
| 17 | Routine Lacking Required Capability |
| 18 | Routine Lacking Capability (Enhancement) |
| 19 | Inaccurate Processing |
| 20 | No Output |
| 21 | Software - Hardware Incompatibility |
| 22 | Valid Data Not Used |
| 23 | Core Storage Exceeded |
| 24 | Software - Documentation Incompatibility |

Table 4-30. Project 5 Software Problem Frequencies by Major Causative and Symptomatic Categories

| Major Causative Error Categories | | 0 | 1 | 2 | 3 | 4 | 5 | 6 | 7 | 8 | 9 | 10 | 11 | 12 | 13 | 14 | 15 | 16 | 17 | 18 | 19 | 20 | 21 | 22 | 23 | 24 | Totals |
|---|---|---|---|---|---|---|---|---|---|---|---|---|---|---|---|---|---|---|---|---|---|---|---|---|---|---|---|
| | | | | | | | | | | | | | Symptomatic Categories | | | | | | | | | | | | | | |
| Computational | (A) | 0 | 0 | 29 | 0 | 0 | 1 | 1 | 1 | 0 | 0 | 1 | 3 | 2 | 0 | 0 | 0 | 0 | 2 | 0 | 2 | 0 | 0 | 0 | 0 | 0 | 42 |
| Logic | (B) | 0 | 0 | 33 | 1 | 1 | 1 | 0 | 2 | 0 | 0 | 4 | 2 | 0 | 1 | 0 | 0 | 1 | 1 | 6 | 0 | 0 | 0 | 1 | 0 | 0 | 54 |
| Data Input | (C) | 0 | 1 | 4 | 0 | 0 | 0 | 0 | 1 | 0 | 0 | 0 | 5 | 1 | 0 | 0 | 0 | 0 | 0 | 0 | 0 | 0 | 0 | 0 | 0 | 0 | 12 |
| Data Handling | (D) | 0 | 2 | 13 | 0 | 0 | 0 | 1 | 1 | 0 | 6 | 3 | 1 | 2 | 0 | 2 | 1 | 0 | 0 | 0 | 0 | 0 | 0 | 0 | 0 | 0 | 32 |
| Data Output | (E) | 0 | 0 | 2 | 0 | 0 | 0 | 0 | 2 | 0 | 0 | 0 | 1 | 0 | 0 | 0 | 0 | 0 | 0 | 0 | 0 | 3 | 0 | 0 | 0 | 0 | 8 |
| Interface | (F) | 0 | 1 | 5 | 0 | 0 | 0 | 0 | 5 | 0 | 0 | 0 | 7 | 4 | 0 | 0 | 1 | 0 | 0 | 0 | 0 | 0 | 0 | 0 | 0 | 0 | 23 |
| Data Definition | (G) | 0 | 0 | 1 | 1 | 0 | 0 | 0 | 0 | 0 | 0 | 0 | 0 | 12 | 1 | 0 | 1 | 0 | 0 | 0 | 0 | 0 | 0 | 0 | 0 | 0 | 16 |
| Data Base | (H) | 0 | 3 | 10 | 0 | 0 | 0 | 0 | 0 | 0 | 3 | 0 | 4 | 28 | 0 | 0 | 4 | 0 | 0 | 1 | 1 | 0 | 0 | 0 | 0 | 2 | 56 |
| Operations | (I) | 0 | 0 | 6 | 0 | 0 | 0 | 0 | 1 | 0 | 0 | 0 | 0 | 0 | 0 | 0 | 7 | 0 | 0 | 1 | 1 | 0 | 1 | 0 | 0 | 0 | 17 |
| Other | (J) | 0 | 0 | 0 | 0 | 0 | 0 | 0 | 0 | 2 | 0 | 1 | 1 | 0 | 0 | 0 | 39 | 4 | 0 | 9 | 0 | 0 | 0 | 0 | 2 | 0 | 58 |
| Documentation | (K) | 0 | 0 | 2 | 0 | 0 | 0 | 0 | 0 | 0 | 0 | 0 | 4 | 0 | 0 | 0 | 0 | 0 | 0 | 0 | 0 | 0 | 0 | 0 | 0 | 0 | 6 |
| Rejection | (X) | 12 | 0 | 6 | 0 | 0 | 0 | 0 | 3 | 1 | 0 | 2 | 5 | 4 | 0 | 0 | 7 | 0 | 0 | 1 | 0 | 0 | 0 | 0 | 0 | 0 | 41 |
| Totals | | 12 | 7 | 111 | 2 | 1 | 2 | 2 | 16 | 3 | 9 | 11 | 33 | 53 | 2 | 2 | 60 | 5 | 3 | 18 | 4 | 3 | 1 | 1 | 2 | 2 | 365 |

## 4.5  Ancillary Investigations

In the course of examining and trying to understand software error data documented during testing, it quickly became obvious that the picture of causes is much more complex than had even been anticipated prior to the beginning of the study.  During the data collection process, it also became obvious that there was a tremendous amount of information available, not all of it test related, that might be useful in understanding the software development cycle as a whole, as well as the test phase.

In the sections which follow  are presented results of several ancillary investigations of Project 3 data which were found to be interesting. Not all investigations attempted are presented here because of inconclusiveness and, in some cases, lack of confidence in the quality or quantity of data.  It will be noted that some of the results presented here are inconclusive, too; similar investigations with other data sets may be more successful.  In each investigation, an attempt is made, where possible, to identify preconceived notions and expected results (hypotheses?) held by the investigators.  An attempt is also made to outline conditions and qualifiers needed to understand results.

### 4.5.1  Personnel Ratings

The objective of this investigation was to determine if personnel rating parameters could be used to explain error rates in the software.  The feeling was that programmer experience*, alone, is a poor indicator of quality or error-freeness of the software.  As was mentioned in Section 2.0 it was further felt that addition of a programmer load factor would improve the correlation between error rates and personnel ratings.

In this investigation only TRW developers were considered.  These individuals (76 in this instance) were expected to design, code, debug, document, test (routine level), and maintain TRWs portion of the software system.  Programmer ratings, a function of knowledge, intelligence, initiative, and responsibility, were assigned by managers.  A workload factor was also determined.

The contention that experience alone is a poor indicator was suggested in a previous study [5] and this result was borne out again in this study.

The contention that programmer rating and load factor would improve the correlation did not hold.  There was no correlation ($r = 0$) between programmer rating and error rates, in errors/100 statements.  One very interesting fact was discovered, however.  In plotting each programmer's error rate against his rating, it was noted that one group of programmers had both high ratings (>16) and high error rates (arbitrarily set at >2.0 errors/100 statements).  Further examination showed that these programmers were mostly technical work unit** managers who had, for one

---

*In the Project 3 environment, at least.

**A work unit should not be confused with a chief programmer team.

reason or another, retained some of the software as their own responsibility. This responsibility, added to the responsibilities of managing
from five to fifteen people, attending technical and management meetings,
finding and allocating needed resources, and generally serving as an interface between the programmers and upper management and the customer,
detracted from their ability to produce error-free code. Figure 4-32
presents error rates vs. programmer rating for both the programmers and
work unit managers. Typically, these work unit managers are successful
programmers who are rewarded with a management position. Dividing the
error rate of each programmer by his load factor helped to bring these
managers into the range of all other programmers, Figure 4-33. The
percent difference between programmer and work unit manager error rates
changes from 34 percent to 12 percent using this technique.

The message here may be to let these technical managers manage and
keep them away from the code. This may be easier said than done in real
world software development situations where time and manpower resources,
as well as tools to assist with tedious tasks, are in short supply.

As far as programmer ratings go, those used in this study were
clearly lacking in their ability to explain error rates. In one specific
instance where a highly rated programmer, not a work unit manager, had a
high error rate it was discovered that this individual was going through
the throes of divorce at the time, and this fact, unknown by anyone at
the time, affected the individual's performance. Any successful programmer rating scheme is going to have to take into account some of the less
tangible characteristics.

### 4.5.2  Errors and Programmer Assignments

The objective of this investigation was to determine if the number of
programmers assigned to work on a particular routine had any effect on the
error rate (actual errors per 100 source statements) for the routine. The
hypothesis in this investigation was that routines suffer higher error
rates as a result of having more than one programmer assigned the responsibility of producing the routine.

Conditions and qualifications which apply in this investigation are
as follows:

- Only TRW routines were examined due to the lack of
  co-contractor personnel data for Project 3.

- Multiple assignments occurred throughout the development cycle. That is, design, coding, and testing
  were all subject to multiple assignments of developers.

- Detailed assignments of percent work completed by each
  programmer for each task were not available. Nor was it
  possible to determine the type of multiple assignment
  very accurately, i.e., whether it was in parallel or
  serial in nature (or some combination of each).

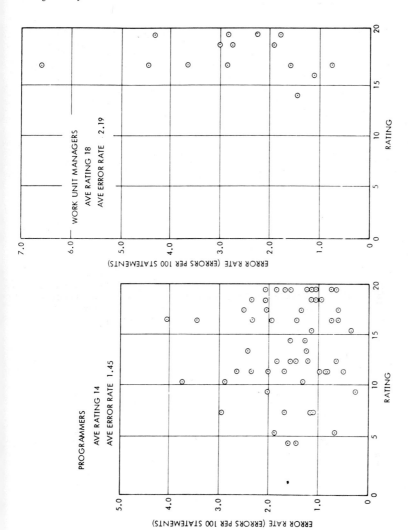

Figure 4-32. Programmer Rating versus Rate per 100 Statements

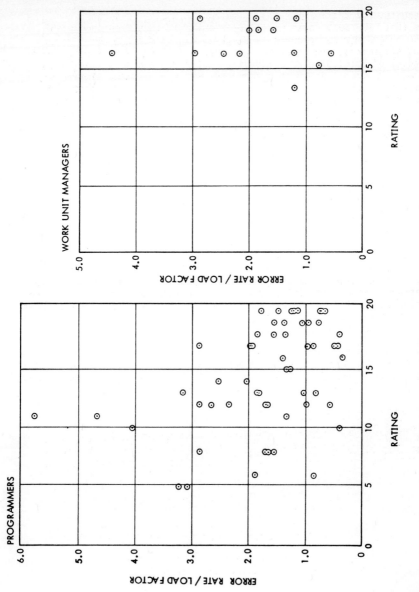

Figure 4-33. Programmer Rating versus Error Rate Load Factor

Results, bearing in mind the above *caveats*, did not support the contention that "too many cooks spoil the stew." In fact, routines with only one programmer assigned had a slightly higher average error rate, 2.87/100 statements, than routines with two and three or more programmers assigned, 1.87 and 1.97 errors/100 statements, respectively (see Figure 4-34). Routines with high error rates (>2.0 errors/100 statements) were typically subject to so many adverse development conditions that it would be difficult to determine just how much influence personnel assignments had. As one Project 3 manager pointed out, assignment of multiple developers may have had a beneficial effect because these assignments were typically made in times of crisis when the fresh viewpoint and added manpower were needed.

Note in Figure 4-35 that multiple programmer assignments were made on the larger routines. An average routine size of 574 statements characterized the routines with three or more programmers assigned, while the average routine sizes for two and one programmer assignments were 430 and 449 statements, respectively.

As part of the investigation of programmer assignment, there was an effort to determine if the highly rated programmers were assigned to the larger and generally more complex, routines. Table 4-31 summarizes the finding that there was a tendency for this to be true with a 13.4% difference between maximum and minimum average programmer ratings. Perhaps the most interesting finding in this investigation, however, was the fact that routines that experienced no problems (i.e., no code change errors discovered) were predominantly the ones smaller than 300 total statements in length.

To improve investigations of this type more data collected in a controlled manner are needed. These data should indicate how programmers are using their time as well as where overlaps and duplication occur.

### 4.5.3  Problem Report Closure Time

The objective of this investigation was to determine the mean time required to close a software problem report. That is, the time required to identify the error, develop and test a fix, and close out the software problem report. Project 3 data are used here because of availability and because of the sense of urgency felt by project performers to find and fix problems as quickly as possible. Additional information needed in this investigation is as follows:

- Validation testing was conducted by software contractors

- Acceptance testing was attended by customer, user, and customer technical assistance personnel.

- Integration testing was conducted by a system integration contractor not colocated with the software contractors who fixed errors.

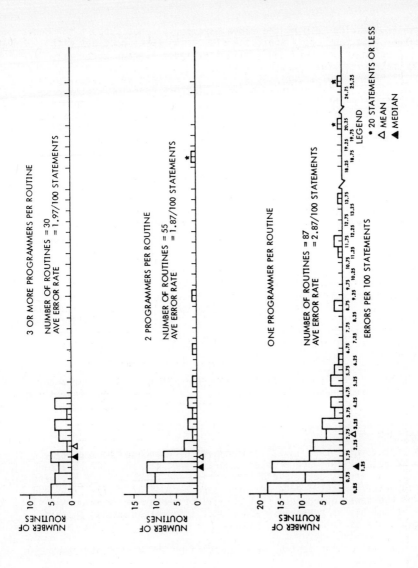

Figure 4-34.  Routine Error Rates for Various Programmer Assignments

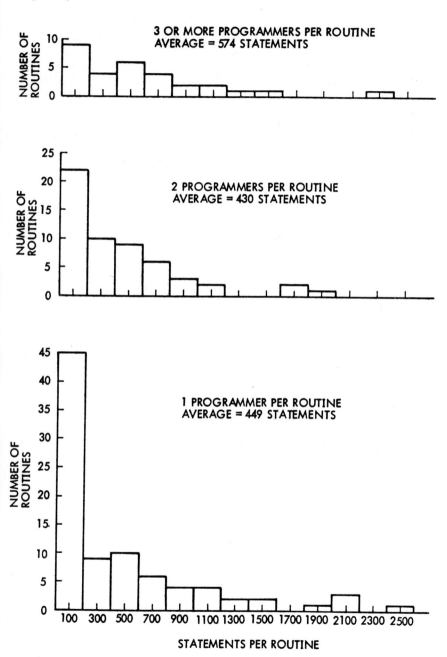

Figure 4-35.  Programmer Assignments by Routine Size

Table 4-31.  Average Programmer Ratings According to Routine Size

| NUMBER OF STATEMENTS PER ROUTINE | NUMBER OF TRW ROUTINES | NUMBER OF ROUTINES WITH NO PROBLEMS | AVERAGE PROBLEMS PER 100 STATEMENTS | AVERAGE PROGRAMMER RATING |
|---|---|---|---|---|
| 0-100 | 51 | 18 | 4.09 | 14.2 |
| 101-200 | 25 | 4 | 1.81 | 15.5 |
| 201-300 | 12 | 2 | 2.22 | 15.8 |
| 301-500 | 23 | 2 | 1.85 | 13.9 |
| 301-400 | 11 | 1 | 1.84 | |
| 401-500 | 12 | 1 | 1.86 | |
| 501-800 | 29 | 1 | 1.52 | 14.9 |
| 501-600 | 13 | 1 | 1.49 | |
| 601-700 | 9 | 0 | 1.61 | |
| 701-800 | 7 | 0 | 1.45 | |
| 801-1500 | 21 | 0 | 1.38 | 16.1 |
| 801-1000 | 9 | 0 | 1.14 | |
| 1001-1500 | 12 | 0 | 1.54 | |
| 1500 + | 11 | 0 | 1.47 | 16.4 |
| 1501-2000 | 6 | 0 | 1.53 | |
| 2001 + | 5 | 0 | 1.39 | |

- Operational demonstration was conducted by S/W contractors working together in the operational environment with user assistance.

- Priorities were assigned to problems according to their impact on the progress of testing.  Since test cases were patterned after operational scenarios, a high priority test problem would, in general, also be a high priority problem in the operational environment.  Priorities were

  HIGH - Problem prevents execution of a test case or seriously impedes demonstration of software requirements.  (Continued)

       MEDIUM - Problem impacts successful execution of a test
                  case but useful output is available and testing
                  can continue.

       LOW     - Problem does not impact demonstration of soft-
                  ware requirements and a workaround exists.

• Not all problem reports received a priority. These data
points were not considered, nor were problem reports
designated as product improvements. The sample size
used here is 1325 SPRs.

The mean times required to close problems followed trends that might
be expected, see Figure 4-36*. In each test phase high priority problems
were closed first. Note that the parameter here is not the Δt to fix the
problem but the Δt between the problem's identification and the time its
fix was checked out and available for use in formal testing. For high
priority problems the inactive time in the queue, when the problem was
open but not being attended to, was minimal because of the pressure to
close all high priority or test limiting problems. Inactive time for
medium and low priority problems was substantial by comparison, although
no data exist to quantify this Δt.

Validation and acceptance test cases and test objectives were basically the same. The mean times to close high and medium priority problems
were virtually the same, too. The increased pressure to correct problems
during acceptance testing (due to customer involvement and impending
delivery dates) probably accounted for the drastic reduction in the time
required to close the generally easier-to-fix low priority problems.

Integration testing occurred some distance from the location of the
problem fixers. The pressure to close problems during integration was
similar to that during acceptance. There was a one day transit time
between the test group and the fixer of the problem, which would explain
the two day** difference between acceptance testing and integration testing for high and low priority problems. The low Δt for medium priority
problems is unexplained.

The operational demonstration concerned itself only with high and
medium priority problems, leaving low priority problems for later closure;
therefore low priority problems were not considered here. The lower mean
on high and medium priority problems is due to fewer total problems to correct, lesser severity of problems encountered, and probably to some extent
the experience the problem fixers had in correcting problems.

---

*Points are connected in this figure to amplify trends.
**One day for delivery of the problem description via SPR and one day for
delivery of the fix.

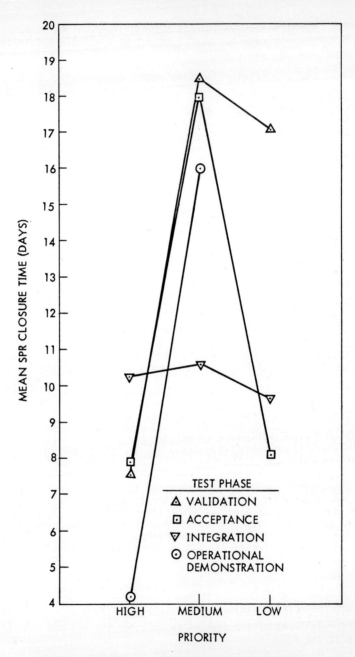

Figure 4-36.   Project 3 Mean Problem Closure Time
as a Function of Problem Priority

Project 5 data was not examined because factors influencing closure time are not so easily identifiable and the pressure to effect closure is not that of a production process, but that of an R&D program.

## 4.5.4 Design Problems and Software Problems

The objective of this investigation was to determine if the number of design problem reports (DPRs) generated during the design review process of Project 3 might serve as an indicator of the number of software problem reports (SPRs) generated in subsequent formal test phases.

In this investigation there were really no preconceived notions concerning the relationship, just a healthy curiosity. The data used were raw counts* of DPRs written against the same software that was subject to SPRs during validation, acceptance, integration, and operational demonstration testing. Also, only TRW software is represented here due to lack of co-contractor DPR data.

Correlation at the function level** was fairly good, r = 0.969 results are graphically presented in Figure 4-37. There was a definite tendency for functions which were criticized during design reviews to also be the subject of test SPRs. One interesting point on Figure 4-37 is the outlier with relatively few DPRs. Further investigation revealed that this function was one believed to be of relatively lower concern because it was similar to software built for other projects, i.e., it wasn't considered "new". This function, C1, was not an outlier in other test data investigations, suggesting that it did not receive as thorough a design review as other functions in the system.

It is believed that much can be gained in terms of developing improvements in the design process by examination of problems documented during design reviews. From the limited analysis of DPRs done in this study and the results of the investigation of principal error sources, Section 4.2, this would seem to be the case. Such examinations should include detailed categorization of the type of error and the design activity that produced the error. Error severity and the amount of review given each particular segment of the design would be data collected to support studies of this type.

---

*No attempt was made to categorize these according to the amount of review given, type of problem they documented, or their severity. This would have involved retrospective analysis of over 5000 DPRs, and time did not permit this.

**At the routine level a linear fit was not as good.

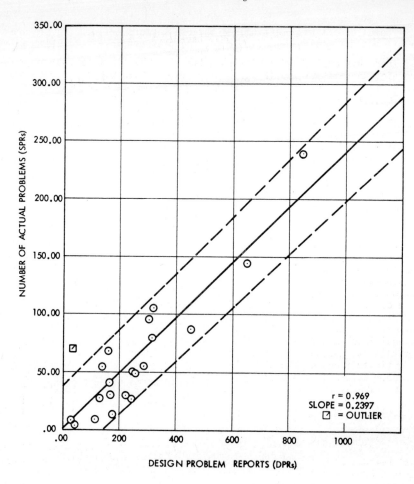

Figure 4-37.  Design Problems and Software Problems (Project 3)

## 4.5.5  Computer Usage vs Software Problem Reports

There has been considerable discussion in the software community concerning the possible relationship between computer usage and the number of resulting software problems, with particular emphasis on developing mean time between failure (MTBF) values applicable to software.

TRW data from Project 3 validation and test phase provided computer time data in order to explore this possibility. Since there was reason to suspect that the distribution of time versus SPRs might be dichotomous, computer time and problem report data were divided into two categories: formal test activity and developer activity. Test activity was all testing performed by the independent test group personnel to specified test procedures. Developer activity was the computer time used for the verification, solution and checkout of software problems.

In the scatter diagram, Figure 4-38, illustrating weekly computer usage and problem reports for both activities, it is apparent, from the pattern formation and the vertical separation of the means of the data sets, that the data represent two populations. This can be explained by examining the nature of the two activities using computer time. The test function operates to a schedule, reporting problems encountered randomly in the course of planned testing. Concurrently, the designers use computer time on an as-needed basis, specifically for the verification of problems, correction and retest, occasionally writing problem reports when additional unrelated problems are encountered or when a problem is not within the designers' jurisdiction. Thus, generally speaking, the test activity finds problems, while the developer activity solves problems. The random nature of the designers' activity is apparent in the scatter diagram, clearly showing no measurable relationship between the variables.

Using a CDC 6500 applications library program, curves were fit to the weekly test activity data (minus one out-lying point) to measure linearity. The best approximation of the curve proved to be the hyperbolic function of the form $Y = A+(B/x)$, Figure 4-39, with the worst point estimation (actual value) being -22.1% from the calculated value. The correlation coefficient (r) was 0.87899 and the index of determination ($r^2$) of 0.77262 implied a 77% dependence of the dependent variable (SPR's) on the amount of computer time used.

The daily test activity was then plotted, Figure 4-40, to determine whether or not the relationship held for daily activity. It is clear that it does _not_, providing no possible estimation of daily SPR activity.

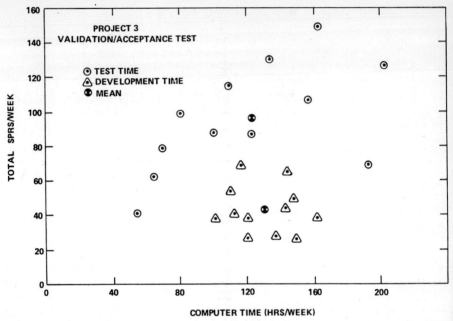

Figure 4-38. Computer Usage vs Total Problem Reports

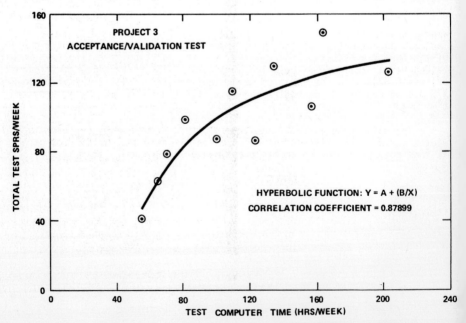

Figure 4-39. Curve Fit to Test Computer Time vs SPRs

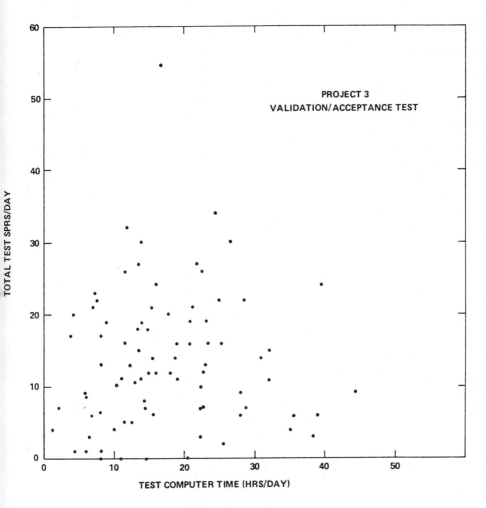

Figure 4-40.  Daily Test Computer Time vs Test SPRs

Extreme caution should be used in projecting this data to other test phases or other software projects. While the statistics imply a strong relationship of the variables on a weekly basis, the relationship was not substantiated by the daily data. Further, there were very few data points on which to generate the curve. Logic for the removal of the out-lying point was based on a number of factors, such as inordinate testing of one section of software, but the extent of actual influence of these factors cannot be quantified.

In addition, the generation of problem reports was not controlled. Writing, or not writing, an SPR was a matter of judgment rather than a defined requirement. Lack of control tended to cause reports to be written which did not reflect true problems. Since the effect cannot be measured, actual, singular problems could not be examined against the actual computer time which produced them.

Observations which can be noted are:

1) There may be a valid relationship between computer usage and resulting problem reports when the data are viewed on a gross basis. This may provide some management insight for planning purposes.

2) The results suggest justification to further explore the relationship and possibly to improve control of problem reports and computer time on future programs.

3) No attempt should be made to establish MTBF values during this test phase. Since the daily data does not corroborate the weekly findings, the relationship is not sufficient to suggest an MTBF could be valid.

4) Analysis for other projects on test phases should consider the possibility of dichotomous data and thus thoroughly examine the circumstances concerning computer usage and the related problem reports.

## 4.5.6  SPR Activity for Project 3

Project 3 SPR Activity during validation/acceptance, integration, and operational demonstration test phases shown in Figure 4-41 provides some food for conjecture. Shown in this histogram are the SPRs per week for TRW and the co-contractor.

During the validation and acceptance period the co-contractor activity was greatly influenced by the availability of the TRW software, which performed the executive and major initialization functions. Gradual build-up of the co-contractor problems as TRW software was validated is evident from the histogram.

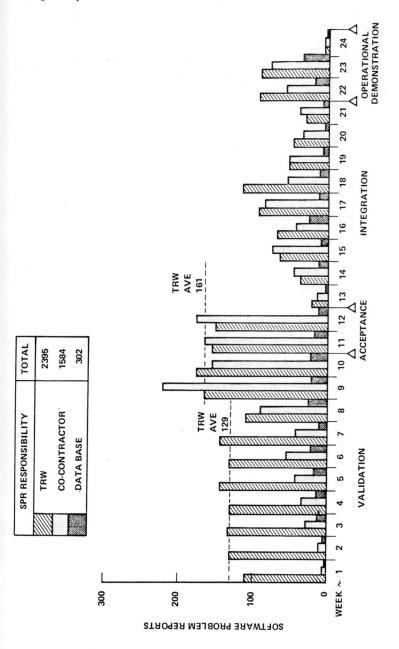

Figure 4-41. Project 3 Total SPR's/Week

Beginning with the 9th week of the validation/acceptance period two factors influenced the SPR output of both contractors. First, the co-contractor delivered a substantial portion of the software. Second, the customer's arrival with an additional force of analysts to prepare for and participate in the forthcoming  acceptance phase. Results of the increased test activity and available manpower are apparant in the sudden increase in SPR activity of both contractors. The "table" effect of the TRW activity suggests saturation. That is, there may be a physical limi-tation to the number of SPRs which can be written, assuming there are so many problems that the simple act of looking for them results in SPRs. The sudden increase in  the average of TRW SPRs/week, along with the availa-bility of customer manpower, and a similar phenomenon for the co-contractor activity may also be evidence to this.

If the above assumption is correct, it might be expected that once the "residual"* errors dropped below the SPRs  saturation level, the number of SPR generated would exhibit a continual decline. The fact that this did not occur on a per contractor basis implies that validation and acceptance testing was stopped prematurely.

Build-up of activity during the integration phase is most likely due to learning curve on the part of the integrating test personnel, and the fact that not all tests are independent of one another. Some tests provide inputs to successive tests, resulting in an increasing number of tests which can be run as time progresses. Tail-off, following the mid-point peak, results from the discovery of errors that the test cases are designed to find.

The operational demonstration test phase is short and merely shows the number of problems discovered during the period by running tests that simulated operational usage. Once these problems were closed, the product was received by the customer for operational use.

---

*Note:  Residual for the specific test cases being examined.

## 4.5.7  Errors and Software Cost

The objective of this investigation was to determine the relationship between the number of problems encountered during Project 3 preoperational testing* and the cost of the software.  That is, did the most error-prone routines also cost the most to produce?  The feeling was that the answer to this would be yes since previous studies showed that cost correlated fairly well with size, too.

Using Project 3 data, routine cost was determined for the entire development period, including the design, coding, development test, and formal test phases.  It should be noted that other project costs such as top level management, configuration management, and the independent test costs were left out of this study since accurate records on how these organizations spent their dollars at the routine level were not available.  Figure 4-42 shows a normalized** plot of the cost as a function of the number of problems documented for the routines in one TRW subsystem.  For this subsystem there was a definite positive correlation, $r = 0.8424$, between cost and the number of problems.  The cost vs. size relationship mentioned earlier is presented in Figure 4-43 for the same Project 3 subsystem where $r = 0.8899$.  Only one subsystem is shown here as an example of this type of analysis.  Other subsystems were similarly correlated.

---

*Validation, acceptance, system integration, and operational demonstration testing.

**Cost normalization was done with respect to the most expensive routine in the subsystem.

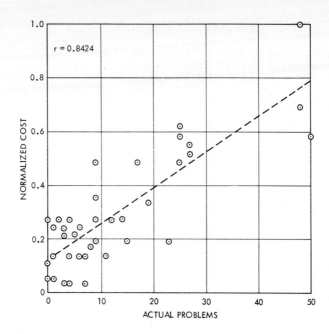

Figure 4-42.  Routine Cost Versus Problems
(Project 3, Subsystem C)

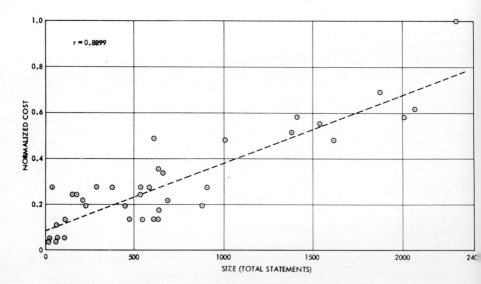

Figure 4-43.  Routine Cost Versus Size
(Project 3, Subsystem C)

## 4.6  Comparison of Data from Different Projects

The temptation to compare data from different projects is great.  Yet
the results of comparison can be misleading unless the differences and
similarities between the projects are well specified in common terms.
Differences between data items and the means of their collection are also
needed.

Our studies have emphasized just how significant the problem of providing a basis for comparison can be.  For example, the work with Project 3
software attributes and metrics, Section 4.3, was thought to be a basis for
comparison of structural characteristics collected from Project 5.  Using
the logical complexity* metric appropriate for describing complexity on
Project 3, we very quickly found Project 5 to be structurally fairly simple.
Project 3 nesting of loops and IFs reached indenture levels frequently
exceeding the fifth level and sometimes reaching as high as the 10th level.
Such nesting was awarded a high complexity rating.  Project 5, on the other
hand, cannot afford this kind of complexity since run time must be minimized.  By comparison, it must be structurally more simple than Project 3.
However, if one were to ask people familiar with both projects to rate the
complexity of each, Project 5 would be rated more complex and descriptions
like "orders of magnitude more complex" would be used.  As might be
imagined, the difference is in something other than the code.  Project 5
is solving a highly complex analytical problem in real time, a problem
being solved with algorithms developed  for the first time.  Project 3,
although highly analytical, solves a problem that is, by comparison, well
understood.

Even comparison of such apparently straightforward attributes as
size can be misleading.  One of the most common measures of size is in
machine language instructions.  This is typically the easiest measure of
size to collect.  However, size at the machine language level is dependent
on the machine.  The conversion factor from source language statements to
machine language instructions can vary considerably.  What we have found
is that both measures of size are necessary, and the source measure should
recognize the difference between executable and nonexecutable code, as well
as comments.  Even then the size picture is not complete for comparison
purposes.  A definition of the product whose size is being measured is
important.  In the case of Project 3 the size of the end product source
code was very nearly** all the code developed.  For Project 5, however,
the end product's size is only a fraction of the code developed, partly
because of the top down approach in which a certain amount of "breakage"
or replacement of code is planned and partly because of the special tools
needed to develop real time code.  In an accurate comparison of error rates
in errors per unit size, or especially in a comparison of programmer productivity, these things must be considered.

---

\*
A measure of complexity based on source code structure.
\*\*
With the exception of nondeliverable debug code.

   The problem, then, is that we're not able to define projects in common terms, and it is this prcblem which keeps us from making many comparisons in this study.  However, based on our studies there is reason to
believe that this·is not an insolvable problem.  Similarities in error
data from more than one project, our only real area for comparison, are
encouraging.  The fact that the error category lists were essentially the
same helped.  When uniform approaches to collecting and analyzing data
are developed and employed in controlled experiments, further comparison
will be possible.

## 4.7 Tools and Techniques

In a general sense, many things can be done to improve the software development and test processes. This is becoming increasingly obvious from recent papers in the trade journals and the objectives of current government R&D programs. Improvements are taking one of two generic forms, either tools or techniques. Their applications are aimed at both managerial and technological improvements during virtually any phase of the software life cycle, from pre-proposal activities, through requirements analysis, design, coding, testing, and into operation and maintenance. Tools are defined for this discussion as computer programs which perform tasks which would otherwise have to be done manually. Techniques are defined as the standards and procedures used in the development and maintenance of the software system. The principal objectives of these tools and techniques may be summarized by the following:

- ● to eliminate errors before they get into the product (code or documentation)

- ● to find those errors that do get into the product earlier

- ● to support project performers in completion of drudgery tasks, freeing them to work on technical problems

- ● to increase communication and enhance common understanding between project performers, the customer, and the user

Since almost any topic dealing with the development of software systems may serve as the target of a brainstorming session on tools and techniques, the full spectrum is understandably (and in this discussion, prohibitively) large [10,11]*. Suggestions given in the following paragraphs are limited, therefore, to those that appear to provide obvious benefit in the Project 3 environment.

Also, a certain economy in selection of tools and/or techniques is suggested by available empirical data and by References [12] and [13]. For example, units conversion errors could be detected with a tool called a Units Consistency Analyzer, but may also be detectable through use of algorithm string tests and design/code inspections or walk-throughs. During Project 3 testing 9.3 percent of the computational errors (0.8 percent of all errors) could have been detected by a units consistency analyzer. Other related computational errors which might have been detected by such a tool boost the percentage to 15.9 percent of the computational errors (1.4 percent of all errors). However, virtually every computational error, including those errors mentioned above (9.0 percent of all errors) would be susceptible to detection by multipurpose design and code inspections and

---

*Reifer in References 10 and 11 provides a very comprehensive summary of tools and techniques (he appropriately calls these aids) that are presently in use, being developed, or under investigation. Viewgraphs shown by Reifer at the 1975 International Conference on Reliable Software present additional information on the subject.

algorithm string tests.  Therefore, the analysis presented here is limited
to that made possible by Project 3 data, i.e., technological improvements
in the form of tools and techniques applicable to the development and test
phases of the software life cycle.  The approach taken in this analysis is
similar to the one suggested by Curry in [12].

### 4.7.1  Techniques

Techniques will be discussed first because quantitative results showed
them to have the greatest potential for improvement.  Data used in this
analysis were the 4519 software problem reports (SPRs) written between
delivery of the code to an independent test team and the completion of an
operational demonstration just prior to turnover to the customer.  As was
noted in Section 4.2, these were categorized according to error type into
20 major categories and 165 detailed categories within the various major
categories.  The sample size was reduced significantly when all SPRs that
did not produce a code change were removed from consideration*.  There
remained 2019 SPRs which produced changes to the code, and these are the
data that were used in the analysis here.

Next, an attempt was made to determine which error categories were
susceptible to several preventive and detective techniques.  It should be
noted that these techniques won't guarantee that the errors will be caught,
but they will tend to make errors visible, i.e., certain types of errors
will be susceptible to prevention or detection with these techniques.

Finally, the terms "preventive" and "detective" are used loosely here.
Any technique (or tool) which is applicable prior to any form of testing is
termed preventive.  Those connected with testing were termed detective.
Table 4-32 presents a summary of general error categories and the percentages of each category susceptible to the various techniques being considered.  Table 4-33 presents the percentages of all errors, by major category, susceptible to the same techniques.  Note that these techniques are
not exclusive in their ability to locate errors, e.g., design standards and
design inspections both have the capability to prevent the same type errors.

### 4.7.1.1  Design Standards

Design standards are particularly appealing in the Project 3 environment because so much is known about the problem to be solved, the requirements, and user needs.  Using the approach outlined above, as high as
28.7 percent of the code change errors found in subsystem and system type
testing were judged susceptible to prevention through some sort of design

---

*SPRs that didn't produce a code change were due to out-of-scope (product
improvement), no-problem, pure documentation, and data base change SPRs.

Table 4-32.  Susceptibility of Project 3 Errors to Preventive and Detective Techniques (Errors Within Major Categories)

| Major Error Categories | | % of Total Code Change Errors | Probable Source % of Each Major Category Design | Code | Preventive Techniques Design Standards | Coding Standards | Design Inspection | Code Inspection | Detective Techniques PATH/ FCL/ DSET Test | DSET (3) | Algorithm Test | Integration Test | Requirement Test |
|---|---|---|---|---|---|---|---|---|---|---|---|---|---|
| Computational | (AA) | 9.0 | 90 | 10 | 53.9 | 15.9 | 65.4 | 46.7 | 87.4 | 52.2 | 73.6 | 0 | 62.6 |
| Logic | (BB) | 26.0 | 88 | 12 | 52.7 | 31.5 | 86.5 | 72.9 | 79.6 | 57.3 | 0 | 24.2 | 52.3 |
| I/O | (CC) | 16.4 | 24 | 76 | 21.7 | 23.5 | 21.7 | 78.6 | 98.5 | 35.2 | 0 | 50.0 | 57.8 |
| Data Handling | (DD) | 18.2 | 25 | 75 | 2.7 | 51.0 | 24.4 | 73.9 | 84.2 | 76.9 | 0 | 63.0 | 58.3 |
| Operating System/System Support Software | (EE) | 0.1 | (1) | | – | – | – | – | – | – | – | – | – |
| Configuration | (FF) | 3.1 | 24 | 76 | 11.1 | 0 | 0 | 0 | 0 | 0 | 0 | 0 | 0 |
| Routine/Routine Interface | (GG) | 8.2 | 93 | 7 | 47.9 | 41.2 | 78.2 | 86.1 | 20.0 | 0 | 0 | 99.4 | 7.9 |
| Routine/System Software Interface | (HH) | 1.1 | 73 | 27 | 27.3 | 0 | 27.3 | 100.0 | 27.3 | 0 | 0 | 100.0 | 0 |
| Tape Processing Interface | (II) | 0.3 | 90 | 10 | 0 | 0 | 90.0 | 0 | 100.0 | 0 | 0 | 100.0 | 100.0 |
| User Interface | (JJ) | 6.6 | 83 | 17 | 12.7 | 0 | 24.6 | 0 | 89.6 | 87.3 | 0 | 100.0 | 12.7 |
| Data Base Interface | (KK) | 0.8 | 10 | 90 | 0 | 0 | 0 | 0 | 100.0 | 0 | 0 | 100.0 | 0 |
| User Requested Change | (LL) | 0 | (2) | | – | – | – | – | – | – | – | – | – |
| Preset Data Base | (MM) | 4.1 | 79 | 21 | 0 | 0 | 0 | 53.7 | 100.0 | 29.3 | 29.3 | 13.4 | 61.0 |
| Global Variable/Compool Definition | (NN) | 0.8 | 62 | 38 | 60.0 | 12.5 | 60.8 | 81.3 | 87.5 | 81.3 | 62.5 | 100.0 | 0 |
| Recurrent | (PP) | 1.3 | (1) | | – | – | – | – | – | – | – | – | – |
| Documentation | (QQ) | 0.8 | (1) | | – | – | – | – | – | – | – | – | – |
| Requirements Compliance | (RR) | 0.4 | 89 | 11 | 0 | 0 | 75.0 | 75.0 | 75.0 | 0 | 0 | 25.0 | 100.0 |
| Unidentified | (SS) | 1.0 | (1) | | – | – | – | – | – | – | – | – | – |
| Operator | (TT) | 0.7 | (1) | | – | – | – | – | – | – | – | – | – |
| Questions | (UU) | 1.1 | (1) | | – | – | – | – | – | – | – | – | – |
| Averages | | 38% | 62% | 38% | | | | | | | | | |

NOTES: (1) Although errors in these categories required changes to the code, their source breakdown of design versus code is not attempted here. Those categories considered encompass 95 percent of all code change errors.

(2) For Project 3 product enhancements or changes to the design baseline were considered "out-of-scope" and, therefore are not present here.

(3) Data Singularity and Extreme Test (DSET)

Table 4-33.  Susceptibility of Project 3 Errors to Preventive and Detective Techniques (All Code Change Errors)

| Major Error Categories | | % of Total Code Change Errors | Preventive Techniques | | | | Detective Techniques | | | | |
|---|---|---|---|---|---|---|---|---|---|---|---|
| | | | Design Standards | Coding Standards | Design Inspection | Code Inspection | PATH/FCL/DSET Test | DSET (1) | Algorithm Test | Integration Test | Requirement Test |
| Computational | (AA) | 9.0 | 4.9 | 1.4 | 5.9 | 4.2 | 7.9 | 5.6 | 6.6 | 1.5 | 5.7 |
| Logic | (BB) | 26.0 | 13.7 | 8.2 | 23.5 | 18.9 | 20.7 | 14.9 | 0 | 6.3 | 13.6 |
| I/O | (CC) | 16.4 | 3.6 | 3.9 | 4.5 | 12.9 | 16.2 | 5.8 | 0 | 8.2 | 9.5 |
| Data Handling | (DD) | 18.2 | 0.5 | 9.3 | 13.5 | 13.4 | 15.3 | 14.0 | 0 | 11.4 | 10.6 |
| Operating System/System Support Software | (EE) | 0.1 | 0 | 0 | 0.1 | 0 | 0.1 | 0 | 0 | 0.1 | 0 |
| Configuration | (FF) | 3.1 | 0.4 | 0 | 0 | 0 | 0 | 0 | 0 | 0 | 0 |
| Routine/Routine Interface | (GG) | 8.2 | 3.9 | 3.4 | 6.4 | 7.1 | 1.6 | 1.6 | 0 | 3.1 | 0.6 |
| Routine/System Software Interface | (HH) | 1.1 | 0.3 | 0 | 0.3 | 1.1 | 0.3 | 0 | 0 | 1.1 | 0 |
| Tape Processing Interface | (II) | 0.3 | 0 | 0 | 0.3 | 0 | 0 | 0 | 0 | 0.3 | 0.3 |
| User Interface | (JJ) | 6.6 | 0.8 | 0 | 1.6 | 0 | 6.0 | 5.8 | 0 | 6.6 | 0.8 |
| Data Base Interface | (KK) | 0.8 | 0 | 0 | 0 | 0 | 0.8 | 0 | 0 | 0.8 | 0 |
| User Requested Change | (LL) | 0 | – | – | – | – | – | – | – | – | – |
| Preset Data Base | (MM) | 4.1 | 0 | 0 | 0 | 2.2 | 4.1 | 1.2 | 1.2 | 0.6 | 2.5 |
| Global Variable/Compool Definition | (NN) | 0.8 | 0.6 | 0.1 | 0.6 | 0.7 | 0.7 | 0.7 | 0.5 | 0.8 | 0 |
| Recurrent | (PP) | 1.3 | 0 | 0 | 0 | 1.2 | 1.2 | 0 | 0 | 0 | 1.2 |
| Documentation | (QQ) | 0.8 | 0 | 0 | 0.7 | 0.7 | 0.6 | 0.2 | 0 | 0.2 | 0.5 |
| Requirements Compliance | (RR) | 0.4 | 0 | 0 | 0.3 | 0.3 | 0.3 | 0 | 0 | 0.1 | 0.4 |
| Unidentified | (SS) | 1.0 | – | – | – | – | – | – | – | – | – |
| Operator | (TT) | 0.7 | – | – | – | – | – | – | – | – | – |
| Questions | (UU) | 1.1 | – | – | – | – | – | – | – | – | – |
| Totals | | | 28.7% | 26.3% | 57.7% | 62.7% | 72.9% | 51.1% | 8.3% | 46.1% | 45.7% |

Note: (1) Data Simularity and Extreme Test (DSET)

standard.  In the computational category these errors fell into the following detailed categories:

- computation of physical and logical entries
- computations related to indices and indexing schemes
- calculating and converting time
- units conversion

Logical categories that might be prevented through design standards were

- handling endless loops
- logic necessary to check for data conditions and flag settings

To varying degrees similar design standards are possible for prevention of I/O, data handling, and interface errors.  Detailed error categories for these are as follows:

-I/O

- tape and data card output formats
- debug output
- error message content

-Data Handling

- setting/using internal variables
- data chaining
- complete processing of input data

-Interfaces

- calling sequences
- communication through correct data block

### 4.7.1.2  Coding Standards

An expansion of existing project coding standards was judged to have as high as 26.3 percent preventive effect on the Project 3 code change errors.  Here the greatest benefit[*] would be in the data handling, logical,

---

[*] Note that standards for structured programming and structured design are not addressed here nor under design standards, respectively.  Although such standards would definitely enhance understandability, testability, maintainability, etc., quantitative benefits were undeterminable.  Use of such standards is believed to be part of the Project 5 success.

I/O, and interface areas.  As might be expected with a Compool and existing coding standards, errors in the global and local variable definition categories were low, less than 0.1 percent of all errors.  Susceptible detailed categories are as follows:

-Data Handling

- initialization and updating of flags and indices
- bit manipulation
- floating point to integer conversion
- definition of local (non-Compool) variables
- data packing/unpacking

-Logical

- limit determination
- loops
- tests of indices and flags

-I/O

- error message formats
- output field size
- output header placement
- line count/page ejects

-Interfaces

- routine calling sequences

## 4.7.1.3  Design and Code Inspections

The design and code inspections described here are basically those suggested by Fagan in [13].  In this report inspections are described as fairly formal "walk-throughs" of, first, the design and later the code. These inspections consist of a presentation of the design or code by the person(s) responsible for each, respectively, to a group of other project performers represented by those knowledgeable in design, coding, testing, interfacing software, and the data base.  Also, there is an inspection chairman who keeps the meeting going according to the agenda, which is made up of standard topics and topics made obvious by errors that are found to be most common.  These inspections are truly working meetings between project performers who are creating the product and should not be confused with the larger and generally higher level preliminary and critical design reviews (PDRs and CDRs) defined in MIL-STD-1521[14].  These should still be held, even with the design and code inspections.

Inspection techniques provide a significant potential for error prevention, 38 percent in the IBM experience [13]* and an estimated 62.7 percent of all errors using the Project 3 data. This is because inspections force a type of communication at the worker level which occurs randomly and in varying degrees of formality on most projects. Similar inspections are being conducted with apparent success in selected groups on Project 5 where it has been found that the essential ingredients needed for these inspections are a) getting all the right people together at the same time, b) defining meaningful agenda items tailored to the specific project, and possibly most important c) allocating time in the schedule to accomplish inspections.

## 4.7.1.4 Path/FCL**/DSET*** and Algorithm Testing

These detective techniques are suggested for use during development testing; i.e., the testing done by the programmer subsequent to achieving an error-free compilation. Although not new, these techniques can provide the greatest single error removal lever in the development cycle because tests are performed on units of code, usually the routine, sufficiently small so that testing can be very thorough. In fact, on Project 5, with its design and coding standards for maximum routine size of 100 executable statements, it is possible to execute all paths during unit testing†. Also, unit tests are performed by the developers, who know best how the unit works and where the potential errors are. Using the Project 3 data, it was determined that 72.9 percent of all errors found were susceptible to a combination of path, functional capability, and data extremes testing. (This assumes enough time to accomplish these tasks in detail.)

Table 4-33 presents the percentage breakdown of this functionally-oriented testing into the 20 Project 3 major categories and shows that 72.9 percent of the errors could have been detected with this combined test strategy. It also shows in a column headed DSET, that 51.1 percent of the errors would require consideration of data singularities and extremes in the testing. These results are particularly interesting in light of discussions of the mathematical theory of software reliability, Sections 5.0 and 6.0.

A functional capability list (FCL) is a detailed list of things a portion of the code must do. These lists may be compiled for virtually any level of modularization, but the level suggested here is the unit or routine level. Ideally, the functional capabilities would be a further breakdown of and treaceable to software requirements. Items on the list become the things that testing of the unit must demonstrate, and for each item test success criteria and expected test results may be specified. In conjunction

---

*     A productivity increase of 24 percent is also reported.

**    Functional Capability List.

***   Data Singularity and Extremes Testing.

†     Where a path through a loop is defined so that it includes at least one traversal of a loop.

with the testing of specific functional capabilities, it also is possible
to accomplish the following generic test objectives.

### Logical Objectives

- Execute every coded statement in the software at least
  once, and execute every source code branch at least
  once

- Utilize every entry point at least once

- Utilize every exit point at least once

- Exercise and validate every error message at least once

- Verify that all decision points within every subroutine
  are executed properly

### Computational Objectives

- Verify every computation using legal input values

- Verify proper handling of extreme values (maximum and
  minimum), singular values, and out-of-bounds values
  for every computation

- Verify proper handling of missing input data associated
  with every computation

(The verification method, e.g., hand calculation versus use of results from
similar but independent programs, may vary with the specific application.)

### Data Handling and I/O Objectives

- Verify that input data are obtained from the proper
  location

- Verify that output data are stored in the proper
  location and format

- Verify that every data conversion is correctly performed

- Verify that incorrect data are properly handled

- Verify that data are not lost nor destroyed

Note the repeated reference to test data in this strategy. The technique of testing with data singularities and extremes, as well as typical
values, representative of actual operational values has been termed DSET
here. An obvious benefit of this type of testing is the early attention
focused on an operational data base for use in validation or operational
type testing at the subsystem or system level. Project 5 application of
this technique has resulted in early identification of operational data
base problems.

Algorithm string testing is a form of simulation involving duplication of algorithms outside the modular structure of the code in order to test data flow, sensitivity to input data, timing and accuracy, and facilitate examination of algorithms in great detail.

### 4.7.1.5   Integration Testing

Integration and integration testing have always been difficult to accomplish due to schedule pressures and the need to begin validation testing.  Examining the Project 3 data again, an estimated 46.1 percent of the errors found in validation testing may have been visible through testing directed at routine/routine, routine/data base, and subsystem level interfaces.  Regardless of the magnitude of the improvement percentagewise, the symptoms of interface errors are particularly troublesome to validation testing because of their severity (e.g., aborts, no-loads, etc.).  A marked improvement would be to schedule (even at the expense of validation test time) a dedicated integration period with test cases specifically designed to detect interface errors.  The test objective would be to make sure that all elements of the code load and cycle together and that the software passes data correctly from start to finish.  The implication that integration testing plays down investigation of all requirements except interface requirements is intended.  Validation test procedures designed to demonstrate functional and performance requirements are typically poorly suited for efficient interface testing.

### 4.7.1.6   Validation, System Integration, and Operational Demonstration

The importance of subsystem and system level testing is obvious from what can be seen in the error data.  Testing to requirements (validation and acceptance testing), assuring that the software performs correctly when played together with the total system (system integration testing), and operational exercises have their own specific test objectives, yet each uncovers errors that should have been discovered earlier.  This appears to be the rule in real-world situations, regardless of the amount of planning and actual testing that may have gone on before.  Using Project 3 as a sample, only about 27 percent of the total number of code change errors that were found during the subsystem and system level testing phases named above were found when they should have been found.

It is apparently the plight of the software developer to be behind schedule.  Typically he has a lot of things going against him, those over which he has little or no control, e.g., resource availability, changing external requirements, and unforeseen technical problems.  The result is that the schedule is compressed in one fashion or other, and the thoroughness of testing is usually the thing that suffers.  Testing is the last item in the schedule.   Although both thorough routine level development testing, and function and subsystem level interface testing were planned for Project 3, the schedule remained inflexible while the technical problems continued to occur.  Forcing subsystem and system level validation testing by an independent test group[*] on a scheduled date actually had a positive

---

[*] This group had liberal help from the software development group in the areas of error correction and test output review.

effect on the progress and quality of the software product.  It tended to
force interface testing to occur, and the additional personnel increased
the number of software problem reports written per unit of time (See
Section 4.5.6).  The penalty that had to be paid was the inefficiency of
discovering errors which should have been found in earlier test phases
through execution of higher level tests designed to demonstrate satisfaction
of requirements in the operational environment.  On the positive side, this
higher level testing was the user's final filter before accepting delivery
of the product.  It allowed him to become involved in operational-like testing which also served as a training session for operational crews.  And,
the error trends seen in preoperational testing are predictors in terms of
numbers of operational errors[*].  Also, the type of errors encountered are
much like those experienced during operational usage.  Involvement in the
error identification and removal process of preoperational system testing
was also an important facet of user training.

### 4.7.2  Tools

Tools may be categorized according to their roles in eliminating specific software errors as being preventive (e.g., an algorithmic simulator)
or detective (e.g., an interface checker).  A third category exists for
those tools which perform a support role (e.g., a dynamic path analyzer)
where the tool supports some development or test technique.  It will be
seen that the benefit of tools is fairly easy to quantify for the first two
categories and less so for the support tools, although it is this third
category which may represent the greatest lever in creating an error-free
software product because of the broad range of errors made visible.  For
example, an algorithmic simulator would be effective in preventing specific
computational errors, maybe as high as 74 percent of the Project 3 computational errors (6.6 percent of all errors).  A dynamic path analyzer, a
support tool, is an obvious benefit to anyone interested in thorough testing, but this benefit is much more difficult to quantify.  The dynamic path
analyzer in this example would typically be used to support functional capability testing at the routine level where the scope of the error detection
activities is not limited to one detailed or even general category of error,
in this case 72.9 percent of <u>all</u> errors.  Without explicit (and controlled)
experimental evidence the best that can be said is that these support tools
greatly assist in performance of techniques with a potential for dealing
with some with some types of errors.

In the discussion which follows tools representing a benefit in the
Project 3 development and test environment are described.  A summary is provided in Table 4-34 for selected preventive and detective tools followed
by short descriptions of these tools and some suggested support tools.

### 4.7.2.1  Simulations

Simulations designed to investigate logical and computational aspects
of the software system would have addressed 9.5 percent and 5.8 percent of
the Project 3 errors, respectively.  A simulation of system data flow, with

---

[*]Correlation coefficient of 0.92 observed for Project 3 (See Section 4.2.4).

Table 4-34. Susceptibility of Project 3 Errors to Preventive and Detective Tools

Each tool column shows two values: *% of Errors in Major Category* / *% of all Code Change Errors*

| Major Error Categories | | % of Total Code Change Errors | Preventive Tools — Simulation | | Preventive Tools — Design Languages | | Detective Tools — Code Standards Auditor | | Detective Tools — Units Consistency Analyzer | | Detective Tools — Set/Use Checker | | Detective Tools — Compatibility Checker | |
|---|---|---|---|---|---|---|---|---|---|---|---|---|---|---|
| | | | Cat | All | Cat | All | Cat | All | Cat | All | Cat | All | Cat | All |
| Computational | (AA) | 9.0 | 64.3 | 5.8 | 35.2 | 3.2 | 15.9 | 1.4 | 15.9 | 1.4 | 0 | 0 | 11.0 | 0.5 |
| Logic | (BB) | 26.0 | 36.7 | 9.5 | 55.9 | 14.5 | 9.2 | 2.4 | 0 | 0 | 9.5 | 2.5 | 9.5 | 2.5 |
| I/O | (CC) | 16.4 | 3.6 | 0.6 | 29.2 | 4.8 | 17.2 | 2.8 | 0 | 0 | 16.6 | 2.7 | 0 | 0 |
| Data Handling | (DD) | 18.2 | 14.2 | 2.6 | 22.1 | 4.0 | 43.9 | 8.0 | 0.3 | 0.1 | 38.4 | 7.0 | 1.4 | 0.3 |
| Operating System/System Support Software | (EE) | 0.1 | 0 | 0 | 100.0 | 0.1 | 0 | 0 | 0 | 0 | 0 | 0 | 0 | 0 |
| Configuration | (FF) | 3.1 | (1) | – | – | – | – | – | – | – | – | – | – | – |
| Routine/Routine Interface | (GG) | 8.2 | 7.3 | 0.6 | 7.9 | 0.6 | 41.2 | 3.4 | 0 | 0 | 14.5 | 1.2 | 78.2 | 6.4 |
| Routine/System Software Interface | (HH) | 1.1 | 0 | 0 | 0 | 0 | 0 | 0 | 0 | 0 | 0 | 0 | 72.7 | 0.8 |
| Tape Processing Interface | (II) | 0.3 | 0 | 0 | 0 | 0 | 0 | 0 | 0 | 0 | 0 | 0 | 0 | 0 |
| User Interface | (JJ) | 6.6 | 10.5 | 0.7 | 54.5 | 3.6 | 0 | 0 | 0 | 0 | 0 | 0 | 2.2 | 0.2 |
| Data Base Interface | (KK) | 0.8 | 0 | 0 | 100.0 | 0.8 | 100.0 | 0.8 | 0 | 0 | 100.0 | 0.8 | 0 | 0 |
| User Requested Change | (LL) | 0 | (2) | – | – | – | – | – | – | – | – | – | – | – |
| Preset Data Base | (MM) | 4.1 | 20.7 | 0.8 | 0 | 0 | 0 | 0 | 0 | 0 | 0 | 0 | 0 | 0 |
| Global Variable/Compool Definition | (NN) | .0.8 | 0 | 0 | 6.3 | 0.1 | 25.5 | 0.7 | 62.5 | 0.5 | 6.3 | 0.1 | 0 | 0 |
| Recurrent | (PP) | 1.3 | (2) | – | – | – | – | – | – | – | – | – | – | – |
| Documentation | (QQ) | 0.8 | (2) | – | – | – | – | – | – | – | – | – | – | – |
| Requirements Compliance | (RR) | 0.4 | 25.0 | 0.1 | 0 | 0 | 0 | 0 | 0 | 0 | 0 | 0 | 0 | 0 |
| Unidentified | (SS) | 1.0 | (2) | – | – | – | – | – | – | – | – | – | – | – |
| Operator | (TT) | 0.7 | (2) | – | – | – | – | – | – | – | – | – | – | – |
| Questions | (UU) | 1.1 | (2) | – | – | – | – | – | – | – | – | – | – | – |
| Totals | | | – | 20.7% | – | 31.7% | – | 19.5% | – | 2.0% | – | 14.3% | – | 10.7% |

Notes: (1) All configuration errors were discovered through use of the compiler.

(2) No attempt is made here to assign these categories. However, 95.1 percent of the total code change errors are addressed here.

consideration of the internal and user interfaces would have helped with another 3.9 percent of all errors.  Computational simulations might also have helped in early determination of preset data base values, accounting for 0.8 percent of all errors.  Here it should be pointed out that the percentage for Project 3 preset data base errors may be very low compared to other systems, especially real time processors and systems with large hardware/software interfaces.  In these systems, like Project 5, simulations can be instrumental in early data base tuning.

#### 4.7.2.2  Design Languages

This generic group of tools represents the largest benefit of any of the tools listed in Table 4-34.  This might be expected from the finding that approximately 64 percent of the Project 3 errors were design errors. The same percentage existed for Project 2.  The chief benefit of design languages is that they specifically address program logic, including the most frequent logic error, missing logic or condition tests, which alone accounted for 12.3 percent of all code change errors (47.6 percent of the logic errors).  An estimated 31.7 percent of all errors were susceptible to prevention through use of design language tools.

#### 4.7.2.3  Code Standards Auditor

The chief benefit of this detective tool is that it enforces adherence to coding standards.  In the Project 5 application this Product Assurance tool has seen eventual acceptance by all development groups, to the point where they use it themselves to verify compliance of code with project standards*.  The result is code that is easy to read, is well documented, and looks as if one person wrote it all.  In addition to the improvements in understandability and code documentation, specific coding errors which can be precluded through adherence to coding standards could be eliminated as part of the pre-compilation process.  An estimated 26.3 percent of the Project 3 errors were susceptible to prevention with project specific coding standards.

#### 4.7.2.4  Units Consistency Analyzer

This tool checks consistency (and compatibility) of stated parameter units within equations and prespecified standard units.  Such a tool could also be expanded to check global variable definitions against accepted project standards.  Although errors detectable by such a tool represent a small portion of the Project 3 data (2.0 percent) this tool is particularly attractive because it could virtually eliminate such errors while at the same time forcing developers to think in great detail about data definitions.

#### 4.7.2.5  Set/Use Checker

This tool's primary function is to identify where certain data items are set and which routines use them.  It also provides information on which routines call or are called by other routines.  It also locates and

---

*Compliance with Project 5 standards can be considered very good, in excess of 95%.  Those not complying must obtain a waiver based on technical merit.

identifies variables, both global and local, that are declared but not
set/used and variables that are used but not declared. This tool (a
similar one was available for Projects 2 and 3) is extremely useful in
detecting data handling errors.

#### 4.7.2.6  Compatibility Checker

Compatibility checker is a general term for a tool which checks for
compatibility between two elements of the code, e.g., calling sequence
definitions. As might be expected, most of these errors were in the interface categories; an estimated 10.7 percent of all errors could be checked
for compatibility with other parts of the code.

#### 4.7.2.7  Dynamic Path Analyzer

A dynamic path analyzer identifies and instruments segments and paths
in the code and monitors execution of the code to determine which portions
of the code were exercised. This support tool is particularly valuable in

- determining a measure of test thoroughness,

- minimizing test redundancy,

- relating specific routine capabilities and allocated software
  requirements to segments and paths in the code,

- determining the extent of retest after a problem is fixed.

It was noted earlier that such a tool should be applied during detailed
development testing at the routine level, the test phase that has the
greatest potential for discovering software errors. It can serve a
valuable function during integration and system level testing in the determination of test thoroughness. It is also particularly useful in confidence
testing subsequent to update of the software. In confidence testing the
objective is to test new code as well as demonstrate the fact that old
capabilities have not been altered.

#### 4.7.2.8  Test Data Generator

A thorough development test strategy involving use of a dynamic path
analyzer would require that all segments (in-line code between branch points)
and all branches be exercised. For some short, non-complex routines it is
even possible to exercise all paths, a Project 5 routine-level test objective. One of the penalties of such a strategy, however, is that the
developer has to carefully examine his code to determine data conditions
that force execution of specific segments or paths. A tool to automate this
data generation process could greatly reduce the amount of work required to
set up and execute tests.

#### 4.7.2.9  Test Case Execution Monitor

For validation and system level testing maintenance of test configurations and creation of test records represents a considerable amount of work

when done manually.  On Project 3 there were in excess of 200 test cases during formal subsystem and system level testing.  Each was executed a number of times* and each required that complete records be kept concerning characteristics of the test environment and the success or failure of the test.

A test case execution monitor would load and execute test decks from tape or disk and could be capable of recording

- test case and software configurations

- the number of test executions and whether they were successful or not

- status of applicable SPRs

- satisfaction of software requirements

Presumably, this monitor might also be capable of inserting debug code at instrumented points in the source program, compiling, and executing with prespecified data.  Such a tool is being used effectively by Project 5 test personnel.

### 4.7.2.10  Generalized Data Base Construction Tool

Software testers have always been plagued by the need to have test data early in the development cycle.  Responses to requests for GFE data are generally late**, and the development groups are reduced to creating data bases by hand, a task of purest drudgery which could be greatly reduced by a tool capable of generating tables and arrays of data*** for development test purposes.  This support tool should have the capabilities of generating values between extremes, creating singularities such as discontinuities, and creating combinations of settings.  It should also have the capability of extracting and reformatting data from blocks on other existing data bases.  Creation of large numbers of entries for simulating maximum data load conditions, as well as tape and punched card output, should be possible with this tool.  The benefit of such a tool would be a freeing of the development personnel to spend more time debugging and testing the code prior to initiation of higher level subsystem and system testing.

### 4.7.2.11  Data Base Comparator

One tool available to the Project 3 test group which proved extremely useful as a test support tool was a data base comparator.  This tool

---

* Actual execution records were part of the "perishable" data that were destroyed after project completion.  A conservative estimate is 3 executions per test case.
** Government suppliers of these data bases also lack tools.
*** Operational data bases would still be required GFE for system **type** testing.

compared data bases, input as well as output, element for element and
flagged differences in values.  It was extremely useful in demonstrating
that changes to the code (e.g., use of debug code for test purposes) did
not alter the software's performance.

### 4.7.3  Reflections on the Project 3 Findings

The obvious message from the preceding analysis of Project 3 data is
that more testing should have been done prior to initiation of formal subsystem and system level testing.  An estimated 72.9 percent of the errors
resulting in a code change should have been found through thorough routine
level, tools-aided testing.

The data also inspire a number of questions.  For instance, was detailed
routine level testing planned, and if so, was it accomplished?  Routine
level testing was planned, although not in the detail suggested in the
preceding paragraphs.  Function level integration testing was also planned.
However, neither type of testing was completely accomplished, nor could
they have been in the seven month schedule prior to delivery of the software
to an independent validation test team.  In the real world of tight schedules, the activity at the end of the cycle suffers when time is limited,
and there simply wasn't enough time to complete routine level testing.

One might also ask if the inability to complete routine level testing
was foreseen, and what was done about it.  The situation was recognized
fairly early in the development cycle.  Evidence of this was in the developers' weekly status reports to management and also in the data available
through recordkeeping activities of the configuration management organization.  Although a number of things were done to help the situation, the
fact that formal subsystem and system tests were not strictly limited to
demonstration of requirements probably did more to assure an acceptable
product at delivery time than any other single thing.  It was this objective
of testing as many capabilities as possible, along with stated requirements,
that made it possible to detect so many non-requirements related errors.

The next question might be how error free was the software in operational use?  Using a simplistic ratio of the number of code change errors
to software size, the operational software experienced 1.7 errors per
thousand total source statements* (0.61 errors per machine language instruction) for intermittent operation over a period of approximately one year.
A rate of 17.5 errors per thousand total source statements (6.3 errors per
machine language instruction) was experienced during preoperational testing.
The operational software was delivered on time and allowed the user to
satisfy his operational needs.  Although not a very efficient approach, the
combination of validation, acceptance, system integration, and operational
testing was effective in the "catch up" detection of errors that should
have been detected at the routine level.  A word of warning, however; all

---

*Total source statements include executable as well as non-executable
statements, but no comments.

software systems are not as visible in a testing sense as the Project 3
batch mode, higher order language software.  To depend on high level test
for some software systems, e.g., real time systems, could be a fatal mis-
take if the nature of the software being tested precludes detection of
errors through introduction of debug techniques.

### 4.7.4  Evaluation of Project 5 Test Techniques

Although comparison of projects is not intended here, Project 5 presents an opportunity to examine the success of detailed routine level testing in a development environment where use of some of the tools and techniques described earlier are a reality.*

For the portion of the Project 5 system described as the applications
software, there is a routine level test requirement that not only all
branches be exercised but all paths as well.**  Project design and coding
standards make this latter requirement realizable.  In particular, routines
can be no larger than 100 executable statements in length, and structural***
simplicity is encouraged to lower execution times.

Although the software is being developed in a top-down, incremental
approach, testing within each increment is a combination of top-down and
bottom-up.  Testing is done by the developers at the routine level using
a dynamic path analyzer tool (PACE) to aid in accomplishing test requirements listed above.  Other test objectives include testing to functional
capabilities, testing with data singularities and extremes, and finally,
integration of routines into functional groups called tasks.  Functional
capabilities are traceable to specific paths through the software and to
the software requirements.  An important feature about Project 5 is that
time has been scheduled for this very detailed testing and tools have
been developed to aid in the test process.

Once the developers complete routine level and task integration testing, the software is turned over to an independent test organization for
process integration, during which the software plays against the real-time
simulator and under control of a real-time operating system.  It is in
this test phase that problem reports are created; these form the data
being used in this study.****

Using 273 problem reports generated during process integration testing
of the real-time applications software, an attempt was made to determine
if the routine level test strategy is effective in detecting errors it was
designed to detect.  Results were divided into three categories: 1) errors
that were found where they should have been found, 2) errors where earlier
detection was debatable, and 3) errors that slipped through routine level

---

*
Comparison to Project 3 results is tempting, but the differences between
two two projects make this unwise.
**
A path through a loop is defined so that it includes at least one
traversal of the loop.
***
Standards also require that the design and code be structured.
****
Formal validation and operational performance testing will eventually
be done at the end of the top-down development cycle.

testing and were discovered in process level integration testing. Results are presented in Table 4-35 for each of the Project 5 major error categories and for the total sample of problem reports.

The "debatable" classification comes about because of the extreme importance of having the simulator available to detect some types of errors. That is, to detect these errors earlier might be possible, but generally impractical.* For this reason the percentage of debatable errors best fits in with the errors that were detected when they should have been detected.

Results show a significant improvement over Project 3 routine level test effectiveness with only 15.7 percent of all the errors slipping through.

Table 4-35.  Effectiveness of the Project 5 Test Strategy

| Project 5 Major Error Categories | Occurrences | Errors Found When They Should Have? (Percent) | | |
|---|---|---|---|---|
| | | Yes | Debatable | No |
| Computational (A) | 42 | 62.0 | 19.0 | 19.0 |
| Logic (B) | 52 | 48.1 | 23.1 | 28.8 |
| Data Input/Output (C/E) | 21 | 76.2 | 9.5 | 14.3 |
| Data Handling (D) | 29 | 62.1 | 20.7 | 17.2 |
| Interface (F) | 27 | 96.3 | 0 | 3.7 |
| Data Definition (G) | 19 | 47.4 | 36.8 | 15.8 |
| Data Base (H) | 54 | 79.6 | 9.3 | 11.1 |
| Other (J) | 29 | 65.5 | 27.6 | 6.9 |
| Totals | 273 | 66.7 | 17.6 | 15.7 |

---

*The scope of this study didn't allow individual resolution of each of these problem reports.

Looking at individual error types, we see that the logical errors had the highest slippage at 28.8 percent and interface errors had the lowest slippage at 3.7 percent. Computational and data handling categories were next highest with 19.0 percent and 17.2 percent, respectively. The relatively low slippage of data base errors stresses the importance of integration testing in data base tuning for Project 5.

Detailed error categories that slipped past routine level development testing were the following:

Computational Errors

  A_100  Incorrect operand in equation
  A_600  Incorrect/inaccurate equation used
  A_800  Missing computation

Logic Errors

  B_100  Incorrect operand in logical expression
  B_400  Missing logic or condition test
  B_600  Loop iterated incorrect number of times
       (including endless loop)

Data I/O Errors

  C_300  Incorrect input format
  E_500  Incomplete or missing output

Data Handling Errors

  D_100  Data initialization not done
  D_200  Data initialization done improperly
  D_500  Bit manipulation done incorrectly

Interface Errors

  F_500  Software/data base interface error

Data Definition Errors

  G_100  Data not properly defined/dimensioned

Data Base Errors

  H_100  Data not initialized in data base
  H_200  Data initialized to incorrect value

Other Errors

  J_900  Software not compatible with project standards

Evidence of the improved effectiveness of Project 5 development and routine level test strategies is also seen in the absence of certain types of errors in the integration test data. For instance, errors in calculating indices, entry numbers, and total number of entries (representing 26.3 percent of the Project 3 computational errors or 3.2 percent of all errors) are virtually nonexistent in the Project 5 data. Errors associated with reading and writing data in the wrong location are also virtually nonexistent for Project 5; Project 3 errors of this type represented 12 percent of the data handling errors or 2.2 percent of all errors. It is felt that these types of errors are being detected in the routine level testing.

At the same time some error types continue to be predominant for both projects, e.g., missing logic and data initialization errors. A summary of percentages for these categories is presented below in Table 4-36.

Table 4-36. Sample Error Type Similarities Between Projects 3 and 5

| | Project 3 | | Project 5* | |
|---|---|---|---|---|
| Error Category | Percent of Major Category | Percent of All Errors | Percent of Major Category | Percent of All Errors |
| Missing Logic Errors | 47.6 | 12.3 | 46.8 | 8.0 |
| Data Initialization Errors | 43.1 | 7.7 | 26.7 | 2.9 |

Although this type of comparison is tempting, too many unknowns exist to pursue further investigation. For example, one project is operational, the other is still in development, i.e., Project 5 data are not complete. And, data being compared are from different types of testing. Any future comparisons should be made using controlled experimental data. However, based on software size and the apparent volume of documented errors alone, Project 5 should, at completion, compare very favorably to similar measures taken on other projects.

---

*Real-time applications software only, but other portions of the Project 5 software exhibit high percentages in these categories as well.

## 4.7.5 Conclusions

The following conclusions are drawn from the foregoing examination of software errors and their susceptibility to elimination by various tools and techniques.

● To be of any practical use in developing or evaluating tools and techniques, errors have to be categorized in considerable detail.

● Detailed error categorization can provide groundwork for specification of requirements for tools. Once the characteristics of errors most frequently encountered are defined, it is a short step to a list of capabilities a tool must have.*

● Error data may be used to justify introduction of new techniques or to direct application of existing techniques in areas known to need attention.

● Although the analysis done here encompassed error data documented during formal subsystem and system testing, the approach used should apply equally well to error data collected during other phases of the software development process, including requirements specification, design, coding, and maintenance phases.

Quantitative results given here should be viewed as peculiar to one development environment. Although major categories used in Projects 2 and 3 are quite similar to those used in Project 5, the detailed characteristics of errors are quite different owing to the differences in operating mode (batch versus real-time), language (JOVIAL versus FORTRAN), and development strategy (one time, everything at once versus top down), just to name a few.

The message here is that software quality (and reliability) can be improved through increased attention to detail and discipline in application of development and test techniques. Tools not only aid in accomplishing tasks which are normally done manually but make it possible to accomplish tasks which would not be done at all if the only way possible was manual. Tools are possibly the only way to achieve the needed discipline and attention to detail within schedule constraints of current software development schedules.

---

*This list of capabilities should still be subject to a critique by the eventual users.

5.0     SOFTWARE RELIABILITY MODELS

5.1     Introduction

This section of the report describes proposed models of software reliability as published in the open literature and government-sponsored reports. Also some recent, previously unpublished, progress in this area by TRW is presented (5.2.4).

The term "software reliability model" mainly refers to a mathematical model constructed for the purpose of assessing the reliability of software from specified parameters which are either assumed known or are measured from observations or experiments on software. It can therefore also refer to the mathematical relationships among the parameters which are considered relevant to software reliability, and not specifically include the reliability parameter itself. For example, the relationship of a logic path to the input data subset exercising that logic path is considered relevant to measurement of reliability, but can be evaluated independently of a reliability measurement. Error rate is another related parameter which has useful meaning in a real time continuously operating system, but which is related to software reliability only indirectly (e.g., by assuming an exponential distribution of time between failures).

Another type of software reliability model to be discussed in this section, for which only a statistical relationship to reliability would be assumed, is the so called *phenomenological* or empirical model. In this approach, it is attempted to quantitatively evaluate those characteristics of software which are sensed as associated with high reliability or the lack of it. For example, "complexity" labels what is considered to be a characteristic leading to low reliability, in that error-proneness (on the part of the programmer) or difficulty of finding and removing errors are believed to be two of many consequences of "complexity". In other terms, the phenomenological model of software reliability attempts to deal with those parameters which when appropriately modified will tend to improve software reliability. Section 4.3 discusses some of the studies and progress made in use of this approach to software reliability.

Software generally can be considered as a subsystem of a computer system.  Avizienis [16] presents a clear discussion of this relationship in terms of providing system design features to assure correct execution of programs in the presence of faults in the computer system.  He goes on in [16] to define software faults as "deviations from correct program execution which are due to errors* occurring during the translation of the original specification of an algorithm to the program being executed". Fault tolerance can be designed into a computer system through the use of redundant hardware or software features.  Software can be designed so that certain classes of software faults can be reduced in frequency or eliminated. The latter is subject matter for *software reliability engineering;* and it is hoped that the current study will contribute to this objective.

Having accepted the definition of "software faults" given above, we can now attempt a definition of software reliability:  as the <u>probability</u> <u>that a software fault which causes deviation from required output by more</u> <u>than specified tolerances, in a specified environment, does not occur dur-</u> <u>ing a specified exposure period.</u>

Let us now discuss this definition in some detail.

There is the implication that not all software faults occurring will reduce the reliability, only those which cause a "deviation from re- quired output by more than specified tolerances."

The specified environment refers to the input data description, which will subsequently be discussed more thoroughly, and the state of the computer system during program execution.  The latter environment will often be described by the amount of fast access storage (core) available, but also will depend on the requirement for the software to operate in the presence of hardware faults.  Here we are referring to features incorporated in the *software* design (e.g., alternate programs, capability of checkpoint

---

* In the following discussion the words "error" or "error type" are de- fined as a cause of a software "fault"; conversely the fault is con- sidered as the manifestation of an error made previously.

restart, etc.) which must work correctly when specified hardware faults
occur.  In general, operating in an environment not included in the specifications and for which the software was not designed, will cause a reduction in reliability.

The specified exposure period is often referred to as the "mission
time."  The concept of a time interval to measure software performance
seems to be most appropriate to a real time situation, in which the number
of executions of any given program and the state of the data base are un-
predictable as of each initiation of a program execution.  The term "operational cycle" or "run" is most apt for a so-called batch environment in
which the state of the system, including the data base is known at the
initiation of execution of a given program.  In general, this will mean
either a return of all storage to its original content prior to re-execution,
or a series of executions which changes the data base in a predetermined
manner.

5.2      Discussion of Models

The discussion of well-documented software reliability models,
such as those attributed to Shooman, Jelinski and Moranda, Wolverton and
Schick, and others, is kept to a minimum in this report.  Hopefully, all
of the essential characteristics are described so that the significance
and relationship to this study can be ascertained without going to the
original reference.

5.2.1     Shooman's Model [17]

The application of this model for reliability estimation depends
upon several assumptions, the most significant of which is the requirement
to use a "system exerciser program", which is not completely defined in
[17].  The remainder of the assumptions are statistical in nature and do
not reflect unique properties of software.  These latter assumptions as
given in [17] can be briefly listed as follows:

A1.  At the start of system integration, there are $E_T$ errors
     present in the software.  Beginning at this point, debug-
     ging time $\tau$ is counted, which is the time spent in test
     ferreting out errors, checkout, etc., exclusive of operating
     time t.  During the debugging time $\tau$, a number $\varepsilon_c(\tau)$ of
     errors per machine language instruction are removed.  Thus
     the number of errors per machine language instruction remain-
     ing after $\tau$ months of debugging is:

$$\varepsilon_r(\tau) = E_T/I_T - \varepsilon_c(\tau)$$

where $I_T$ is the total number of machine language instructions (assumed constant).

A2.  It is then assumed that the hazard function z(t) is propor-
     tional to the number of errors remaining in the software
     after debugging time $\tau$, i.e.:

$$z(t) = C\varepsilon_r(\tau)$$

and if t operational hours are then counted from the point
at which t = 0, and $\tau$ stays fixed, then the reliability
function, or probability of no failure during the operation
time interval (0,t) is:

$$R(t,\tau) = \exp( -C( E_T/I_T - \varepsilon_c(\tau) )t )$$

If k tests are made following periods $(0,\tau_1)$, $(0,\tau_2)$,
$(0,\tau_k)$ of debugging where $\tau_1 < \tau_2 < -- < \tau_k$, it can be
shown that if $k \geq 2$, two equations for the maximum likelihood
estimators $\hat{C}$, $\hat{E}_T$ of the two parameters C, $E_T$ exist:

$$\hat{C} = \sum_{j=1}^{k} n_j \Big/ \sum_{j=1}^{k} ( \hat{E}_T/I_T - \varepsilon_c(\tau_j) ) H_j$$

and

$$\hat{C} = \left( \sum_{j=1}^{k} n_j / (\hat{E}_T / I_T - \epsilon_c(\tau_j)) \right) / \sum_{j=1}^{k} H_j$$

where $n_j$ = number of runs terminating in failure in the $j^{th}$ test

$H_j$ = total time of successful and unsuccessful runs in the $j^{th}$ test

The asymptotic (for large $n_j$'s) variances are given by

$$\text{Var}(\hat{C}) \approx \frac{1}{\dfrac{\sum n_j}{C^2} - \dfrac{(\sum H_j)^2}{\sum \dfrac{n_j}{\epsilon_r^2(\tau_j)}}}$$

$$\text{Var}(\hat{E}_T) \approx \frac{I_T^2}{\sum \dfrac{n_j}{\epsilon_r^2(\tau_j)} - \dfrac{C^2 (\sum H_j)^2}{\sum n_j}}$$

and the correlation coefficient by

$$\rho(\hat{C}, \hat{E}_T) \approx \sum \frac{n_j}{\epsilon_r(\tau_j)} \Bigg/ \left[ \sum n_j \sum \frac{n_j}{\epsilon_r^2(\tau_j)} \right]^{1/2}$$

The usefulness of the asymptotic variances and correlation co-efficient is in the construction of a confidence region for the parameters $C$, $E_T$ based upon normal distribution theory.

Regarding the system exerciser program, it is not emphasized in [17] that this program must present to the subject software input data which represents the operational situations. We will term it an "operational profile", and it is defined essentially by the probability distribution of the input data variables. More will be said on this point in 5.2.4.1 and 5.2.4.2 where some recent work by TRW on a mathematical theory of software reliability is discussed.

## 5.2.2   The Jelinski - Moranda Model [18]

This software reliability prediction model is actually a special case of the Shooman model, as pointed out in [17]. It can be expressed directly as follows. Assume that the amount of debugging time (Shooman's nomenclature) between error occurrences has an exponential distribution, with error occurrence or failure rate (hazard function) proportional to the number of errors remaining in the software. Each error discovered is immediately removed from the software, decreasing the number of errors remaining by one. Consequently, the density function for the time of discovery of the $i^{th}$ error, measured from the time of discovery of the $i-1^{th}$ error is:

$$p(t_i) = \lambda_i e^{-\lambda_i t_i}$$

where

$$\lambda_i = \phi (N - i + 1)$$

and where N is the number of errors originally present. Based upon a sequence of observations $t_1, t_2 \ldots, t_k$, it is shown in [19] that the maximum likelihood estimators for N and $\phi$ as well as their asymptotic variances and correlation coefficient are given by the following formulas.

To find the maximum likelihood estimators, labeled $\hat{N}$, $\hat{\phi}$, solve the two equations:

$$\sum_{i=1}^{k}(\hat{N} - i + 1)^{-1} = k/(\hat{N} + 1 - \theta k)$$

$$\hat{\phi} = \frac{k/A}{\hat{N} + 1 - \theta k}$$

where

$$\theta = B/Ak$$

$$A = \sum_{i=1}^{k} t_i$$

$$B = \sum_{i=1}^{k} i t_i$$

The asymptotic variances and correlation coefficient are given by:

$$Var(\hat{N}) \approx k/\phi^2 D$$

$$Var(\hat{\phi}) \approx S_2/D$$

$$\rho(\hat{N},\hat{\phi}) \approx - A\phi/[kS_2]^{1/2}$$

where

$$D = kS_2/\phi^2 - A^2$$

and

$$S_2 = \sum_{i=1}^{k} (N - i + 1)^{-2}$$

To obtain numerical values of the above quantities, the numerical values of the estimators $\hat{N}$, $\hat{\phi}$ are substituted wherever N, $\phi$ occur. A detailed example is shown in [19].

It is worthwhile to note the modification in the Jelinski - Moranda model suggested by Wolverton and Schick [20]. The modification is to assume that the error rate is not only proportional to the number of errors present, but also to the time spent in debugging, so that the chance of discovery increases as time goes on.

### 5.2.2.1   Generalization of the J-M and S-W Models

Both the Jelinsky - Moranda and Schick - Wolverton models may be generalized by allowing more than one error to occur in a time interval of interest, with no corrections being made until after the end of the time interval.

The likelihood function is slightly different from that of Reference [19] as the observations are now the number of errors occurring in prespecified time intervals, rather than the waiting times to each of the observed errors. All the errors occurring in a specified time interval are then assumed to be removed before resuming testing. Nevertheless, the equations for the solutions of the estimators $\hat{\phi}$ and $\hat{N}$ are quite similar. The details of the derivation are not given here, only the results; the changes to the equations given previously and the reinterpretation of parameters where necessary are pointed out.

The two equations to solve for $\hat{\phi}$, $\hat{N}$ become:

$$\hat{\phi} = \frac{K/A}{\hat{N} + 1 - K\Theta}$$

and

$$\frac{K}{\hat{N} + 1 - K\Theta} = \sum_{i=1}^{M} \frac{M_i}{\hat{N} - n_{i-1}}$$

where

$$A = \begin{cases} \displaystyle\sum_{i=1}^{M} t_i & \text{Jelinsky - Moranda} \\[2em] \displaystyle\sum_{i=1}^{M} t_i \, (T_{i-1} + t_i/2) & \text{Schick - * Wolverton} \end{cases}$$

$$B = \begin{cases} \displaystyle\sum_{i=1}^{M} (n_{i-1} + 1) \, t_i & \text{Jelinsky - Moranda} \\[2em] \displaystyle\sum_{i=1}^{M} (n_{i-1} + 1) \, t_i \, (T_{i-1} + t_i/2) & \text{Schick - * Wolverton} \end{cases}$$

---

* The primary difference between this and the model of Reference [20] is that here it is assumed that the error discovery rate $\lambda_i$ is constant during the time interval $t_i$, so that

$$\lambda_i = \phi \, (N - n_{i-1}) \, (T_{i-1} + t_i/2)$$

i.e., $\lambda_i$ is proportional to the number of errors remaining following the $i$-1st time interval, but also proportional to the total time previously spent in testing (including an "averaged" error search time during the current time interval $t_i$).

$$t_i = \text{Length of time interval in which } M_i \text{ errors are observed}$$

$$T_{i-1} = \text{Cumulative time through } i\text{-}1^{st} \text{ interval}$$

$$= \sum_{j=1}^{i-1} t_j \; ; \; T_0 = 0$$

$$n_{i-1} = \text{Cumulative number of errors observed up through the } i\text{-}1^{st} \text{ time interval}$$

$$n_i = \sum_{j=1}^{i-1} M_j$$

$$n_0 = 0$$

$$M = \text{Total number of time intervals}$$

$$K = \sum_{i=1}^{M} M_i = n_M = \text{total number of errors observed}$$

$$\Theta = B/AK$$

The two equations to solve for $\hat{\phi}$, $\hat{N}$ reduce to their previous counterparts, when $M_i = 1$. In that case $M = K$ (= k in Reference [19]). Also $n_{i-1}$ then becomes simply i-1. The only remaining change is that

$$S_2 \qquad \text{becomes} \qquad \sum_{i=1}^{M} \frac{M_i}{(N - n_{i-1})^2}$$

### 5.2.3    Other Models

Two models which were formulated to deal with the problem of predicting reliability growth in complex systems are briefly described here.
They were chosen from among many for various reasons, primarily for
simplicity of assumptions, but also for variety of other factors considered,
and because they are considered more or less an original contribution.
Finally, some of the concepts expressed and developed should have useful
application to software reliability predictions.

### 5.2.3.1    The Weiss Model [21]

This model (one of three described in [21]), besides assuming an
exponential distribution of time-to-failure, considers that there are M
sources of failure at the beginning of a development process.  Trials are
made (at unspecified points in time) each lasting time $T_t$ and success or
the time of failure is recorded.  The failure rate is assumed to be different for each source of failure and is expressed by an *a priori*
probability distribution of failure rates.  When a failure occurs on a given
trial there is a probability $p_c \leq 1$ that the failure is corrected.  Most
of the consequences of these assumptions are worked out in some simple
examples, the primary outcome being the predicted reliability function
following the removal of errors in a given number of trials.  The author
observes that the mean time to failure can, for the complex model just
described, be fitted by an exponential function of trial number, showing
a constant percentage increase with trial number.

The model described may be useful to evaluation of software reliability if it and the assumptions are modifiable as follows:  Each of the M
sources of failure represents a software error type, e.g., "specified
array size not large enough," which may have several occurrences throughout
the software.  For some error types, such as the above example, once the
error is discovered, there is a high probability that all other occurrences
of this error type will be removed at once.  For other error types, a
relatively small fraction of its occurrences elsewhere in the software will

be discoverable and corrected once discovered. This fraction corresponds to the parameter $p_c$ in the described model except that its value would generally be different for each error source and would be estimated from previous data.

As with all reliability prediction models conceived originally in terms of hardware performance, for software the "test time" must be associated with the degree of representativeness of input data. That is to say, testing for a long time using only a limited region of the input data space will result in unbiased reliability predictions only if the probability of the remaining region of input data being presented to the program is essentially zero. This point was made earlier in reference to the system exerciser program mentioned in [17].

## 5.2.3.2 Models Proposed by Corcoran, et al [22]

The referenced models are mentioned here because they deal with varying probabilities of failure for different error sources and also correspondingly varying probabilities of corrective action. Another reason is that they are relatively simple mathematically and seem capable of simple interpretation to software error data. The models ignore time of test and merely consider the outcome of N trials, in which $N_i$ errors of the $i^{th}$ type (failure source) are observed. Following the N trials, the $i^{th}$ observed error type is corrected with probability $a_i$. As a result of this process, the reliability can be inferred to be larger than the observed success ratio by an amount depending upon the occurrence of errors and their probabilities of removal. One of the reliability estimators labeled as $p_7$ in [22] is:

$$p_7 = N_0/N + \sum_{i=1}^{K} y_i (N_i - 1)/N$$

where $N_0$ is the number of successful trials in N trials, K is the *a priori* known number of error types, and

$$y_i = \begin{cases} a_i & \text{if } N_i > 0 \\ 0 & \text{if } N_i = 0 \end{cases}$$

It is shown in [22] that $p_7$ is unbiased asymptotically for large N, and its variance approaches zero for large N. An exact expression for the expected value of $p_7$ and an approximate expression for the variance of $p_7$ are also shown.

Again, in this model the $a_i$ must be estimated from prior information or data, and to be useful for software reliability estimation, each trial, or at least the collection of N trials must represent the submission to the program of input data regions in accordance with the operational profile.

## 5.2.4    The Nelson Model [23]

The Nelson model was developed at TRW as a mathematical theory of software reliability (MTSR) to provide a foundation for investigating software reliability, viz:

- precise, mathematical definitions of the basic elements of software reliability,

- mathematical relations on these elements, and

- mathematical methods for manipulating the elements to derive new aspects of software reliability.

The model is described in this section and compared with the other models. Work performed on application and extension of MTSR is reported in Section 6.0.

## 5.2.4.1    Description of the Nelson Model

The intuitive definition of software reliability given in 5.1 can be changed into a precise, although statistical, definition by making use of the following primitive concepts:

- A computer program p may be defined [24] as a specification of a computable function F on the set E;

$$E = (E_i : i = 1,2,\ldots,N)$$

of all input data values, each $E_i$ being the collection of data values needed to make a run of the program.

- Execution of p produces, for each input $E_i$, the function value $F(E_i)$.

- The set E defines all the computations which p can make; i.e., each input $E_i$ corresponds to a possible run of p and each run corresponds to an input $E_i$.

- Owing to imperfections in the implementation of p, p actually specifies a function F', which differs from F, the function the program is intended to specify.

- For some $E_i$, the deviation of the actual execution output $F'(E_i)$ from the desired output $F(E_i)$ is within an acceptable tolerance $\Delta_i$ ; i.e.,

$$| F'(E_i) - F(E_i) | \leq \Delta_i$$

- For all other $E_i$, which form a subset $E_e$ of E, execution of p does not produce acceptable output; i.e., either:

$$| F'(E_i) - F(E_i) | > \Delta_i, \text{ or}$$

- execution terminates prematurely, or
- execution fails to terminate.

Such occurrences are called "execution failures".

Each $E_i$ is a possible combination of the values which can be assigned to the input variables (the variables whose values must be presented to p to enable p to execute). The number N of possible $E_i$ is very large, but it is finite because only a finite number of different values can fit in a fixed-sized computer word.

The process of presenting $E_i$ to p and executing p to produce the output $F'(E_i)$ or an execution failure is called a run of p. Note that all of the values that compose $E_i$ do not have to be presented to p simultaneously.

The probability P that a run of p will result in an execution failure is therefore equal to the probability that the input $E_i$ used in the run will be chosen from $E_e$. If $n_e$ is the number of $E_i$ in $E_e$, then:

$$P = \frac{n_e}{N}$$

is the probability that a run of p with input $E_i$ selected from E at random with equal *a priori* probability will result in an execution failure and

$$R = 1 - P = 1 - \frac{n_e}{N}$$

is the probability that a run of p with input $E_i$ selected from E at random with equal *a priori* probability will produce acceptable output.

In operational use of a program, however, the inputs are not usually selected from E with equal *a priori* probability. Rather, they are selected according to some operational requirement. This requirement may be characterized by a probability distribution $p_i$, $p_i$ being the probability that $E_i$ is selected. The set of $p_i$'s is called the "operational profile". P may be expressed in terms of $p_i$ by defining an "execution variable" $y_i$, which is assigned the value 0 if a run with $E_i$ computes an acceptable function value, and which is assigned the value 1 if a run with $E_i$ results in an execution failure. Then

$$P = \sum_{i=1}^{N} p_i y_i$$

is the probability that a run of p with input $E_i$ chosen according to the probability distribution $p_i$ will result in an execution failure, and

$$R = 1 - P = \sum_{i=1}^{N} p_i (1 - y_i)$$

is the probability that a run with input $E_i$ chosen according to the probability distribution $p_i$ will result in correct execution.

Since R is the probability of p not resulting in an execution failure in a single run made with input selected according to $p_i$, the probability of there being no execution failures in n runs with each of the inputs selected independently according to $p_i$ is:

$$R(n) = R^n = (1 - P)^n$$

Thus a mathematical definition of the reliability of a computer program is:

- The probability that the program has no execution failure in n runs.

The unit of exposure of a program is therefore the run.

In operational use, the inputs for n runs usually are not selected independently but in a definite sequence, such as, i.e., ascending values of some input variable or in a sequence determined by some real input, as in the case of a real time program. Then the operational profile must be redefined to be $p_{ji}$, the probability that $E_i$ is chosen as the input to the $j^{th}$ run in a sequence of runs. Then the probability $P_j$ that run j results in an execution failure can be written:

$$P_j = \sum_{i=1}^{N} p_{ji} y_i$$

The reliability R(n) of p is the probability that no execution failure occurs in a sequence of n runs:

$$R(n) = (1-P_1)(1-P_2) \cdots (1-P_n) = \prod_{j=1}^{n} (1-P_j)$$

This formula may be written in exponential form:

$$R(n) = e^{\sum_{j=1}^{n} \ln(1-P_j)}$$

Some of the properties of $R(n)$ may be exhibited by making approximations

- for $P_j \ll 1$

$$R(n) = e^{-\sum_{j=1}^{n} P_j}$$

- if $P_j = P$ for all $j$

$$R(n) = e^{-Pn}$$

$R(n)$ may be expressed in terms of the execution time $t$ by making the substitutions:

- $\Delta t_j$ denotes the execution time for run $j$

$$t_j = \sum_{i=1}^{j} \Delta t_i \quad \text{denotes the cumulative execution time through run } j$$

$$h(t_j) = - \frac{\ln (1-P_j)}{\Delta t_j}$$

$$R(n) = e^{-\sum_{j=1}^{n} \Delta t_j h(t_j)}$$

If $\Delta t_j$ is considered to approach zero as $n$ becomes large, the sum in the exponential becomes an integral, producing the formula:

$$R(t) = \exp\left[-\int_0^t ds\ h(s)\right]$$

which is familiar from hardware reliability theory. In the case $P_j \ll 1$, $h(t_j)$ may be interpreted as the "hazard" function, which when multiplied by $\Delta t_j$ is the conditional probability of failure during the interval $(t_j, t_j + \Delta t_j)$ given no failure prior to $t_j$.

## 5.2.4.2 Measurement of Software Reliability

The reliability of a computer program can be measured by running the program with a sample of n inputs and caluclating $\hat{R}$, the measured value, from the formula

$$\hat{R} = 1 - \frac{\hat{n}_e}{n}$$

where $\hat{n}_e$ is the number of inputs for which execution failures occurred. If the n inputs in the sample are chosen from E at random according to the probability distribution $p_i$, the measured value $\hat{R}$ is an unbiased estimate of R in the sense that the expectation of $\hat{R}$ over the sample probability distribution is equal to R, for $p_i \ll 1$. This can be shown by introducing a "sample variable" $z_{ij}$ which is defined so that:

$$z_{ij} = 1 \text{ if } E_i \text{ is in sample } j$$

$$z_{ij} = 0 \text{ otherwise}$$

The number of distinct inputs $\hat{n}_j$ obtained in a sample j may be less than n, since the same $E_i$ can be selected more than once by the random process.

$$\sum_{i=1}^{N} z_{ij} = n_j$$

However, in most cases the number of possible inputs N is so much larger than the sample size that it is very unlikely that any repetition of inputs would occur. If $s_j$ is the probability that sample $j$ is chosen and M is the number of possible samples:

$$\sum_{j=1}^{M} z_{ij}\, s_j = 1 - (1-p_i)^n$$

Since $\hat{R}$ can be written in the form:

$$\hat{R}_j = \frac{1}{n} \sum_{i=1}^{N} (1-y_i)\, z_{ij}$$

The expectation of $\hat{R}$, $E(\hat{R})$, is:

$$E(\hat{R}) = \sum_{j=1}^{M} s_j \hat{R}_j$$

$$= \frac{1}{n} \sum_{j=1}^{M} s_j \sum_{i=1}^{N} (1-y_i)\, z_{ij}$$

$$= \frac{1}{n} \sum_{i=1}^{N} (1-y_i) \sum_{j=1}^{M} s_j z_{ij}$$

$$= \frac{1}{n} \sum_{i=1}^{N} (1-y_i)\, [1 - (1-p_i)^n]$$

$$= \sum_{i=1}^{N} (1-y_i)\, p_i \quad \text{for } p_i \ll 1$$

$$= 1 - P$$

$$= R$$

In order to carry out a measurement of R, the operational profile $p_i$ must be determined. In actual practice, this is done by dividing the ranges of the input variables into subranges and assigning probabilities that an input will be chosen from each subrange, based on an estimate of the occurrence of inputs in the operational use for which the reliability is being measured. The probabilities $p_i$ having been determined in this way, a sample of n inputs can be chosen at random -- e.g., with the aid of a random number generator -- in accordance with the $p_i$. When the n runs of the measurement are made, the outputs for some of the inputs will be found to be correct while execution failures may occur for other inputs. When an execution failure occurs, the measurement process should not be stopped and the error corrected. Instead the entire sample of n runs should be made without correcting any of the errors which caused the execution failures and the value of $\hat{R}$ can be calculated from the measurement data.

This approach to measuring software reliability was tested at TRW by applying it to two programs, each written by a different person from the same specifications. A profile $p_i$ was established to approximate what could be expected in operational use of the program. A sample of 1000 inputs was selected from this profile with the aid of a random number generator and 1000 runs made with each program. The output for each run was examined and the runs which resulted in execution failures were identified. Three execution failures were obtained for one of the programs and 35 for the other. The measured reliability, $\hat{R}$, was caluclated to be .997 for the first program and .965 for the second. The program having the higher reliability had the simpler structure, supporting the notion that complex structure leads to reduced reliability.[7].

### 5.2.4.3   Comparison with Other Models

Both the Shooman model and the Jelinski-Moranda models use time as the unit of exposure and an exponential formula for R(t):

$$R(t) = e^{-ht}$$

The hazard function h is assumed constant during operational time and changes only when an error is found and removed, after which t must be reset to zero. Since this formula can be derived from the Nelson model by making certain approximations, the approximations required may be used to define the conditions under which the Shooman and Jelinski-Moranda models are valid; viz:

- t should be interpreted as cumulative execution time from a specified starting time;

- t should be large compared to the average execution time $\Delta t$ per run;

- the inputs for successive runs should be chosen at random according a probability distribution approximating that expected in the type of use for which the reliability prediction is made.

Both Shooman and Jelinski-Moranda attempt to extend their models by assuming that the hazard function is proportional to the number of errors remaining in the program and then to apply their models to the testing of programs.

The Weiss model and the Corcoran models were developed to describe reliability improvement during testing and attempt to incorporate the effect of there being several sources of errors present in a program.

All of these models are limited in their applicability because they were not developed to correspond closely to the properties of programs and how they are used and tested. They rely principally on general principles of probability, such as the exponential dependence of reliability on exposure, and on simplistic assumptions about the affect of errors. Although the exponential dependence is well established, the other aspects of these models appear to be, at best, rough approximations to software properties.

The Nelson model was developed from the basic properties of computer programs and uses probability theory to deal with those aspects for which incomplete information is available -- e.g., what input will be chosen in the next run. Where approximations are made, they are well-defined and the limits of their applicability are known. Because of its foundation on software properties, it can be extended systematically to describe in more detail other aspects of software reliability. Some of the extensions which have been made are described in Section 6.0. Because of its broader foundation and extensibility, it is referred to there as a mathematical theory of software reliability rather than a reliability model.

## 6.0 APPLICATION AND EXTENSION OF THE MATHEMATICAL THEORY OF SOFTWARE RELIABILITY

The basic elements of the mathematical theory of software reliability (MTSR) are described in Section 5.2.4.* This section reports on work done in the Software Reliability Study to apply and extend the theory so that it has become a broad conceptual framework for exploring, comprehending, and analyzing the development and testing of reliable software, with mathematical tools for conducting quantitative analysis.  MTSR was applied to:

- Analyze software reliability data (6.1)
- Investigate specific problems (6.2)
  - Input data set partitioning (6.2.1)
  - Reliability measurement uncertainty (6.2.2)
  - Effect of software error removal (6.2.3)
  - Effect of program structure (6.2.4)
  - Estimating reliability from test results (6.2.5)
  - Program safety effects (6.2.6)
- Develop improved techniques for writing reliable programs (6.3)
- Develop improved software testing methods (6.4)

### 6.1  Application of MTSR to Project 5 Test Data

Test data from several routines developed and tested on Project 5 were analyzed with the aid of MTSR.  The nature of this analysis can be illustrated by showing how it was performed on one of the Project 5 routines which will be called "routine A".

Routine A is written in FORTRAN and has 20 executable statements.  Its code is:

```
      IF(GN.NE.0.) GOTO 10
      IF(CN.LT.CT) GOTO 5
      IE = 1
      GOTO 25
    5 IE = 0
      GOTO 25
```

*Some of the notation used in this section has been defined in Section 5.2.4.

```
10  IF(CN.LT.TR) GOTO 20
    IE = 1
    GOTO 25
20  IE = 0
25  IF(IE.NE.1) GOTO 40
    JE = JE+1
    KI = JD
    KM = 2
    KR = 3
    KB = JA
    KE = JB
    JV = JV + KI + 1
    KG = 1
40  RETURN
    END
```

The analysis of routine A began with identification of the input variables, their types and ranges. The variables to which values must be assigned in order for routine A to execute are:

- GN,CN,CT,TR : real data type

- JA,JB,JD,JE,JV : integer data type

For both data types, the variables range over the values which can be stored in a computer word.

The testing performed on routine A involved four test cases. The values assigned to the real variables were:

- Test Case 1:  GN = 0.
  CN = 5.
  CT = 4.
  TR = 6.

- Test Case 2:  GN = 1.
  CN = 8.
  CT = 4.
  TR = 6.

- Test Case 3:  GN = 0.
  CN = 3.
  CT = 4.
  TR = 6.

● Test Case 4:  GN = 1.
                 CN = 5.
                 CT = 4.
                 TR = 6.

The values assigned to the integer data were the same for all 4 test cases and are not listed here.

Next the logic paths which are executed by each of the test cases were determined as well as the set of inputs which cause each logic path to execute.

In test case 1, the value 0 assigned to GN causes the branch test (GN.NE.O.) in the first IF statement to be evaluated false, so execution proceeds to the second IF statement, where the value 5 assigned to CN and 4 to CT cause the branch test (CN.LT.CT) to be evaluated false. Next the internal variable IE is assigned the value 1 and execution transfers to the fourth IF statement, where the test (IE.NE.1) is evaluated false and execution continues down to the RETURN statement. This logic path is executed for the input variable GN = 0 and for values of CN which are greater than or equal to the value of CT. Note that the real variable TR and all of the integer variables are not involved in any computation for this logic path. Therefore the set $G_1$ of input data values which will cause this logic path to execute are completely defined by:

$$G_1: \quad GN = 0$$
$$CN \geq CT$$

A similar analysis shows that test case 2 executes a different logic path, which is defined by the set $G_2$ of input data values:

$$G_2: \quad GN \neq 0$$
$$CN \geq TR$$

The variable CT and the integer variables are not involved in any computations.

Test case 3 executes a third logic path, which is defined by the set $G_3$ of input data values:

$$
\begin{aligned}
G_3: \quad & GN = 0 \\
& CN < CT \\
& JA = I \\
& JB = I \\
& JD \quad I \\
& JE = I \\
& JV = I
\end{aligned}
$$

Where I denotes any integer value. The variable TR is not involved in any calculations.

Test case 4 executes a fourth logic path, which is defined by the set $G_4$ of input data values:

$$
\begin{aligned}
G_4: \quad & GN \neq 0 \\
& CN < TR \\
& JA = I \\
& JB = I \\
& JD = I \\
& JE = I \\
& JV = I
\end{aligned}
$$

The variable CT is not involved in any computations.

There are no other logic paths. The set E can be defined as the union of the four sets $G_1$, $G_2$, $G_3$, $G_4$.

$$
E = G_1 \cup G_2 \cup G_3 \cup G_4
$$

Note that this is not equal to the cartesian product of the sets over which the input variables range, for the possible values of input variables are constrained by the relations used in defining the subsets $G_j$, including the nonutilization of some of the variables in each $G_j$.

Each test case is from a different $G_j$ and causes execution of a different logic path. Collectively, they exercise all the logic paths. No logic path was executed by more than one test case.

A logic diagram can be constructed for routine A in terms of the branch tests $B_i$:

$$B_1 : GN.NE.O.$$
$$B_2 : CN.LT.CT$$
$$B_3 : CN.LT.TR$$
$$B_4 : IE.NE.1$$

and the code segments $S_i$:

$$S_1 : IE = 1$$
$$S_2 : IE = 0$$
$$S_3 : IE = 1$$
$$S_4 : IE = 0$$
$$S_5 : JE = JE + 1$$
$$KI = JD$$
$$KM = 2$$
$$KR = 3$$
$$KB = JA$$
$$KE = JB$$
$$JV = JV + KI + 1$$
$$KG = 1$$
$$S_6 : RETURN$$

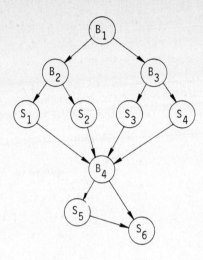

From this logic diagram, it would appear that there are 8 logic paths; however, 4 of these apparent paths are not executable. For each of the four paths leading into $B_4$, the outcome of the branch test $B_4$ is predetermined; i.e., for all inputs that can cause execution of a specific path leading to $B_4$, the test in $B_4$ will result in the same truth value, allowing only one of the branches to be taken.

The partitioning of the input data set E into subsets $G_j$ that correspond to logic paths was done for four Project 5 routines. For all of them, the test cases belonged to different $G_j$. This was not surprising since TRW's software test tool PACE was used to aid in developing the test cases. PACE analyzes the routine structure and provides information to aid in developing a set of test cases which will collectively exercise all segments and branches in the routine. For some of the routines, the number of test cases needed to exercise all segments and branches is less than the number of $G_j$'s, because in most routines, in particular the larger ones, all segments and branches can be exercised by executing a subset of the set of all logic paths.

Additional results of the application of MTSR to Project 5 routines are reported in the following sections.

## 6.2   Extension of MTSR

The capabilities of MTSR were extended by investigating several software reliability problem areas, applying MTSR concepts to them, and developing new mathematical tools and techniques as needed to perform the indicated analysis.

### 6.2.1   Input Data Set Partitioning

For more detailed analysis of software reliability, it is convenient to partition the set E into disjoint subsets $S_j$:

$$E = S_1 \cup S_2 \cup \ldots \cup S_k = \underset{j}{\cup} S_j$$

$$S_i \cap S_j = \phi, \quad \text{for} \quad i \neq j$$

$\phi$ denotes the null set. The probability $P_j$ that an input $E_i$ is chosen from $S_j$ is:

$$P_j = \sum_{E_i \epsilon S_j} p_i$$

$$\sum_{j=1}^{k} P_j = 1$$

Each subset $S_j$ can be further partitioned into two subsets $S_j'$ and $S_j''$ such that any input from $S_j'$ results in correct execution and any input from $S_j''$ results in an execution failure.

$$S_j' \cup S_j'' = S_j$$

$$S_j' \cap S_j'' = \phi$$

$$S_j'' = \left\{ E_i \epsilon S_j \ : \ y_i = 1 \right\}$$

$$S_j' = \left\{ E_i \epsilon S_j \ : \ y_i = 0 \right\}$$

where $y_i = 0(1)$ if input $E_i$ results in correct execution (execution failure).

The probability $P_j'$ that an input is a member of $S_j'$ is:

$$P_j' = \sum_{E_i \epsilon S_j} (1 - y_i) \ P_i$$

and the probability $P_j''$ that an input is a member of $S_j''$ is:

$$P_j'' = \sum_{E_i \epsilon S_j} y_i \ P_i$$

$$P_j' + P_j'' = P_j$$

The reliability formula can be expressed in terms of $P'_j$ or $P''_j$:

$$R = 1 - \sum_{i=1}^{N} y_i \, P_i$$

$$= 1 - \sum_{j=1}^{k} \sum_{E_i \epsilon S_j} y_i \, P_i$$

$$= 1 - \sum_{j=1}^{k} P''_j = \sum_{j=1}^{k} P'_j$$

One type of partitioning of E is that into the subsets $G_j$ associated with the logic paths $L_j$, as was done in the analysis of routine A in Section 6.1. $P_j$ is then the probability that logic path $L_j$ will be executed and $P'_j/P_j$ is the probability that, having selected an input from $G_j$, $L_j$ will be executed correctly.

Since the code sequence of a logic path $L_j$ is itself a program, $L_j$ may, in accordance with the mathematical definition of a program, be interpreted as a specification of a function $F_j$ on $G_j$. For all inputs $E_i \epsilon G_j$, the same code sequence $L_j$ is executed and there is no branching outside of $L_j$; therefore $F_j$ may be considered to have a degree of continuity over $G_j$. Correct execution of $L_j$ for a particular input, say $E_k$, from $G_j$ verifies that the program computes $F_j(E_k)$ correctly. Because of the continuity argument, one may infer from the correct execution of $L_j$ for input $E_k$ that $L_j$ will also, with high probability, execute correctly for most of the other $E_i$ which are in $G_j$. The following argument tends to reinforce the intuitive feeling that this probability is high. $L_j$, in fact, specifies a function, which may be denoted by $F_j'$, and which is intended to be $F_j$. Correct execution of $L_j$ with input $E_k$ means that:

$$|F_j'(E_k) - F_j(E_k)| \leq \Delta_k$$

where $\Delta_k$ is the acceptable tolerance. The notation indicates that the tolerance $\Delta_k$ could be different for each input $E_k$, although in general it will have the same value for a subset of $G_j$. When the tolerance must be met uniformly for the function $F_j$, the notation $\Delta_j$ would be used.

Many of the types of errors that can be made in code $L_j$ will result in $L_j$ specifying a function $F_j'$, the values of which will deviate from the corresponding values of $F_j$ by more than the acceptable tolerance $\Delta_j$ for all the points in $G_j$. There are, however, known types of errors for which $F_j'$ can equal $F_j$ at one or more points and deviate from it at all other points; e.g.:

- The assignment statement Y = X*2 + A at the point X = 2 assigns the same value to Y as the statement Y = X**2 + A, but assigns substantially different values at all other points.

- In the assignment statement, Y = (Q(X) - Q_0)P(X) + R(X), at the point X such that Q(X) = Q_0, any error in P(X) will not affect the value assigned to Y, but errors in P(X) may significantly affect the values assigned to Y for other values of X.

In order for such errors to lead to $|F_j'(E_t) - F_j(E_t)| \leq \Delta_t$ for the execution of test case $E_t$, not only must such an error be present in $L_j$ but also the input $E_t$ chosen for the test case must be the same, or very near the same, point at which the evaluation coincidence occurs. Developing an expression for the probability of such an occurrence would involve developing a measure for the functions $F_j'$ specified by erroneous $L_j$ and the subset of this measure associated with those functions $F_j'$ for which $|F_j'(E_k) - F_j(E_k)| \leq \Delta_k$ for some points $E_k$ in $G_j$.

These considerations can be investigated further by defining the probability of acceptable execution:

$$Pr(|F_j'(E_t) - F_j(E_t)| \leq \Delta_t)$$

with the function $F'_j$ considered to be a random variable owing to the random
occurrence of errors which cause the specified $F'_j$ to differ from the
intended $F_j$.  Then, if the effects of errors do not have a bias — i.e.,
the expectation, $\mathcal{E}(F'_j(E_t)) = F_j(E_t)$ — a form of the generalized Tchebycheff
Inequality may be applied, which states that if $g(x)$ is a non-negative
function of the random variable $x$, then for any $k > 0$,

$$Pr(g(x) \le k) > 1 - \frac{\mathcal{E}(g(x))}{k}$$

Since the expected value of the square of the difference between a random
variable and its expected value is by definition the variance of the random
variable:

$$\mathcal{E}\left[\left(F'_j(E_t) - F_j(E_t)\right)^2\right] \equiv Var\ (F'_j(E_t))$$

then replacing $k$ by $\Delta_t^2$,

$$Pr(|F'_j(E_t) - F_j(E_t)| \le \Delta_t) > 1 - \frac{Var\ (F'_j(E_t))}{\Delta_t^2}$$

If:

$$Var\ (F'_j(E_t)) < \Delta_t^2\ (1-\gamma)\ ,$$

then:

$$Pr(|F'_j(E_t) - F_j(E_t)| \le \Delta_t) > \gamma \tag{*}$$

which if $\gamma$ is sufficiently close to 1, say 0.9, the probability of correct
execution is acceptably high.

The previous results can be further refined by accounting for the probability distribution of the Input Data point, $E_t$. The following is true, approximately:

$$\text{Var}\ (F_j'(E_t)) \simeq \left[\frac{\partial F_j'(E_t)}{\partial E_t}\right]^2 \text{Var}\ (E_t) + V_j'$$

where $V_j'$ = variance of $F_j'(\mathcal{E}(E_t))$, and $\partial F_j'(E_t)/\partial E_t$ is evaluated at $E_t = \mathcal{E}(E_t)$, which measures the relative rate of change of the specified function $F_j'$. Thus

$$V_j' + \left[\frac{\partial F_j'(E_t)}{\partial E_t}\right]^2 \text{Var}\ (E_t) < \Delta_t^2\ (1-\gamma)$$

implies (*).

When N executions of the program are made using a random sample of $E_t$ selected from the Input Data Subspace $G_j$, it is easily shown that:

$$V_j' + \left[\frac{\partial F_j'(E_t)}{\partial E_t}\right]^2 \text{Var}\ (E_t) < \Delta_t^2\ (1-\gamma)N$$

implies (*).

Owing to the factor N, this condition becomes easier to meet as N gets larger. Thus, for all other quantities being fixed, as N increases the probability level $\gamma$ for any Input Data point $E_t$ resulting in a correct functional output within a given tolerance also increases.

In general, since the Input Data point $E_t$ is a member of a multi-dimensional space: $E_t(X_1, \ldots, X_n)$, the previous expressions need to be replaced by their n-dimensional analogues. The previous inequality generalizes to

$$\frac{1}{N}\left\{\sum_{k=1}^{n}\left[\frac{\partial F_j'(E_t)}{\partial X_k}\right]^2 \text{Var}\ (X_k) + V_j'\right\} < \Delta_t^2\ (1-\gamma)$$

which implies (*).

For simplicity, it is assumed in the previous expression that the $X_k$ are
independently selected, so that the covariances of the $X_k$ are not included.

There are also types of errors which affect only one point which can
occur frequently enough to warrant special care to be taken to check for
them; e.g.:

- Divide by zero. It is possible to automatically identify all
  statements in which this could occur.

- Wrong branch operator, such as, e.g., using .LE. for .LT. in
  the second statement of routine A (Section 6.1).

## 6.2.2 Reliability Measurement Uncertainty

In 5.2.4.2, a method of measuring the reliability of a program was
described which involved making runs with a sample of n inputs chosen at
random from E in accordance with the probability distribution $p_i$. There
are other methods of sampling which may be more appropriate for particular
situations. Some of these methods were investigated, making use of the
partitioning of E into subsets $S_j$, and developing expressions for the
variance and confidence limits on the reliability measurements obtained
using the sample.

### 6.2.2.1 Sampling Theory

Assume that a preassigned number $n_j$ data points are sampled from $S_j$,
for each j. The sampling is assumed to be simple random; i.e., selection
of any point of $S_j$ is unaffected by selection of any other point*, and each
has the same chance of being chosen. We merely observe whether a selected
point belongs to $S_j'$ or $S_j''$ so that this type of sampling is also known as
simple binomial; i.e., the probability assigned to a sequence of $n_j$ points
sampled from $S_j$ is $(P_j'')^{f_j}(P_j')^{n_j-f_j}/P_j^{n_j}$, where $f_j$ is the number of points
selected from $S_j''$ — those evoking software failure.

There are various other sampling methods, such as sampling until a
specified number of points from $S_j''$ are selected, thus making $n_j$ rather than
$f_j$ a random variable, but these will not be discussed further.

---

*There are so many points in $S_j$ that the effect of replacement or nonre-
placement on the probabilities of selection can be neglected.

## Estimation for R

In general not all $S_j$ may be sampled. If this is the case the estimator $\hat{R}$ defined below will be biased. Thus if T is the collection of indexes of subsets $S_j$ of the partition which are sampled ($\overline{T}$ will denote the remaining j's),

$$\hat{R} \equiv 1 - \sum_{T} (f_j/n_j) P_j \qquad (1)$$

and the expected value of $\hat{R}$, denoted by $\mathcal{E}(\hat{R})$ is

$$\mathcal{E}(\hat{R}) = 1 - \sum_{T} (P''_j/P_j) P_j = 1 - \sum_{T} P''_j \geq 1 - \sum_{j} P''_j = R \qquad (2)$$

where the latter summation is over *all* j = 1,2, ... ,K. Therefore, when sampling is incomplete, $\hat{R}$ will be biased on the high side. By apportioning just one data point sample to each of the $S_j$ in $\overline{T}$ (but keeping the total sample size $\sum_{j} n_j = \sum_{T} n_j = n$ constant) the bias in the estimator $\hat{R}$ would be removed. We now need a measure of the precision of $\hat{R}$.

One such measure is the variance, abbreviated as V( ). Thus, since $V(f_j) = n_j P'_j P''_j/P_j^2$ , it can be shown that

$$V_T(\hat{R}) = \sum_{T} P'_j P''_j/n_j \qquad (3)$$

Since, however, $\hat{R}$ is biased for incomplete samples, a better measure is the mean-square error, defined by $\mathcal{E}\left[(\hat{R} - R)^2\right]$. We have

$$\mathcal{E}\left[(\hat{R} - R)^2\right] = \sum_{T} \frac{P'_j P''_j}{n_j} + \left(\sum_{\overline{T}} P''_j\right)^2 \qquad (4)$$

Thus the mean-square error can never be less than the number

$$\left(\sum_{\overline{T}} P''_j\right)^2$$

even should the $n_j$ all become large. This makes $\mathcal{E}\left[(\hat{R} - R)^2\right]$ a measure of sampling completeness in a certain sense; however there is no way of calculating it, for although we have information on the sizes of $P'_j$ or $P''_j$ for $j \in T$, nothing is known about $P''_j$ for $j \in \overline{T}$, except the crude bounds $0 \leq P''_j \leq P_j$. Now it is easy to show that

$$\mathcal{E}\left(\sum_T \frac{f_j (n_j - f_j)}{n_j^2 (n_j - 1)} P_j^2\right) = V_T(\hat{R}) \tag{5}$$

and therefore, using the crude bounds on $P''_j$ for $j \in \overline{T}$, an approximate set of numerical* lower and upper bounds on the mean-square error are

$$\sum_T \frac{f_j (n_j - f_j)}{n_j^2 (n_j - 1)} P_j^2 \leq \langle\!\langle \mathcal{E}\left[(\hat{R} - R)^2\right]\rangle\!\rangle \leq \sum_T \frac{f_j (n_j - f_j)}{n_j^2 (n_j - 1)} P_j^2 + \left(\sum_{\overline{T}} P_j\right)^2 \tag{6}$$

The existence of the above unbiased estimator for $V_T(\hat{R})$ evidently requires that every $n_j \geq 2$.

Minimization of Variance

Since the variance of

$$\hat{R} = 1 - \sum_j (f_j/n_j) P_j$$

---
*"$\langle \ \rangle$" denotes a numerical estimate of the quantity within.

for a complete sample is given by

$$V(\hat{R}) = \sum_j \frac{P_j' P_j''}{n_j} \qquad (3')$$

The question arises whether the $n_j$ can be chosen in some manner to make $V(\hat{R})$ as small as possible. Thus for a given

$$n = \sum_j n_j, \quad \text{if we write}$$

$$W = \sum_k \frac{P_k' P_k''}{n_k} + \lambda^2 \left(\sum_k n_k - n\right)$$

then solve the set of equations $\partial W/\partial n_j = 0$ for all j together with the constraint

$$\sum_k n_k = n,$$

we may obtain an extremal solution for the $n_j$ which can then be shown to yield a minimum $V(\hat{R})$. Thus

$$\frac{\partial W}{\partial n_j} = -\frac{P_j' P_j''}{n_j^2} + \lambda^2 = 0$$

Consequently

$$\lambda = \frac{1}{n} \sum_k \sqrt{P_k' P_k''}$$

Therefore

$$n_j \approx \frac{n\sqrt{P'_j P''_j}}{\sum_k \sqrt{P'_k P''_k}} \tag{7}$$

(The "$\approx$" is used since $n_j$ is an integer.)

This choice of $n_j$ will yield a minimum since $\partial^2 W/\partial n_j^2 > 0$ for all subsets for which $P'_j, P''_j > 0$. Thus, substituting the solutions for the $n_j$, the minimum value of the variance becomes

$$V_{min}(\hat{R}) = \frac{1}{n}\left(\sum_j \sqrt{P'_j P''_j}\right)^2 \tag{8}$$

Of course, unless the values of $P''_j$ are known before sampling takes place, the optimum choice of the $n_j$ cannot be deliberately made. If a preliminary sample were taken however, and assuming no significant change in the value of $P''_j$ (e.g., as a result of correcting the detected faults), the final sample of $n_j$ from each subset $S_j$ could be chosen to yield a near-minimal variance estimate.

A numerical example will illustrate the relationships discussed.

$$\text{Let } P_1 = 0.5, \quad P_2 = 0.3, \quad P_3 = 0.2$$

$$\text{Let } P_1'' = 0.1, \quad P_2'' = 0.1, \quad P_3'' = 0$$

$$\text{(and therefore) } P_1' = 0.4, \quad P_2' = 0.2, \quad P_3' = 0.2$$

Assume that $n = 100$, and that $n_j$ are chosen proportional to $P_j$ so that $n_1 = 50$, $n_2 = 30$, $n_3 = 20$. Then

$$V(\hat{R}) = \frac{(0.1)\,(0.4)}{50} + \frac{(0.1)\,(0.2)}{30} + 0$$

$$= 0.00080 + 0.00067 = 0.00147$$

On the other hand, if the $n_j$ had been chosen to yield $V_{min}(\hat{R})$,

$$n_1 = \frac{\sqrt{0.04}\,(100)}{\sqrt{0.04} + \sqrt{0.02}} = \frac{0.2\,(100)}{0.3414} = 58.7 \approx 59$$

$$n_2 = \frac{0.1414\,(100)}{0.3414} = 41.3 \approx 41$$

$$n_3 = 0$$

Then

$$V_{min}(\hat{R}) = \frac{0.04}{59} + \frac{0.02}{41} \quad \underline{or} \quad \frac{(\sqrt{0.04} + \sqrt{0.02}\,)^2}{100}$$

$$= 0.00068 + 0.00049$$

$$= 0.00117$$

## Sampling Representativeness

A measure of sampling representativeness was proposed in [25]. It is

$$x^2 = \sum_j \frac{(n_j - n\,P_j)^2}{n\,P_j} \tag{9}$$

Assume sampling incomplete, so that for $j \, \epsilon \, \overline{T}$, $n_j = 0$, and

$$\sum_{j \, \epsilon \, T} n_j = n \; , \quad \text{where} \quad T \, U \, \overline{T} = (\text{all } j)$$

What choice of $n_j$ will minimize $\chi^2$?

To determine the $n_j$, we set up the function

$$W = \sum_j \frac{(n_j - n \, P_j)^2}{n P_j} - 2\lambda \left( \sum_{j \, \epsilon \, T} n_j - n \right)$$

$$= \sum_{j \, \epsilon \, T} \frac{(n_j - n \, P_j)^2}{n P_j} + n \sum_{j \, \epsilon \, \overline{T}} P_j - 2\lambda \left( \sum_{j \, \epsilon \, T} n_j - n \right)$$

Set

$$\frac{\partial W}{\partial n_k} = \frac{2(n_k - n \, P_k)}{n P_k} - 2\lambda = 0$$

Hence

$$\lambda = \frac{1}{\displaystyle\sum_{k \, \epsilon \, T} P_k} - 1$$

Therefore

$$n_j \approx \frac{n \, P_j}{\displaystyle\sum_{k \, \epsilon \, T} P_k} \qquad (10)$$

The minimized value of $\chi^2$ is then

$$\chi_{min}^2 = \sum_{j \in T} \frac{\left( \dfrac{n\, P_j}{\displaystyle\sum_{k \in T} P_k} - n\, P_j \right)^2}{n\, P_j} + n \sum_{j \in \overline{T}} P_j$$

$$= \sum_{j \in T} n\, P_j \left( \frac{1}{\displaystyle\sum_{j \in T} P_j} - 1 \right)^2 + n \sum_{j \in \overline{T}} P_j$$

$$= n \left( \frac{1}{\displaystyle\sum_{j \in T} P_j} - 2 + \sum_{j \in T} P_j \right) + n \sum_{j \in \overline{T}} P_j$$

and finally

$$\chi_{min}^2 = n\, \frac{\displaystyle\sum_{j \in \overline{T}} P_j}{\displaystyle\sum_{j \in T} P_j} \tag{11}$$

Thus the minimum possible value of $\chi^2$ is proportional to the ratio of the sum of probabilities for those subsets not sampled to the sum of probabilities for those subsets that are sampled.

## Confidence Limits for R

Several measures of "confidence" in the measure of software reliability may be developed from the sampling theory presented in the previous sections. The term "confidence" applied in a technical sense to software reliability means a measure of how closely the reliability is estimated based on a series of test outcomes and a prespecified rule for estimating the reliability from the outcomes. "Confidence" has also been used to denote degree of representativeness, thoroughness, etc.; of the test strategy or sampling technique as discussed in [25].

If V denotes an estimator for the variance of $\hat{R}$, then based on asymptotic normality arguments,

$$\hat{R} \pm \lambda_{\frac{1-\gamma}{2}} \sqrt{V}$$

will be an approximate confidence interval covering R with confidence $\gamma$, where $\lambda_\alpha$ is the standard normal deviate exceeded with probability $\alpha$. The above confidence interval would be expected to be more correct when the numbers of tests $n_j$ for each subset $S_j$ were large. For smaller numbers of tests $\lambda_{(1-\gamma)/2}$ should be replaced by $t_{n;(1-\gamma)/2}$, the Student t-deviate with n degrees of freedom, exceeded with probability $(1-\gamma)/2$. The latter confidence interval is wider than the former and as all $n_j$ get large it will approach the "normal" confidence interval. For example $t_{30;0.05} = 1.697$; $t_{120;0.05} = 1.658$; whereas $\lambda_{0.05} = 1.645$.

We are generally interested in one-sided confidence intervals of the form $\hat{R}_L < R < 1$, where $\hat{R}_L$ is called the lower confidence limit on R. For $\gamma$ confidence, the one-sided intervals for the previous cases would then be

$$\hat{R} - \lambda_{1-\gamma} \sqrt{V} \quad \text{or} \quad \hat{R} - t_{n;1-\gamma} \sqrt{V} \tag{12}$$

In any of the above cases, if sampling were incomplete the intervals cover

$$R = \sum_{T} P'_j \quad \text{which} \quad \leq \sum_{j} P'_j$$

Consequently the true value of R would be covered by the confidence interval with probability $\gamma' \leq \gamma$.

The magnitude of the difference between $\gamma$ and $\gamma'$ is not easily estimated; however, a "safety margin" could be incorporated by using slightly higher values of $\gamma$ in determining $\lambda_{1-\gamma}$ or $t_{n;1-\gamma}$. These differences are not likely to be important however in that the whole procedure already has many elements of approximation.

The approach to finding lower confidence limits on reliability given in the next section avoids the asymptotic normality assumption, and can be termed an "exact" method. Some additional background on previous results in this area is provided.

## Background on Exact Methods

Since about 1958, many papers have been written on the problem of constructing statistical confidence limits on the reliability of a system based upon observed failure data on the components of the system [26]. A typical problem is: A system is serial with respect to failures of its two components which make up the system; i.e., if either component fails, then the system fails. If the failure of either component has no influence on success or failure of the other, i.e., the events $failure_1$, $failure_2$ are statistically independent, then the reliability of the system is $R = R_1 * R_2$. Given $n_1, n_2$ tests of each component and $f_1, f_2$ failures observed, where $0 \leq f_1, f_2 \leq n_1, n_2$, the Neyman definition [27] leads to construction of a system of lower confidence limits $\hat{R}_L$ ($f_1, f_2; n_1 n_2, \gamma$); i.e., such that Prob $(\hat{R}_L \leq R) \geq \gamma$ where $\gamma$ is the specified confidence coefficient (e.g., 0.50, 0.90, 0.95) and R is the actual (but unknown) reliability of the System.

This particular problem was addressed originally in [28] and [29] and subsequently in [30].

For the software reliability model since the actual reliability with respect to the $j^{th}$ subset of a partition is $P_j'/P_j \equiv R_j$ the problem becomes one of determining a system of lower confidence limits on the quantity

$$R = \sum_j R_j P_j \qquad (13)$$

for all possible outcomes $f_j$ and given sample sizes $n_j$, $j = 1, 2, \ldots, K$.

## Neyman Confidence Limits

Since the general formulation of the Neyman or classical confidence limits problem is cumbersome, the formulas will be given only for the case in which there are two subsets in the partition.

In this case

$$R = R_1 P_1 + R_2 P_2 \qquad (14)$$

where

$$P_1 + P_2 = 1$$

Based upon [28], a lower confidence limit on R for observed numbers of failures $f_1, f_2$ out of $n_1, n_2$ tests respectively is obtained by minimizing (with respect to $X_1, X_2$) the function $X_1 P_1 + X_2 P_2$ with the following equality constraint:

$$\sum_{i_1, i_2 = 0}^{f_1, f_2} \binom{n_1}{i_1} X_1^{n_1 - i_1} (1 - X_1)^{i_1} \binom{n_2}{i_2} X_2^{n_2 - i_2} (1 - X_2)^{i_2} = 1 - \gamma \qquad (15)$$

and also by the inequalities

$$0 \leq X_1, X_2 \leq 1$$

where $\gamma$ is the confidence coefficient.

The resulting lower confidence limit is denoted by

$$\hat{R}_L(f_1,f_2;n_1,n_2,\gamma)$$

The quantity summed in (15) is the product of the probabilities of observing exactly $i_1$ failures out of $n_1$ tests and $i_2$ failures out of $n_2$ tests, where sampling is from the respective subsets $S_1, S_2$ and are independent observations (both within each subset and between subsets). Not apparent in the summation is a prescribed ordering of the sample outcomes $(f_1,f_2;n_1,n_2)$. The ordering is not unique as shown in [28], but there are various ways of choosing an ordering which is "more or less" optimum. Here, the meaning of "optimum" is that for every $f_1,f_2$, each of the confidence limits $\hat{R}_L(f_1,f_2;n_1,n_2,\gamma)$ for the prescribed ordering are at least equal to the corresponding $\hat{R}'_L(f_1,f_2;n_1,n_2,\gamma)$ obtained from some other ordering; i.e., all other things being equal, the larger confidence limits are better.

One way of ordering the sample points is: for any observed $(f_1,f_2; n_1,n_2)$ to include in the summation the probabilities of all points $(i_1,i_2; n_1,n_2)$ such that $0 \leq i_1 \leq f_1; 0 \leq i_2 \leq f_2$. This ordering will be satisfactory except when $n_1$ and $n_2$ are very different. A better ordering is obtained by including all sample points $(i_1,i_2;n_1,n_2)$ for which the estimated reliabilities have the relationship.

$$\frac{n_1 - i_1}{n_1} P_1 + \frac{n_2 - i_2}{n_2} P_2 \geq \frac{n_1 - f_1}{n_1} P_1 + \frac{n_2 - f_2}{n_2} P_2$$

which should result in values of $\hat{R}_L$ which are ordered in the same way as the estimated reliabilities, although this assertion could not be verified. In any suitable ordering, however, the sample outcome $(0,0;n_1,n_2)$ will be the first point, corresponding to the largest $\hat{R}_L$ for the set of possible outcomes.

For this case (15) becomes simply

$$X_1^{n_1} X_2^{n_2} = 1 - \gamma \tag{15'}$$

It is easy to show* that the minimum value of $X_1 P_1 + X_2 P_2$ subject to the constraints (15') and $0 \leq X_1, X_2 \leq 1$ is

$$\hat{R}_L = n(1 - \gamma)^{1/n} \left(\frac{P_1}{n_1}\right)^{n_1/n} \left(\frac{P_2}{n_2}\right)^{n_2/n} \tag{16}$$

where $n = n_1 + n_2$ and $P_1 + P_2 = 1$. The generalization to K subsets in the partition, in which case the problem is to minimize

$$\sum_{j=1}^{K} X_j P_j \tag{17}$$

subject to

$$\prod_{j=1}^{K} X_j^{n_j} = 1 - \gamma \tag{18}$$

and the requirement that each $X_j$ satisfy $0 \leq X_j \leq 1$, is also easy, and we have

$$\hat{R}_L = n(1 - \gamma)^{1/n} \prod_{j=1}^{K} \left(\frac{P_j}{n_j}\right)^{n_j/n} \tag{19}$$

_____

*Using the method of Lagrange multipliers.

Examples: (Both examples are based upon the hypothetical data of Reference [25]).

1-a) $n_1 = 2, n_2 = 1, n_3 = 1, n_4 = 1$     Hence     $n = 5$

$P_1 = 0.5, P_2 = 0.33333, P_3 = 0.1, P_4 = 0.06667$

Therefore

$$\hat{R}_L = 5(1-\gamma)^{0.2} (0.25)^{0.4} (0.33333)^{0.2} (0.1)^{0.2} (0.06667)^{0.2}$$

$$= 0.83616 \ (1-\gamma)^{0.2}$$

For

$$\gamma = 0.50 \qquad 0.90 \qquad 0.95$$

$$\hat{R}_L = 0.7367 \quad 0.5340 \quad 0.4649$$

1-b) $n_1 = 6, n_2 = 3, n_3 = 1, n_4 = 1$     Hence     $n = 11$

The $P_j$ are the same as in Example 1-a).

Therefore

$$\hat{R}_L = 11(1-\gamma)^{0.090909} (0.08333)^{0.54545} (0.11111)^{0.27273}$$

$$(0.1)^{0.090909} (0.066667)^{0.090909} = 0.98781 \ (1-\gamma)^{0.090909}$$

For

$$\gamma = 0.50 \qquad 0.90 \qquad 0.95$$

$$\hat{R}_L = 0.9275 \quad 0.8012 \quad 0.7523$$

When sampling is proportional to the probability of the subset; i.e., $n_j = nP_j$, then

$$\hat{R}_L = n(1-\gamma)^{1/n} \frac{1}{n} = (1-\gamma)^{1/n} \tag{20}$$

which is the usual lower binomial confidence limit on reliability obtained when n tests are made with zero failures. This is of course equivalent to the case when there is only one subset.

The formulation of a method for construction of Neyman confidence limits in general is apparently very difficult. However, the Neyman confidence limits do not require the assumptions of an *a priori* probability distribution as does the Bayesian method, to be presented below, so they are in a sense to be preferred over the system of confidence limits generated by the latter approach. Nevertheless, the relative ease of determining Bayesian confidence limits may be sufficient to dictate abandonment of the Neyman confidence limits. As indicated later in the Conclusions, however, a compromise is recommended.

The following sections present one Bayesian method for constructing lower confidence limits on software reliability and show how numerical solutions may be obtained in general.

## Bayesian Confidence Limits

The *a posteriori* probability density of the reliability $R_j$ for the $j^{th}$ subset, given $f_j$ failures in $n_j$ tests and assumed uniform *a priori* probability density of $R_j$ is given by the well-known formula

$$\text{Prob } (r_j < R_j < r_j + dr_j) = \frac{\Gamma(n_j + 2)}{\Gamma(n_j - f_j + 1)\,\Gamma(f_j + 1)} \; r_j^{n_j - f_j} (1 - r_j)^{f_j} \; dr_j$$

which is a Beta density function.

Once the distribution of

$$R = \sum_{j=1}^{K} P_j R_j$$

is found, the lower $\gamma$ confidence limit is defined as the value of r for which Prob $(R \geq r) = \gamma$. Thus the problem is to find the distribution of a weighted sum of independent Beta distributed random variables.

This problem is formidable analytically.* However, an approximate solution is to assume that the random variable R itself has a Beta distribution and determine its parameters by matching the moments of R with those of $\sum P_j R_j$, which are readily calculated.

The mean of $R_j$, denoted by $\mathcal{E}(R_j)$ is easily found to be

$$\mathcal{E}(R_j) = \frac{n_j - f_j + 1}{n_j + 2} \tag{21}$$

The variance of $R_j$, denoted by $V(R_j)$ is

$$V(R_j) = \frac{(n_j - f_j + 1)(f_j + 1)}{(n_j + 2)^2 (n_j + 3)} \tag{22}$$

We have

$$\mathcal{E}(R) = \sum_{j=1}^{K} P_j \mathcal{E}(R_j) \tag{23}$$

---

*A Monte Carlo evaluation may be suitable, particularly for large values of K. See Reference [34].

and since the $R_j$'s are independent

$$V(R) = \sum_{j=1}^{K} P_j^2 \, V(R_j) \tag{24}$$

Thus if the density of R is given by the Beta distribution with parameters p,q

$$\text{Prob } (r < R < r + dr) = \frac{\Gamma(p+q)}{\Gamma(p)\Gamma(q)} \, r^{p-1} \, (1-r)^{q-1} \, dr \tag{25}$$

then we equate

$$\frac{p}{p+q} = \mathcal{E}(R) = \sum_{j=1}^{K} \frac{n_j - f_j + 1}{n_j + 2} \, P_j \tag{26}$$

$$\frac{pq}{(p+q)^2 (p+q+1)} = V(R) = \sum_{j=1}^{K} \frac{(n_j - f_j + 1)(f_j + 1)}{(n_j + 2)^2 (n_j + 3)} \, P_j^2 \tag{27}$$

Since

$$p = \frac{q \, \mathcal{E}(R)}{1 - \mathcal{E}(R)} \tag{28}$$

and

$$p + q = \frac{q}{1 - \mathcal{E}(R)} \tag{29}$$

Equation (27) yields

$$q = (1 - \mathcal{E}(R)) \left[ \frac{\mathcal{E}(R) \, (1 - \mathcal{E}(R))}{V(R)} - 1 \right] \tag{30}$$

and Equation (28) results in

$$p = \mathcal{E}(R) \left[ \frac{\mathcal{E}(R)\,(1 - \mathcal{E}(R))}{V(R)} - 1 \right] \tag{31}$$

Tables of the Beta distribution [31] or a computer program can then be used to determine the value of r such that Prob $(R \geq r) = \gamma$.

Examples:

2-a)  We use the same data as in the previous Example 1-a).

|  | j = 1 | j = 2 | j = 3 | j = 4 |
|---|---|---|---|---|

$$\frac{n_j - f_j + 1}{n_j + 2} = 0.75000 \quad 0.66667 \quad 0.66667 \quad 0.66667$$

$$X$$

$$P_j = 0.37500 + 0.22222 + 0.06667 + 0.04444$$

$$\therefore \mathcal{E}(R) = 0.70833$$

$$\frac{(n_j - f_j + 1)(f_j + 1)}{(n_j + 2)^2 (n_j + 3)} = 0.03750 \quad 0.05556 \quad 0.05556 \quad 0.05556$$

$$X$$

$$P_j^2 = 0.009375 + 0.006173 + 0.000556 + 0.000247$$

$$\therefore V(R) = 0.016350$$

$$p = 8.2421$$

$$q = 3.3939$$

The values of r corresponding to Prob $(R \geq r) = \gamma$ where R has a Beta distribution with parameters $p = 8.2421$, $q = 3.3939$ are given below:

$$\gamma = 0.50 \qquad 0.90 \qquad 0.95$$

$$\hat{R}_L = 0.7206 \qquad 0.5334 \qquad 0.4780$$

2-b) We use the same data as in the previous Example 1-b).

$$j = 1 \qquad j = 2 \qquad j = 3 \qquad j = 4$$

$$\frac{n_j - f_j + 1}{n_j + 2} = 0.87500 \quad 0.80000 \quad 0.66667 \quad 0.66667$$

$$X$$

$$P_j = 0.43750 + 0.26667 + 0.06667 + 0.04444$$

$$\therefore \mathcal{E}(R) = 0.81528$$

$$\frac{(n_j - f_j + 1)(f_j + 1)}{(n_j + 2)^2 (n_j + 3)} = 0.012153 \quad 0.026667 \quad 0.055556 \quad 0.055556$$

$$X$$

$$P_j^2 = 0.0030382 + 0.0029630 + 0.0005556 + 0.0002469$$

$$\therefore V(R) = 0.0068037$$

$$p = 17.2310$$

$$q = 3.9042$$

The values of r corresponding to Prob $(R \geq r) = \gamma$ where R has a Beta distribution with parameters p = 17.2310, q = 3.9042 are given below:

$$\gamma = 0.50 \qquad 0.90 \qquad 0.95$$

$$\hat{R}_L = 0.8253 \qquad 0.7032 \qquad 0.6640$$

The results of the Neyman and Bayesian methods compare closely in Examples 1-a) and 2-a), but in Example 2-b) the Bayesian lower confidence limits are significantly smaller; i.e., more conservative, than the Neyman limits of Example 1-b).

The preceding analysis considered that the distribution of $\sum P_j R_j$ could be approximated by a Beta distribution using the first two moments of the distribution of each $R_j$ and the known formulas for the first two moments of a sum of random variables. Reference [32] presents a technique which provides correction terms to a fitted Beta distribution; however, at the expense of calculating more moments of each $R_j$ and a considerably more difficult computation.

Mr. J. E. Wolf of TRW had previously developed the technique of [32] for application to a slightly different problem [33]. A brief description of the application to the present problem is given in the following paragraphs.

The basic idea is to fit a curve of the form

$$g(x) = a_o x^\alpha (1 - x)^\beta (1 + a_1 x + \ldots + a_k x^k) \tag{32}$$

to the probability density function for $\sum P_j R_j$. When just the constant term $a_o$ is present, we have the previous case of fitting the density function to a Beta density, with $a_o = \Gamma(\alpha + \beta + 2)/\Gamma(\alpha + 1)\,\Gamma(\beta + 1)$ (Equation (25) with $p = \alpha + 1$, $q = \beta + 1$).* In general when all terms through $a_k x^k$ are to

---

*Note that the requirement for the area under the curve between 0 and 1 to be unity, essentially determines one of the parameters.

be used, the first $k + 2$ moments of each $R_j$ are required. The $i^{th}$ ordinary moment, or moment about the origin for the distribution of $R_j$ is given by

$$m_i^{(j)} = \frac{\Gamma(n_j + 2)}{\Gamma(n_j - f_j + 1)\ \Gamma(f_j + 1)} \int_0^1 x^{n_j - f_j + i}\ (1 - x)^{f_j}\ dx$$

or

$$m_i^{(j)} = \frac{\Gamma(n_j + 2)\ \Gamma(n_j - f_j + 1 + i)}{\Gamma(n_j - f_j + 1)\ \Gamma(n_j + 2 + i)} \tag{33}$$

The next step is to determine the ordinary moments $M_i$ of the random variable

$$\sum_{j=1}^K P_j R_j$$

The first moment $M_1 \equiv \mathcal{E}(R)$ was already given by (23). The second central moment was given by (24). The second ordinary moment is given by:

$$M_2 = \sum_j m_2^{(j)} P_j^2 + 2 \sum_{j<k} m_1^{(j)} m_1^{(k)} P_j P_k \tag{34}$$

the third ordinary moment is given by

$$M_3 = 3M_1 M_2 - 2M_1^3 + \sum_j m_3^{(j)} P_j^3 - 3 \sum_j m_1^{(j)} m_2^{(j)} P_j^3 + 2 \sum_j (m_1^{(j)} P_j)^3 \tag{35}$$

The fourth ordinary moment is less straightforward and is too complicated to be given here.

Using the higher moments (which are relatively easy to compute) the table below gives the computed lower confidence limits corresponding to several higher order fits of Equation (32) to the density function for $\sum_j P_j R_j$, for the previous Example 1-b).

| | $\gamma = 0.50$ | 0.90 | 0.95 |
|---|---|---|---|
| $a_0$ | 0.8253 | 0.7032 | 0.6640 |
| $a_0, a_1$ | 0.8263 | 0.7027 | 0.6626 |
| $a_0, a_1, a_2$ | 0.82629 | 0.70301 | 0.66248 |
| $a_0, a_1, a_2, a_3$ | 0.82620 | 0.70310 | 0.66281 |

The example indicates that the zero[th] order (only two moments used), or possibly the first order approximation may be adequate in general. The next example of the Bayesian method includes the case where there is a failure.

Example 3-a)   $n_1 = 6$, $n_2 = 3$, $n_3 = 1$, $n_4 = 1$

$$P_1 = 0.5, \; P_2 = 0.33333, \; P_3 = 0.1, \; P_4 = 0.066667$$

$$f_1 = 0, \; f_2 = 1, \; f_3 = 0, \; f_4 = 0$$

| | $\gamma = 0.50$ | 0.90 | 0.95 |
|---|---|---|---|
| $a_0$ | 0.7563 | 0.6261 | 0.5863 |
| $a_0, a_1$ | 0.7560 | 0.6259 | 0.5867 |
| $a_0, a_1, a_2$ | 0.75552 | 0.62651 | 0.58815 |
| $a_0, a_1, a_2, a_3$ | 0.75536 | 0.62698 | 0.58873 |

Example 3-b)  Sample as Example 3-a) except

$$f_1 = 0, \ f_2 = 0, \ f_3 = 0, \ f_4 = 1$$

| | $\gamma = 0.50$ | 0.90 | 0.95 |
|---|---|---|---|
| $a_o$ | 0.8016 | 0.6816 | 0.6439 |
| $a_o, a_1$ | 0.80384 | 0.68020 | 0.64058 |
| $a_o, a_1, a_2$ | 0.80436 | 0.68045 | 0.64027 |
| $a_o, a_1, a_2, a_3$ | 0.80372 | 0.68115 | 0.64068 |

Both Examples 3-a) and 3-b) indicate that the first or even zero[th] order approximation is adequate, except possibly for high confidence coefficients.

## 6.2.2.2  Conclusions

The Bayesian approach to determine lower confidence limits on software reliability, based upon the approximate solution developed by Wolf, affords a method for handling almost all situations — any number of subsets, sample sizes and failures.  As indicated by comparing Examples 1-b) and 2-b), however, the Bayesian method may in some cases be conservative, i.e., yield lower confidence limits on reliability which are smaller than those obtained by the Neyman method; or may be optimistic, i.e., yield lower confidence limits which are larger than those obtained by the Neyman method.

Consequently, the Neyman method should be investigated, possibly only for two or three failures in total, in order to keep the analysis and programming manageable.  Further comparison could be made with the Bayesian method, which could then be "corrected" to correspond to the Neyman method. Thus a more optimum system of confidence limits could then be obtained from the easily calculated Bayesian confidence limits.

### 6.2.3  Effect of Software Error Removal

When an error is detected — e.g., by the occurrence of an execution failure and analysis of the code to determine the source of the failure — the failure probability P and the reliability R of the program p are changed.  To investigate the nature of these changes, the combined effect of several errors will be derived.  First, the failure probability $P_1$ for the effect of a single error may be represented as:

$$P_1 = \sum_{i=1}^{N} P_1 y_{1i}$$

$$y_{1i} = 1, \text{ if error 1 causes an execution failure for } E_i$$

$$= 0, \text{ otherwise}.$$

The execution variable $y_{1i}$ has been doubly subscripted to show that it represents the effect of error number 1.  Similarly, the failure probability $P_2$ for two errors is:

$$P_2 = \sum_{i=1}^{N} P_1 (y_{1i} + y_{2i} - y_{1i} y_{2i})$$

$y_{2i}$ is the execution variable for the effect of error number 2.  The combined effect of two errors is not simply additive for they both can affect the execution of p for the same inputs.  The term $y_{1i} y_{2i}$ compensates for the inputs affected by both errors.

The expression for more than 2 errors can be developed by introducing a new indexed variable $z_{ji}$ , which is defined recursively by:

$$z_{1i} = y_{1i}$$

$$z_{2i} = y_{1i} + y_{2i} - y_{1i}y_{2i} = 1 - (1 - y_{1i})(1 - y_{2i})$$

$$z_{ji} = y_{ji} + z_{j-1,i} - y_{ji}z_{j-1,i} = 1 - \prod_{k=1}^{j}(1 - y_{ki})$$

The change in program failure probability when an error (assumed to be error j) is detected and corrected is:

$$P_j - P_{j-1} = \sum_{i=1}^{N} P_i (y_{ji} - y_{ji}z_{j-1,i})$$

$$= \sum_{i=1}^{N} P_i y_{ji} (1 - z_{j-1,i})$$

$$= \sum_{i=1}^{N} P_i y_{ji} \prod_{k=1}^{j-1}(1 - y_{ki})$$

In the development of this formula, it has been assumed that the errors in a program can be identified and enumerated.

The equation for $P_j - P_{j-1}$ can be solved for cases in which the right hand side has a simple dependence on j. The simplest case is obtained by setting it equal to a constant, say a.

$$P_j - P_{j-1} = a$$

and therefore

$$P_j = aj + b$$

Since

$$P_0 = 0$$

$$b = 0$$

$$P_j = aj$$

This case of constant decrease in failure probability corresponds to the case where all errors have approximately a constant effect, which may not be a good approximation to reality. It is the case used in the Shooman and Jelinsky-Moranda models.

The case of a linear change can also be solved:

$$P_j - P_{j-1} = cj + d$$

and if $P_0 = 0$,

$$P_j = \frac{c}{2} j^2 + (d + \frac{c}{2})j$$

$$= \frac{c}{2} j (j + 1) + dj$$

It corresponds to a situation in which the error having the largest effect is detected and corrected first and the error having the least effect is detected last. This seems to be a better approximation to reality.

An important problem in developing reliable software has been the introduction of new errors in the process of correcting detected errors. An error is detected by observing an execution failure for a run with a specific input, $E_k$. The source of the failure is sought by examining the code. When an error is found, that error is corrected by changing some of the code and the effect of the change is tested by running the program with input $E_k$. If the program executes correctly for input $E_k$, the error is assumed to be corrected; however, experience has shown that execution failures occurring later may be due to the change made in correcting the code to make the case with input $E_k$ run correctly.

Analysis of the correction process with the aid of concepts from
MTSR has led to a test procedure which should reduce the occurrence of
correction-induced errors. A correction is made by changing the code in
one or more segments, a segment being a sequence of contiguous executable
statements which contains no branch. The logic path executed by the test
case $E_k$ is composed of a sequence of segments. The segments which were
changed in the error correction process may also be part of other logic
paths. The changes involved in the correction may also change the execution results of the other logic paths and unless the effect of the changes
on these other logic paths is taken into account in making the correction,
the changes could cause execution failures. To guard against this happen-
ing, whenever an error is corrected, the changed code should be tested not
only by the original test case but also by a test case chosen so that it
causes another logic path containing the changed segments to be executed.
If this is done, most of the errors introduced in correcting errors will
be detected and the resultant correction should have a low probability of
having introduced new errors and correction of the error will, in fact,
have increased the reliability of the program.

Correction of the error will, in some cases, involve a change in a
branch statement such that the segment or segments to which the branch
transfers execution is changed. If this is the case, the changed program
will have a changed set of logic paths and the partition of E into the
input subsets associated with each logic path will also be changed.

## 6.2.4  Use of Structural Information in the Analysis of Reliability

The structure of a program p may be characterized by the logic paths
$L_j$, the input subsets $G_j$ associated with each logic path, the segments $S_i$
of which the logic paths are composed, and the branch tests $B_k$ which cause
transfers from one segment to another during the execution of a logic path.

Most errors are confined to a single segment; some are spread over
several segments; and others involve one or more branches. Each error will,
however, affect the execution of only a few logic paths — viz., those logic
paths that contain the affected segments and/or branches. It will not
affect the execution of those logic paths that do not contain the erroneous code. Thus the error will not be detected by test cases that do not

cause the erroneous code to be executed. A necessary condition for the detection, by testing, of all the errors in a program is that all segments and branches be executed in the testing. Then all the components of the program — all the segments and all the branches and therefore every executable statement — will have been exercised in the testing and there will be no component that has not been subject to test. Satisfaction of this condition is, however, *not sufficient* to ensure detection of all errors, as shown in the discussion in Section 6.2.1.

If S is the set of segments, $S_i$ is an arbitrary segment, and m is the total number of segments in program p — i.e.,

$$S = \{S_i : i = 1,2, \ldots , m\}$$

then execution of p with input $E_k$ from the input subset $G_j$ will cause execution of the segments in a subset of S defined by the logic path $L_j$. If L is the set of all logic paths and n is the number of logic paths; i.e.,

$$L = \{L_j : j = 1,2, \ldots , n\}$$

then L includes all segments and executing all logic paths will guarantee execution of all segments; however, all segments are contained in subsets of L, which, for most programs, have fewer members than L. A subset of L which contains the smallest number of $L_j$ that collectively contain all segments is called a set of "characteristic paths". For a given program, there may be more than one set of characteristic paths. The number of paths in such a set is usually sufficiently small that it is practical to identify them — e.g., with the aid of a test tool such as PACE — and execute all of them during testing.

Since each logic path corresponds to a set of segments, the set of segments corresponding to logic path $L_j$ will be contained in a subset $C_j$ of a set C of characteristic paths and all the segments in $L_j$ will be exercised by the test cases that execute all members of $C_j$. Thus if all the logic paths in C have been executed in the testing, all logic paths will have had a degree of testing in the sense that all of their segments will have been exercised in the testing.

A branch is equivalent to an ordered pair of segments, $(S_i, S_j)$. Since only a few of the possible pairs of segments correspond to branches, in most programs, the number of branches is usually substantially less than $m(m-1)/2$, the number of possible pairs of segments. Thus it is also practical to identify — with the aid of test tools such as PACE — and test all branches. Owing to the definition of a branch, executing all branches will guarantee that all segments have been executed. Thus, testing which executes all branches will have exercised all the segments and pairs of segments that occur in all logic paths. It will also have exercised a substantial number of the possible higher order ($\geq 3$) segment sequences. This explains the high reliability/(low incidence of execution failures) in operational use of the programs which have been tested, with the aid of test tools, so that all branches have been exercised in the testing.

Routine A of Project 5, which was discussed in Section 6.1, has 10 segments (the 6 segments composed of assignment statements plus the 4 branch statements), 13 segment pairs, and 4 logic paths. In the case of this routine, the set of characteristic paths is equal to the set of logic paths and the minimum number of test cases needed to exercise all segments also execute all segment pairs and all logic paths.

A second routine, "routine B", has 17 segments, 24 segment pairs, and 9 logic paths. All segments are contained in 5 logic paths and all segment pairs are contained in 6 logic paths. Thus only 5 test cases are needed to exercise all segments and 6 test cases are needed to exercise all segment pairs, but 9 test cases are needed to exercise all logic paths.

## 6.2.5 Estimating Software Reliability from Test Results

The method of measuring the reliability of a program described in Section 5.2.4.2 involves defining an operational profile $p_i$ and making n runs with the inputs for the runs chosen at random according to the probability distribution $p_i$. In Section 6.2.2, alternative methods based on choosing samples in various ways were defined. Since testing consists of making a series of runs and examining the output of each run to determine whether or not an execution failure occurred, the question can be raised as to whether the data available from testing can be used to develop an estimate of the reliability of the program as of the end of the testing.

Testing differs significantly from the prescribed conditions for making a good reliability measurement. The runs are not made with inputs chosen at random. Test cases are generally chosen to find errors rapidly, based on the experience and intuition of the test team, the functional capabilities the program must have, or on the use of a test tool, such as PACE. Thus the test cases do not usually form a representative sample of the inputs expected in operational use of the program. Additionally, after an execution failure is detected in the testing, the source of the failure is sought and, after the error is found, it is corrected; so the reliability of the program is changing during the testing.

Making use of the concepts developed in the preceding sections, the following procedure was developed to provide a rough estimate of R from the test data.

- Define the input set E.

- Analyze E into the $G_j$ associated with logic paths.

- Define, for the anticipated operational usage, the $P_j$ for each $G_j$.

- Determine the $G_j$ to which each test case belongs.

- Detérmine the segments and pairs of segments which were exercised in the testing and those that were not exercised.

● Compute for each j:

$$P'_j = a_j P_j$$

with $a_j$ determined by the following rules:

● 0.99, if more than one test case belongs to $G_j$,

● 0.95, if only one test case belongs to $G_j$,

● 0.90, if no test case belongs to $G_j$ but all segments and segment pairs in $L_j$ have been exercised in the testing,

● 0.80, if all segments but not all segment pairs in $L_j$ have been exercised in the testing,

● 0.80-0.20 m, if m segments $(1 \le m \le 4)$ of $L_j$ have not been exercised in the testing, and

● 0, if more than 4 segments of $L_j$ have not been exercised in the testing.

● $\hat{R} = \displaystyle\sum_{j=1}^{k} P'_j$, where k is the number of logic paths, is then a rough estimate of R.

The values of the $a_j$ given above were assigned intuitively, based on the analysis performed in this study and on experience in testing. For specific programs and specific testing, it may be possible to develop a better assignment of values to the $a_j$'s.

To develop a better estimate of R, a measurement based on a suitable sampling technique should be performed.

## 6.2.6  Program Safety Effects

The definition of software reliability given in 5.2.4.1 is dependent
on the definition of the function F which the program is intended to specify.  F is usually defined in the program specification; however, the specification itself may contain errors, so F is ultimately defined by the
physical problem the program is intended to solve.  The reliability definition can accommodate itself to any definition of F.  A changed definition
of F changes the definition of an execution failure, but the changed definition of an execution failure can be used in the other formulas of the
reliability theory without any change in the formulas.

This same approach can be used to adapt the theory to deal with the
safety of a program.  Such a question can arise in the guidance program in
a missile, where an error could cause a missile control failure resulting
in the missile striking a populated area.  Another case is that of the
process control computer in a chemical process plant, where a software
error could lead to control action that could result in an explosion or a
fire.

The safety condition $S(E_i)$ needs to be expressed so that safe execution of the program can be defined, e.g., as:

$$F'(E_i) \leq S(E_i)$$

and this definition is used in place of the previous definition of correct
execution.  Whether or not a premature termination or failure to terminate
is considered a safety violation will depend on the system behavior which
can result from them, and it must be determined for each such system.

With this definition of safe execution and non-safe execution, all
the reliability formulas can be used to calculate the safety of a program.
Note that unreliable operation of a program will not necessarily lead to
safety violations.

## 6.3 Guidelines and Techniques to Minimize Error Introduction During Software Development

It is generally agreed that one of the major contributors to the large number of errors which are found in most computer programs is the logical complexity of the program. This complexity is manifested in the large number of logic paths, even in small programs, and in the high inter-connectivity of the paths. Dealing with the complexity has been compounded by the fact that some of the paths indicated on a logic diagram are unexe-cutable or "phantom paths"; i.e., they cannot be caused to execute by any choice of input values; e.g., in the program, routine A, which was analyzed in Section 6.1, 4 of the 8 indicated paths are phantom paths. Some programs have been found to have more phantom paths than they have executable or "real" ones. Thus the actual structure of a program tends to be veiled in a web of phantom paths, which obscures the actual structure so that it is not readily visible in the program text. Owing to the phantom paths, the program text does not continually "cue" the programmer on the actual struc-ture as he writes the program. A programmer has to keep a "map" of the structure in his mind as he is writing a program. If the program is more than a few statements long, this can be quite difficult, and he will make errors. Additionally, he cannot easily see the errors in the text he has written; consequently, he does not catch the errors, and they remain in the program until they are found in testing or show themselves in the form of execution failures in operational use of the program.

It is therefore apparent that the number of errors could be reduced if programs could be written in such a way that they contain no phantom paths. To verify this, routine A was rewritten in the form:

```
      IF(GN.NE.O.) GOTO 10
      IF(CN.LT.CT) GOTO 30
      GOTO 20
10    IF(CN.LT.TR) GOTO 30
20    JE = JE + 1
      KI = JD
      KM = 2
      KR = 3
      KB = JA
```

```
        KE = JB
        JV = JV + KI + 1
        KG = .1
30   RETURN
     END
```

This new form of routine A contains four paths, all of which are executable.
Both branches of each branch test — (GN.NE.O.), (CN.LT.CT), and (CN.LT.TR) —
can be taken irrespective of the outcome of the evaluation of previous
branch tests. Therefore the programmer can make local checks of the logic
in the program without having to trace the logic path back to its initial
point. The rewritten routine not only has a simpler and more visible
structure, it also has fewer executable statements, 13 as compared to 20
in its original form.

Several other routines of Project 5 were analyzed and found to contain phantom paths. All of them were rewritten in a form containing no
phantom paths. The new forms of the routines all contained fewer executable statements than their original forms. Two of the Project 5 routines
were found to contain no phantom paths, as originally written. They were
principally in-line code. Each contained only one branch test.

The interpretation of a program p as a specification of a function F
can also be used to aid in reducing error introduction during software
development. F defines the information processing problem which the program p is intended to solve. It is defined by what are usually called the
"requirements" on the program. The representation of F by a collection of
functions $F_j$ defined on sets $G_j$, each of which is associated with a logic
path $L_j$ of p, establishes a relationship between the logic path structure
of the program and the requirements. Each $F_j$ defines the portion of the
information processing task concerned with computing values from the inputs
in the set $G_j$; thus $F_j$ defines the requirements on p for operating on $G_j$.
Each $F_j$ can therefore be interpreted as a "functional requirement" associated with a logic path $L_j$.

Expression of the requirements in the form $(F_j, G_j)$ and association
of each functional requirement with a logic path can aid in the detection
of errors. This is particularly true if the program is written in a form

such that all its logic paths are executable. Then each functional requirement can be checked against the code of its corresponding logic path. In fact, a form of this type of testing is being performed on Project 5. Software requirements are allocated to portions of the software system and from these the functional capabilities of individual routines may be determined. These functional capabilities then form the basis for developing the routine level test cases which must also exercise all segments. The importance of this test strategy and a more detailed description of the techniques involved are presented in Section 4.8.

## 6.4   Improved Methods of Software Testing

A fundamental problem in software testing is how to choose test cases so that from their correct execution one can infer that the program tested will execute correctly for almost all inputs. Traditionally, software testing has concentrated on verifying that the functional capabilities of the program are the ones it was intended to have. This has involved preparing test cases to demonstrate that the program has certain defined functional characteristics. Additional test cases were then generated, based on the experience and intuition of the test team, until scheduled test time and/or budget ran out. In spite of large amounts of money spent in testing in this manner, the results were generally unsatisfactory, for the tested software tended to have a high incidence of execution failures in operational use.

The development of test tools, such as the PACE test tool of TRW, shifted the focus of testing to assuring that the test cases exercised all structural elements — i.e., all segments or branches — of the program. Usage of these tools effected a dramatic reduction in the number of execution failures in software tested with them (Section 4.0).

MTSR explains why these test tools work as well as they do and it shows how to use them more effectively. The test tools analyze program code into segments and branches. They instrument the program so that, during test execution, the frequency of segment (or branch) exercising is recorded. Those segments (or branches) not exercised are identified and data is provided to aid in developing test cases to exercise them. In Sections 6.2.1, 6.2.3 and 6.2.5, it was shown that correct execution of a program for one test case can be used as a basis for inference that the program will execute correctly for almost all inputs in the subset $G_j$ to which the test case belongs.  Correct execution of test cases which exercise all segments and branches was shown to remove the errors having the largest effect (number of inputs affected), to provide an effective test of a set of characteristic paths, and to provide a degree of testing (exercising of their segments and branches) of all other logic paths.  Any remaining errors will, in most cases, each affect a relatively small number of inputs.

In the discussion in Section 6.2.5, it was noted that most of the errors introduced in correcting a detected error can be detected by executing the program with inputs chosen such that they exercise the code changed in the error correction process and they exercise a different logic path than the one exercised by the test case that detected the original error.  It turns out that, for many programs, the set of test cases that exercise all segments will also result in most segments being exercised by two or more test cases.  However, investigation of what is done in actual testing has shown that, as each error is detected, it is corrected, but that, at the end of testing, it is rare that the program is run with all of the test cases to verify that with all of the error corrections performed it exe-cutes correctly for all test cases.

Based on the concepts developed in MTSR, the following test strategy is proposed:

- Test the program until all segments and branches have been exer-cised and the program executes correctly for all test cases.

- For each error corrected, all segments and branches modified by the correction should be tested (if possible) by at least two test cases which exercise the modified segments and branches and which cause execution of different logic paths.

- Identify the input data subset $G_j$, logic path $L_j$, and functional requirement $F_j$ for each test case.

- Identify any functional requirements not directly verified by the test cases and develop test cases for them.

- Check the code for occurrences of all known types of errors — e.g., divide by zero, branch test boundary errors, variable name misspelling, etc.

- Reduce residual errors remaining after the preceding testing by choosing a sample of inputs at random from the operational profile.

The first element is a necessary condition for the testing to detect all errors. The second solves, to a large degree, the problem of errors introduced in correcting errors. It requires only a few more, if any, test cases than those used in the first element. The third and fourth elements assure that the testing verifies that the functional requirements are met, a necessary ingredient in any practical test process. The fifth element catches known error types. The sixth reduces residual errors and also provides a measurement of the reliability of a program.

## 7.0  DATA COLLECTION

Learning how to collect software reliability data is an iterative process.  Each time we try to use data subsequent to its collection there is the familiar sound of palm hitting forehead and the accompanying oath concerning "the next time."  Early planning produces long lists of information to be collected, but not until the analysis begins does the list of desired yet unavailable parameters start to grow.  The data are all there as a by-product of the software development process; the trick is in knowing what to collect and, generally more important, when to collect it.  The approach often taken is to collect anything that isn't nailed down.  This approach works fairly well for parameters that are purely descriptive (routine size) and poorly for parameters which result from evaluation (resources required in closing a problem).

In this section we will briefly discuss data collection, recounting some of the lessons learned and problems identified while performing the Software Reliability Study.  Some suggestions for improvement are also presented.

### 7.1  Observed Realities

Software projects have the potential for creating a tremendous amount of data, and as mentioned above, these data are largely a by-product of the software development process.  Even though the duration of this study allowed a certain amount of planning and implementation of data collection procedures to suit our purposes, availability of data resulted principally from project activities other than reliability oriented studies.  Specifically, data used in the SRS was the result of rigorous configuration management and quality assurance practices.  The reliability data collection was necessarily done on a non-interference basis.  The point to be made, here, is that mechanisms for collecting software data already exist in most disciplined software development projects.  This can easily be seen, for example, in the records resulting from configuration control during testing.  These are the problem reports, the test execution logs, and the records of updates to the software configuration generated in an attempt to control testing.  But testing is only one phase, usually the last one, in the software development process.  What about the rest of the development cycle?  One of the first wishes of the analyst trying to explain test data is to know what went on prior to testing.

Figure 7-1 illustrates a typical software development project by phase and points out when various types of data can become available.  Ovals indicate error or problem data that can be produced and collected.  These are the data most useful in the study of software quality and reliability.  They form a continuum of problems and solutions starting as early as the requirements specification phase and extending into the operational portion of the system life cycle.  Ancillary data, shown below the phases of the development cycle, become available roughly at the times indicated, are absolutely necessary to the understanding of the error histories, and can be extremely useful in assessing on-going project performance.  Triangles along the base of Figure 7-1 denote points at which snapshots of the software structural characteristics can be taken to gain a picture of the volume of change.

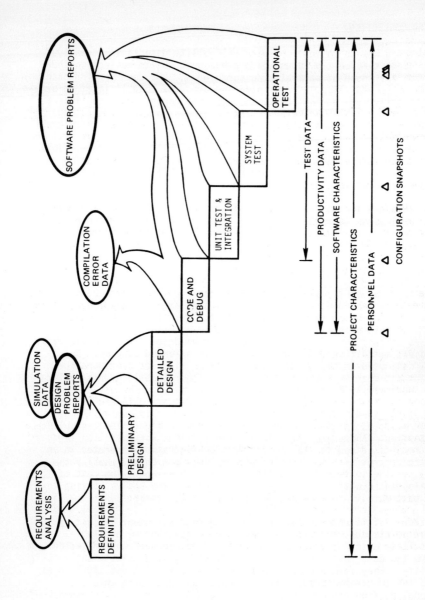

Figure 7-1. Data Availability Throughout the Software Development Cycle

There is the implication in Figure 7-1 that problem reports can be written during virtually every phase of the development cycle. This implication is intended, with one exception--problem reporting during the coding and debug phase, when the programmers are attempting to create an error-free compilation. During this phase manual data collection techniques can represent a counter-productive, extra task to perform.*

Also implied in Figure 7-1 is the fact that the mechanism for collecting data, including manpower, procedures, and tools, must exist prior to the appropriate phase in order to capitalize on the freshness (and accuracy) of the data. In the case of software requirements problems this may mean having the collection mechanism ready prior to contract go-ahead.

## 7.1.1 Data Collection Techniques

A project's ability to provide data will depend largely on the data collection techniques it can apply. Experience has shown that manual techniques tend to be the easiest to implement in the sense that they are readily adjustable to changing project demands. However, they require manpower committed to the task of collection. Automated techniques ease the pain of the collection task but do not necessarily reduce the amount of work involved since they increase the scope of the job, making possible work that was previously not possible through manual techniques. Automated techniques also tend to be less flexible in response to changes in project demands. An additional aspect is the cost of implementation. Not all projects can support full blown data collection tasks.

In conjunction with its configuration management and quality assurance activities TRW has applied both manual and automated data collection, storage, and reporting techniques. The earliest attempts to collect data were entirely manual and centered around software problem reports (SPR) written during testing. These reports were written at the routine level, if possible, and remained "open" until a second form documenting the corrective action "closed" the problem. This second form, the software modification record (SMR), was actually a vehicle for delivering an update to the software configuration. This two form approach to software problem documentation has been and continues to be used successfully by many software contractors.**

A second, equally successful software problem documentation scheme is also employed on Project 5. A one document form, the discrepancy report (DR), is used to document the identification of a software problem and, through update procedures, the closure of the problem. Examples of these forms and other problem reporting forms are presented in Appendix B.

---

*However, it is during this phase that automated error data collection is most easily accomplished through the compiler.

**A similar problem closure form is the modification transmittal memorandum or MTM used on Projects 2 and 3.

Both the one document and two document forms work as vehicles for controlling changes to the software configuration. As vehicles for software error data collection they also work - if certain steps are taken to assure data accuracy and completeness. That is, it is possible to have a description of the software problem (its symptoms), a description of the change to the software (the fix), and evidence that the problem was fixed (test output) and to still not know what the actual software error was. This phenomenon was noted in a review of Project 3 software problem reports. Although forms were adequate to cover configuration management concerns, they failed to provide adequate data for thorough software error analysis. The Project 5 form was designed specifically to provide sufficient information about both concerns.

As may be seen in Figure 7-1, much more data exist than are documented by various types of problem reports, and some are extremely difficult or virtually impossible to col<sup>1</sup>~ct with manual techniques. For example, software structural characte. stics are determined by examining the source code and tabulating the occurrence of such structural elements as loops, branch statements, etc. For very small software programs this information can be obtained manually, but even for small software systems, the job is too big and tedious to attempt using manual techniques.

As far as data analysis goes, our experience in the course of this study showed that having the data in machine readable form is imperative. The volume of information handled and the number of approaches to analysis typically needed to bring out the results make purely manual techniques very ineffective.

## 7.1.2 Cost and Schedule Impact of Data Collection

The actual collection of data represents a considerable amount of work. When contributions are requested from project performers, this work may be counter-productive to the development of the software product. This work can be translated into both cost and, possibly, schedule impacts to the project. Depending on the project, these impacts could represent significant drawbacks.

In collecting data for the SRS only Project 5 afforded the opportunity to tailor the data collection to study needs and to ask for real-time assistance from project performers in categorizing software problems. Aside from a healthy amount of grumbling about the added nuisance, cooperation was very good. In the retrospective analysis of data from Projects 2, 3, and 4, there was also very good cooperation from project performers. Apparently, our limited data collection activities did not adversely affect any of these projects because we were allowed to continue our work.

The only attempt made to assess the impact of our data collection activities was to determine how much time it took to assign an error category to a problem report. This was the only area where we enlisted the help of project performers on a continuing basis.

It was determined that it takes an average of 1.2 minutes for a knowledgeable* analyst to assign an error category to a software problem report if he does it long after the problem is fixed. An unknowledgeable analyst takes an average of 1.6 minutes** to assign the error category in this after-the-fact fashion. If the fixer of the problem assigns the category at the time he documents the fix, the time is considerably less than a minute and the results are considerably more accurate.

The cumulative time just to categorize the software problems from Project 3 is in excess of 60 manhours, assuming a one minute assignment time by a knowledgeable programmer when the problem is fresh on his mind. On the other hand, as is pointed out in Section 7.3, this may be a worthwhile project expenditure in terms of increased software quality and potential improvements in the development and test processes.

### 7.1.3  Specific Data Collection and Analysis Problems

One of the principal problems encountered in analyzing Project 3 data was identifying the software error. As mentioned in 7.1.1, it was possible to have the SPR, the MTM, the source code fix, and results from test cases demonstrating problem closure and to still not know exactly what the error was. This is due to the fact that the MTM, as its name implies, was designed chiefly to deliver or transmit modifications of software routines to the master configuration. Although the MTM makes provision for descriptions of the error and the fix, this form was used principally to satisfy CM requirements, leaving the reliability analyst at the mercy of the MTM's author, who is thinking only of closing the problem. The collection forms require redesign to guarantee configuration management control and reliability data as <u>equal</u> data collection objectives. Luckily, these objectives are not incompatible, and collection techniques can be tailored to satisfy both objectives. Such was the case with the Project 5 discrepancy report or DR.

Another major problem concerns availability of resources during the data collection process. Many parameters are not considered for collection by virtue of the fact that they are difficult to collect and, once collected, they are not easily stored. For example, the amount of code exercised by a test case is extremely difficult, and in most cases impossible, to determine without the aid of automated tools; yet this parameter is believed to be essential to determination of error freeness. A series of software tools designed to automatically collect and store certain reliability related parameters is essential.

---

*A programmer who either developed the software or is responsible for fixing it.

**These times include time required for familiarization with the list of error categories and assume all problem documentation is available.

Manpower resources are also essential to the collection process. There is a tendency to reduce the scope of data collection to a level necessary to support immediate contract and project obligations. If reliability data collection is not one of the project's principal objectives, the best of attempts is liable to be shelved in the first schedule of manpower pinch.

The next problem is one of education. Here the situation is similar to that experienced in the early days of hardware reliability data collection; initially the idea was a foreign one, while today data is collected as a matter of course. In the collection of data for Projects 2 and 3 it was discovered that programmers would have been more or less willing to provide detailed information about errors had they known that such information was of value and had they been given guidelines for its provision. Project 5 experience bore this out.

Related to this problem is the necessity of benchmarking the data, i.e., collecting data sets that are compatible with one another in an evolutionary or time sense. Many parameters, especially the software structural characteristics, change over the span of the design, development, and test phases. This change can also be prevalent during the operational usage of software systems. Although intuitively desirable, a considerable amount of planning is required to establish all the required resources and identify the data to be collected. Depending on the software and the project development or operational characteristics, these benchmarks may be planned for almost any plateau in the software evolution; typically, they can be established subsequent to the preliminary design, prior to formal testing, and at delivery for operational use.

Any attempt to collect data quickly points to a long list of problems. Such a list, based on SRS experience in collecting, storing and analyzing software data from source projects, is presented in Table 7-1. Although this is a fairly comprehensive list, it is short in that it deals in generalities. For instance, entry 4 mentions that certain valuable data items are perishable. The solution to preserving this data is to collect the data items as they become available. An example of this is the error category that can be assigned to a report of a software problem. In a closer look at the requirements for accurately providing these data we find that the "who" of the collection is just as important as "when" the data is collected. Typically, it is the fixer of the software problem alone that can assign such a category, and he must do the collection and associated analysis when the error is fresh in his mind. The problem is further compounded when it is realized that some very successful projects, owing to variations in project structure, do their data collection in a time driven mode (data collected periodically in time) rather than in an event driven mode (data collected as it is generated). Here we see that the opportunity to collect perishable data depends on another problem, the ability of a project to provide certain types of data (entry 16).

We encountered virtually all of these problems during performance of the SRS. Our solutions to these problems were, admittedly, not always successful, but successful solutions are possible and will be forthcoming as more of these studies are attempted in the software community.

Table 7-1.   Data Collection and Analysis Problems

1.  Projects, the software, and the data vary considerably and
    are not describable in common terminology.

2.  Data collection can represent cost, schedule, and manpower
    impediments to software development projects.  The impact
    or cost considerations of data collection, although real,
    are not fully appreciated.

3.  Data collection is a lot of work.  The tools and techniques
    for collecting data are not available.

4.  Certain data items are perishable and must be collected <u>and</u>
    analyzed when they become available, not after the fact.

5.  Performers, project management, and even the buyers of soft-
    ware are sensitive about providing data that might be used
    to adversely evaluate the project by external agencies.

6.  Some projects produce data that are classified.

7.  Analysis techniques and questions to ask of the data are not
    well known.

8.  There is no guarantee that data will be collected (i.e., no
    requirement for projects to collect data).

9.  Data accuracy is a chronic question.

10. Analysis is often incomplete or inaccurate if proper communi-
    cation with project performers is not established.

11. Contractor and customer representatives of project manage-
    ment are not aware of the benefits of data analysis and
    therefore tend not to support it.

12. Project structure is generally not tailored to use available
    data (i.e., the mechanism for analyzing data and folding
    results back into the project is not provided).

13. The fervor of data collection inspires data gathering that
    is non-supportive of the software development process.

14. Some data elements require protection to preserve the privacy
    of the contributor (e.g., cost data).

15. Data collection is commonly thought to be "not necessary"
    to a properly managed project.

16. Project organizational structure and resources vary, making
    consistent, multi-project data collection questionable.

17. Definition of which parameters are needed and meaningful to
    collect is in its infancy.

18. Presently implemented data collection schemes often fail to
    gather data in sufficient detail, making results of analysis
    questionable.

## 7.2 Recommendations for Improvement of Data Collection

From the considerable practical experience gained in collecting
and compiling data it is obvious that a major change in philosophy is
needed to guarantee a successful data collection process. Once we are
committed to the need for such information we need to support this commitment on all fronts. In this regard the following recommendations can
be made:

- Problem reports and closure reports should be problem oriented,
  providing the symptoms of the problem, an accurate statement of
  the problem, and a detailed description of the necessary fix.
  An ideal situation would be total separation of the problem
  closure and the vehicle for delivering modifications to the
  software, i.e., two separate formats, one to document closure
  and explain the fix, the other to deliver the source code of
  the fix.

- Data collection and analysis should be preceded by standards
  specifying procedures and formats. These procedures and
  formats must satisfy configuration management and reliability
  data collection requirements.

- All project performers should be made aware of the objectives
  of the study. The necessity of their making the error and the
  correction "perfectly clear" cannot be over-stressed.

- Further work to generate reliability data collection tools is
  necessary. These should be made general purpose wherever
  possible.

- To guarantee the collection process, dedicated manpower should
  be allocated to monitor the data as it is generated.

- The data collection must be started early in the software
  development cycle; the pre-code stage of development is rife
  with information.

Each of these points was addressed by the Project 5 discrepancy
reporting system which was maintained and monitored by a quality assurance
organization, and each is feasible in the Project 5 environment. Of
particular help in the data collection process was the involvement of the
project performers who were guided by formal project standards.

### 7.2.1 Meaningful Data Items

The "parameters we wish we had" is an ever growing list. This is
especially true when the object of analysis is problems discovered during
testing. They reflect all the technical, managerial, and political problems that preceded the test phase. A short list of data items which
appear to be meaningful to the analysis of software problem reports is
given in Table 7-2.

Table 7-2. Information Useful on Analyzing Software Problem Reports

| Parameter | Description |
|---|---|
| Requirements and Design Problems | Descriptive information concerning the type and frequency of problems encountered during the requirements and design periods. |
| Problem Criticality | An assessment of the importance of the problem to the success of software operation or "mission" completion. |
| Test Stress | Quantitative assessment of the amount of code, number of segments, variation of data conditions, etc. treated by each test case in a test program. |
| CPU Time | CPU time tied accurately to specific development and test jobs. |
| Difficulty of a Problem Closure | Relative difficulty encountered in closing a problem accompanied by a reason. |
| Problem Independency Factor | Identification of a problem that is introduced as a result of a fix to another problem. |
| Coding Load Factor | Accurate count of number of lines of code during a given period of time. |
| Before and After Difficulty Ratings | Subjective assessment of difficulty to design, code, test, document, and implement a routine made at first definition of the routine and, later, after the routine reaches operational status. |
| Manhour Availability | Accurate account of number of developer, test, customer personnel manhours. |

Finally, information that was found very helpful in analyzing Project 3 data was the textual "related experience" information which was collected to explain analyses of outliers in the metric studies of Section 4.0. Developers were able to provide much useful information when asked to verbalize what made their software difficult or easy. Even though this information was subjective, there was surprising commonality in terminology between developers.*

## 7.2.2  The Data Set Concept

Data that can be collected during the development process may be categorized generically into data types, e.g., design data, productivity data, test data, etc.  Within each of these generic categories are detailed parameters which support various paths of analysis, allow decisions to be made concerning project status, indicate software quality, etc.  However, the ability to provide data from each category will vary from project to project.

A particularly attractive approach to data collection was made obvious by attempts to compare projects in work done on the SRS.  This would require, first, that quantifiable descriptions of generic analyses be defined and, second, that the minimal number of parameters sufficient to support these descriptions be identified.  The resulting minimal data sets would be applicable to varying degrees in virtually any project; large projects could supply data to many data sets, while smaller projects might be limited to one or two data sets.  Parameters would be consistent from project to project, however.

## 7.3  Benefits of Data Collection and Analysis

Assuming that information is collected and available, what can we expect to gain from its analysis?  The long range benefits are the most obvious.  We will learn, for example, how large a software module can be without affecting understandability and how small it can be before partitioning problems are encountered.  Specific tools and techniques to improve the development process will also be identified.  These are all things that can be applied in the future, to the next project.  But, what about the near term payoff for the project supplying the data?  Project managers, when asked to contribute to the data collection and analysis activities, will invariably ask two questions:  (1) What is the impact of such a study on my project? and (2) How will the study benefit my project?

The answer to the first question determines largely what the answer to the second question will be.  Done properly, manpower <u>and</u> schedule relief would be provided for collection of data throughout the life of the project; much of the useful data is perishable and must be collected as it is created.  Even if this is not done project involvement is required in the analysis because individual performers alone are able to provide some of the data with sufficient accuracy (e.g., causative error data).  Access to project experience is essential to accurate interpretation, even if the analysis is done independently.  The more project commitment there is to such a study, the greater the impact on project resources and the greater the yield of usable information.  The extent of this commitment must be determined for each individual project.

---

*For that one project.

The benefit to the on-going project comes from increased awareness of problems and better control over the development process. This is particularly true if the project is of sufficient duration to allow findings to be folded back into the project in the form of improvements. For example, results of analysis of Project 5 integration test data were used in a briefing to project performers on improvement of test techniques. In this briefing it was recommended that unit level test case preparation include special emphasis on "what if" thinking in selecting data to exercise routine logic. Put another way, this calls for the test designer to ask what will happen if various input data, including extremes, singularities, and combinations of parameter settings, are presented to the software. Will the test cases demonstrate the software's ability to handle these data scenarios? This recommendation was in response to the most common logical error, missing logic or condition tests*, Incidentally, this feedback of results to project performers also provides an excellent opportunity to point out positive findings and specific successes, as well as areas needing improvement.

Another benefit of data collection and analysis may be in the way project performers view their errors. Several Project 5 programmers admitted that, although they didn't particularly enjoy categorizing their own errors, this task helped register the error in their memories, and they tended not to repeat errors of the same type.

In summary, data collection and analysis on software development projects has been beneficial in the following ways.

- It has helped us to better understand the various factors and difficulties characterizing the software and the development process.

- It has given us a benchmark for estimating certain parameters, such as size and cost, during the proposal stage of new work.**

- It has shot down some and confirmed others of our intuitive notions about software and its development. It has also given us some surprises.

- It has given us a healthy respect for the difficulties of collecting and interpreting data.

- Probably most important, it has demonstrated a potential for benefit to the project supplying the data.

---

*One development group admitted use of this sort of common sense approach not only in creating test cases but also in design. They then challenged the authors to find a missing logic error in the integration test data. None were found.

**Where this new work is similar to the projects studied.

Data collection is truely on its infancy.  We've identified some significant problems and have some project-specific solutions for these problems.  Overall the experience has been a positive one and the benefits are real.

## 8.0 CONCLUSIONS AND RECOMMENDATIONS

Our first finding on the Software Reliability Study was that software projects have a potential for creating tremendous amounts of useful data. And, in a disciplined software development or maintenance environment, data can be a by-product of all project phases and activities. To guarantee data quality, however, the collection process should be event driven, i.e., information should be collected as events create it, not after the fact. This means that the collection mechanism must be planned and ready in advance, and that data items must be well defined prior to their collection.

Analysis of error data showed that most of our errors were design and requirements errors, as opposed to coding errors and errors made during the correction of other errors. Although software development projects typically expend much effort in requirements and design reviews, these sources of error were shown to represent major portions of the total errors detected during formal testing. For one project it was also shown that the ratio of requirements and design errors to coding errors may well decrease with project maturity in the top-down, multiple increment development process. These results suggest that further detailed analyses of requirements and design errors is necessary and that there is a need for aids, either tools or techniques, to assist the developer in creating both the requirements and the software design.

A detailed look at error types showed that logic errors were, percentagewise, the most frequent errors in each of the projects examined. Of these logic errors, the most frequent error was the one where logic to handle a specific data condition was missing. Again, this supports the need for requirements and design aids to describe the need and the design solution, respectively. Next, in order of occurrence, were the data handling or computational errors, depending on the type of software being analyzed. Data base errors and changes due to tuning also represented a significant percentage of the total error history.

One very positive outcome of this study was the similarity in frequency of occurrence of various error categories for nonsimilar projects. Although comparison of projects was discouraged in this study, the near equivalent (i.e., standardized) error category lists used in the analysis made these similarities visible. Standardized data description and analysis techniques should make future project comparisons possible in a number of areas. Since many of the investigations pursued in this study were improved by grouping the software by function (e.g., data base management) or by purpose (e.g., computational) it is recommended that future work be aimed at standardizing these categories for project comparison purposes.

Error categorization may be symptomatic or causative. To perform categorization, three pieces of information are needed: The symptoms of the problem, a description of the cause, and a description of the fix. Two pieces of additional information are also needed: error criticality, because all errors are not equal in a reliability sense, and the effort required to correct each error. It is recommended that criticality be keyed to "mission" success, where the following criteria dictate the error's criticality.

| | |
|---|---|
| Critical | - user's mission cannot be completed |
| High | - user's mission can be continued but performance is degraded |
| Medium | - workaround is available, performance not degraded |
| Low | - performance not affected |
| Noncritical | - product improvement |

The amount of effort required to fix an error should take into account 1) time to find the error, 2) time to create a fix, and 3) time to test the fix. It should be noted that collection of this information is <u>not</u> trivial and implies availability of individuals qualified to provide the information*.

Although investigations of the effects of size on reliability showed a good linear fit for preoperational software, indicating no preferable size to minimize errors, operational data show a tendency for large routines, say >1000 total source statements, to be more error-prone in the operational environment. That is, it is possible to thoroughly test and remove all errors from the smaller routines.

Standard measures of test thoroughness are also needed. Work in connection with the Mathematical Theory of Software Reliability are particularly attractive since this model treats not only a measure of the amount of code exercised in a test but also variation of the input data space and functional capabilities of the software.

Two important modifications to the standard regression analysis were used in the course of the study of software attributes and metrics. The first was the application of the constraint of non-negativity to all influence coefficients of parameters assumed to exert a positive influence

---

*Criticality and effort to fix were sufficiently difficult to collect accurately that they were not available for this study. They were, however, identified repeatedly as information that is needed.

on numbers of problems. This was used as a screening technique only since standard statistical analyses cannot be applied with these constraints on the estimation process. The second modification was to make another structural constraint on the linear regression model to exclude undefined parameters; in other words to eliminate the free constant usually assumed in linear regression analyses. Another way of stating the same thing is that the regression plane was forced through the origin. This assumption appeared to be substantially borne out, in that plots of number of problems versus each parameter tend to form a "ray" from the origin. The imposition of this assumption on the regression analysis estimation procedure usually results in a higher multiple correlation coefficient than if the constant term is left in.

Use of test error data in suggesting improvements in development and test techniques was shown to be possible. Similar studies using data from other software development activities, such as requirements and design reviews, should also be possible.

Finally, when work was started on the Software Reliability Study, opinions from investigators (and from performers on projects supplying the data) were mixed concerning whether the data would show anything at all. The only precedent at the time was a study done for the CCIP-85 Study Group [5] which, for all of its data, was not very productive in terms of final results. The skeptics pointed to this initial attempt and predicted similar inconclusive results for this study. Yet, for those S.R.S. investigators who worked on the projects supplying data to both study projects, it seemed that the data had to be indicative of what happened during the software development process and of the reliability of the software itself.

One of the first things we learned in our study was that the earlier investigators had developed useful techniques, laying the groundwork for subsequent investigations. These techniques were their results. In the S.R.S. we altered definitions, collected needed data not previously available, and refined the techniques, but the basic approach to investigation of empirical data was the one suggested by Reference [5] . It was a valuable first step, and we didn't have to start from scratch. To this we added techniques suggested by other investigators, again altering and modifying where improvements were necessary. We conclude, then, that the analysis of empirical data is in its infancy, and no single "best" approach has yet been identified. We recommend that future investigators not discard techniques that, for others, have proven inconclusive. Rather, techniques should be considered as modifiable candidates for future investigations. Those presented in this study should be no exception.

# 9.0 BIBLIOGRAPHY

## 9.1 References

1. B. W. Boehm, et al, "Characteristics of Software Quality," TRW Software Series TRW-SS-73-09, 28 December 1973.

2. B. W. Boehm, "Software and Its Impact: A Quantitative Assessment," Datamation, Vol. 19 - No. 5, May 1973.

3. W. Amory and J. A. Clapp, "A Software Error Classification Methodology," MITRE Technical Report No. MTR-2648, Volume VII, 30 June 1973.

4. M.L. Shooman and M.I. Bolsky, "Types, Distribution, and Test and Correction Times for Programming Errors," Proceedings 1975 Conference on Reliable Software, April 21-23, 1975, IEEE Catalog No. 75, CH0940-7CSR, pp. 347-362.

5. C. A. Bosch and W. L. Hetrick, "Software Development Characteristics Study for the CCIP-85 Study Group," TRW Systems, Volumes A and B, Report 4851.1-003, 8 October 1971.

6. R. J. Rubey, and R. D. Hartwick, "Quantitative Measurement of Program Quality," Proceedings, ACM National Conference, 1968, pp. 671-677.

7. TRW Software Series TR-SS-73-06, in press January 1976. Revised from earlier report published as Report No. SD1776, "The Quantitative Measurement of Software Safety and Reliability," August 24, 1973.

8. A. V. Fiacco and G. P. McCormick, Nonlinear Programming: Sequential Unconstrained Minimization Techniques, John Wiley & Sons, Sons, Inc.. New York, 1968.

9. C. L. Lawson and R. J. Hanson, Solving Least Squares Problems, Prentice-Hall, Inc., Englewood Cliffs, New Jersey, 1974.

10. D. J. Reifer, "Automated Aids for Reliable Software," An Invited Tutorial at the 1975 International Conference on Reliable Software, 21-23 April 1975.

11. D. J. Reifer, "Interim Report on the Aids Inventory Project," Technical Report SAMSO-TR-75-184, 16 July 1975.

12. R. W. Curry, "A Measure to Support Calibration and Balancing of the Effectiveness of Software Engineering Tools and Techniques," Science Applications, Inc., Technical Report BRS-15, 14 October 1975.

13. M. E. Fagan, "Design and Code Inspections and Process Control in the Development of Programs," IBM Technical Report TR 21.572, 17 December 1974.

14. Military Standard; Technical Reviews and Audits for Systems, Equipment, and Computer Programs; MIL-STD-1521 (USAF), 1 September 1972.

15. R. W. Wolverton, "The Cost of Developing Large Scale Software," TRW Software Series TRW-SS-73-01, March 1972.

16. A. Avizienis, "The Methodology of Fault-Tolerant Computing," First USA-Japan Computer Conference, 1972.

17. M.L. Shooman, "Operational Testing and Software Reliability Estimation During Program Development," Record, 1973 IEEE Symposium on Computer Software Reliability, April 30 - May 2, 1973, IEEE Catalog No. 73, CHO741-9CSR, pp. 51-57.

18. Z. Jelinski and P. B. Moranda, "Applications of a Probability-Based Model to a Code Reading Experiment," Proceedings, IEEE Symposium on Computer Software Reliability, April 30 - May 2, 1973, p. 78.

19. M. Lipow, TRW Report No. 2260.1.9-73B-15, "Maximum Likelihood Estimation of Parameters of a Software Time-To-Failure Distribution," June 1973.

20. R. W. Wolverton and G. J. Schick, "Assessment of Software Reliability," TRW Software Series, TRW-SS-73-04, September 1972.

21. H. K. Weiss, "Estimation of Reliability Growth in a Complex System with a Poisson-Type Failure," Operations Research, Vol. 4, No. 5, October 1956, pp. 532-545.

22. W. J. Corcoran, H. Weingarten and P. W. Zehna, "Estimating Reliability After Corrective Action," Management Science, Vol. 10, No. 4, July 1954, pp. 786-795.

23. E. C. Nelson, "A Statistical Basis for Software Reliability Assessment," TRW-SS-73-03, March 1973.

24. E. K. Blum, "The Semantics of Programming Language," Part I, TRW-SS-69-01, December 1969.

25. J. R. Brown and M. Lipow, "Testing for Software Reliability," Proceedings 1975 International Conference on Reliable Software, April 21-23, 1975, IEEE Catalog No. 75, CHO940-7CSR, pp. 518-527.

26. M. Lipow, "Measurement of Over-all System Reliability Utilizing Results of Independent Subsystem Tests," Space Technology Laboratories Report No. GM-TR-0165, October 1958.

27. J. Neyman, "Outline of a Theory of Statistical Estimation Based on the Classical Theory of Probability," Phil Trans. Royal Society, London, A., Vol. 236 (1937) p. 333.

28. R. J. Buehler, "Confidence Intervals for the Product of Two Binomial Parameters," J. Amer. Stat. Assoc., Vol. 52, pp. 482-493 (1953).

29. G. P. Steck, "Upper Confidence Limits for the Failure Probability of Complex Networks," Sandia Corporation Research Report, December 1957.

30. D. K. Lloyd and M. Lipow, Reliability: Management, Methods, and Mathematics, Prentice Hall, Inc., Englewood Cliffs, New Jersey, 1962, pp. 224-229.

31. H. L. Harter, New Tables of the Incomplete Gamma - Function Ratio and of Percentage Points of the Chi-Square and Beta Distributions, Aerospace Research Laboratories, USAF, 1964. Obtainable from NTIS, Springfield, VA. 22161.

32. E. Pinney, "Fitting Curves with Zero or Infinite End Points," Ann. Math. Stat., Vol. XVIII, No. 1, March 1947, pp. 127-313.

33. J.E. Wolf, "Reliability Assessment from Test Data," Proceedings 1976 Annual Reliability and Maintainability Symposium, Jan. 20-22, 1976, IEEE Catalog No. 76, CH01044-7RQC, pp. 441-449.

34. D. T. Gillespie, "The Monte Carlo Method of Evaluating Integrals," Report No. NWC TP5714, Naval Weapons Center, China Lake, CA 93555, February 1975. Obtainable from NTIS, Springfield, VA 22161.

## 9.2 Other Material Surveyed in this Study

1. E. F. Miller, Jr., "Methodology for Comprehensive Software Testing," Interim Report, Rome Air Development Center, RADC-TR-75-161, June 1975.

2. J. A. Clapp and J. E. Sullivan, "Automated Monitoring of Software Quality," 1974 AFIPS National Computer Conference Proceedings, pp. 337-342.

3. E. A. Youngs, "Error-Proneness in Programming," Doctoral Thesis in Computer Science, University of North Carolina 1970.

4. R. D. Avery and J. C. Hoyle, "Evaluating Computing Personnel," Datamation, Vol. 19 - No. 7, July 1973.

## APPENDIX A
### GLOSSARY OF TERMS

CDR — Critical Design Review (as described in MIL-STD-1521).

CM — Configuration Management

COMPOOL — An operating system capability which provides single source data base definition and structure for global variables.

Delivery — The point at which the software package is turned over to a customer for use in the operational environment.

Development Cycle — A series of tasks performed in serial order (for the projects in this study) to create the deliverable software product and its documentation. These tasks consist of requirements analysis, preliminary and detailed design, coding and checkout, and formal testing. It is appropriately called a cycle because it may be applied iteratively, as in the Project 5 top-down development approach. (See Section 7.0)

Direct Interface — An interface immediately between two software elements

```
| Routine 1 |<--->| Routine 2 |<--->| Routine 3 |
```

In the example here Routine 1 interfaces directly with Routine 2 and indirectly with Routine 3.

DPR — Design Problem Report - used to document problems in the design for preliminary and critical design reviews.

DR — Discrepancy Report - the Project 5 software problem report

DUT — Document Update Transmittal

FOC — Final Operational Configuration

Formal Testing — Testing conducted according to test procedures which are documented and approved by contractor and customer.

Function — A grouping of routines which performs a prescribed function (structural elements of Projects 2 and 3).

GLOSSARY OF TERMS (Continued)

| | |
|---|---|
| Instructions | Machine instructions (machine dependent parameter). |
| Internal Delivery | The point at which the software as an entire package is given to the independent test group. |
| IOC | Initial Operational Configuration. |
| Metric | A measure of the extent or degree to which the software possesses and exhibits a certain characteristic, quality, property, or attribute. |
| MTM | Modification Transmittal Memorandum (Projects 2 and 3). |
| MTSR | Mathematical Theory of Software Reliability |
| Operational | The status given a software package once it has completed contractor testing and is turned over to the eventual user for use in the applications environment. |
| OS | Operating System. |
| PA | Product Assurance. An organizationally independent group charged with specifying and enforcing adherence to software quality standards in the areas of requirements design, coding, all phases of testing, and management. |
| PDR | Preliminary Design Review (as described in MIL-STD-1521). |
| Routine | Smallest group of compilable code |
| SMR | Software Modification Record |
| SPR | Software Problem Report |
| S.R.S. | Software Reliability Study |
| S/S | Subsystem |
| Statements | Programming Language at the Source Code Level |
| S/W | Software |
| User | The individual at the man/machine interface who is applying the software to the solution of a problem, e.g. test or operations. |

APPENDIX B

SAMPLE DATA COLLECTION FORMS


This appendix presents blank examples of data collection forms actually used and forms similar to those used to collect error data for the Software Reliability Study.

Three software problem reports are presented first.  These are the forms used to document software errors during testing.  Both the one and two piece of paper approaches, discussed in Section 7.0, are represented by the SPR and DR, respectively*.

Used on Projects 2 and 3, the SPR (page B-2) opens the problem by identifying the symptoms of the error, the test configuration, and if appropriate, a proposed solution.  The problem remains open until it is closed by a modification transmittal memorandum or MTM (page B-3) which explains and delivers the fix.  Hence the reference to a two piece of paper approach.

The discrepancy report, or DR (page B-4), is used in an approach where one form documents the error and later the fix.  This form was used on Project 5.

A third example of a software problem report is also given.  This form and its companion closure form, the Software Modification Record (SMR), are presented on pages B-5 through B-12.  Both were designed during the early part of the Software Reliability Study for application on Project 5.  The project eventually selected as Project 5 was not the one for which the SPR/ SMR pair was developed, and since it already utilized the DR as a successful problem reporting form, no attempt was made to impose the SPR/SMR pair.  Incidentally, the SPR/SMR pair was used successfully on the project for which it was designed.

A sample of the Design Problem Report (DPR) is presented on page B-13.

---

*Note:   SPR - Software Problem Report
         DR - Discrepancy Report

| **MTM** | TO: CONFIGURATION MANAGEMENT | PAGE 1 of _____ | SCND CONTROL NUMBER _____ |
|---|---|---|---|

```
MTM | TO: CONFIGURATION MANAGEMENT          PAGE 1 of _____ | SCND CONTROL
     |                                                       | NUMBER _____
─────┴───────────────────────────────────────────────────── ├──────────────────
FROM:                                                        | DATE LOGGED ___ ___
  NAME _____ DATE _____ ├──────────────────
─────────────────────────────────────────────────────────── | ORIG. CONTROL
MODIFICATION SUBMITTED:          SUBSYSTEM _____ _____  | NUMBER
PROGRAM NAME _____ MID _____ MOD _____    |
────────────────────────────────────────────────────────────┴──────────────────
DOCUMENT TITLE _____ IDENT. NO. __ _____
RESPONSE TO SPP(S) _____ SUPPLEMENTS MTM _____
─────────────────────────────────────────────────────────────────────────────
REASON FOR SUBMITTAL:  □ DELIVERY      □ SPR EXPLANATION    □ SPR STATUS
TYPE OF DELIVERY:  □ PRE CAPABILITY   □ MIN CAPABILITY   □ VAL CAPABILITY (IMS5)
□  SPR FIX      □ COMPOOL       □ DATABASE      □ COMPOOL COMPATIBILITY
─────────────────────────────────────────────────────────────────────────────
PROBLEM ANALYSIS: _____
_____
_____
_____
_____
_____
_____
_____

CHANGE DESCRIPTION: _____
_____
_____
_____
_____
_____
_____
_____
_____ ANALYST _____ DATE _____
─────────────────────────────────────────────────────────────────────────────
CHANGE IMPACT:
□ NO PROBLEM   CCR NO. _____ DBCR NO. _____ DUT NO. _____ ECP NO. ____
─────────────────────────────────────────────────────────────────────────────
SUBMITTAL INSTRUCTIONS FOR PROGRAM DELIVERIES:
  INPUT MID (VERSION)_____ MOD _____ SOURCE TYPE _____ TAPE NO._____ REEL NO._____
─────────────────────────────────────────────────────────────────────────────
VERIFICATION / AUTHORIZATION:
  MTM APPROVED BY _____ DATE _____ CONCURRENCE _____ DATE _____
─────────────────────────────────────────────────────────────────────────────
DISPOSITION:
  INCORP. AMT ___ _____ BY _____ DATE _____ VERIF. BY SCND ____
```

**PUNCH ALL CARDS**

C.C.

| (2-9) |
|---|
| 0 0 0 0 |

# DISCREPANCY REPORT

**1** 2-9 | (10-15) RUN DATE YR / MO / DY | (16-27) LIBRARY NAME | CY NO. (28-41) TEST PROCEDURE ID AND REVISION NUMBER

(42-53) ORIGINATOR | (54-58) PHONE | LOCATION (59-61) | TEST LEVEL (62-64) | (65-73) L.Ø.Ø.P.

**2** 2-9 | (10-16) PROGRAM MNEMONIC | MOD NO. (17-18) | DATE BASE (19-23) | MNEMONIC (24-25) | MOD NO. | (26-41) NOTES BUILD, RELEASE, ETC.

**3** 2-9 | (10-41) DISCREPANCY

(42-73)

**4** 2-9 | (10-41)

(42-73)

**5** 2-9 | (10-41)

(42-73)

**6** 2-9 | (10-41)

(42-73)

**7** 2-9 | (10-41) PROPOSED SOLUTION

(42-61) | (62-73) ROUTE TO TEST DIRECTOR

— DISCREPANCY

**8** 2-9 | (10-41) ACTUAL FIX/DISPOSITION

(42-73)

**9** 2-9 | (10-41)

(42-73)

**A** 2-9 | (10-41)

(42-73)

**B** 2-9 | (10-41)

(42-46) | (47-58) ASSIGNED ANALYST | (59-64) ASSIGNED DATE YR / MO / DY | (65-70) FIX DATE YR / MO / DY | INITIALS

**C** 2-9 | (10-41) NEW PROGRAM NAME AND MOD NUMBER (9 CHARACTERS) UP TO 6 PROGRAMS

(42-63) | (64-73) SCO NUMBER

**D** 2-9 | (10-14) DEFECT CAT | (15-24) DOCUMENT AFFECTED | (25-33) DPR NUMBER | (34-41) REFERENCE DR NUMBER

(42-73) OTHER DOCUMENTS AFFECTED

**E** 2-9 | *SIGNATURE OF WM OR LOCAL TEST DIRECTOR | (20-25) DATE YR / MO / DY | *PA CONCURRENCE | (36-41) DATE YR / MO / DY

— DISPOSITION

(42-53) WORKING LIBRARY UPDATE ID CY NO. | (54-59) WLU DATE YR / MO / DY | INITIALS | (63-73) TEST DESCRIPTION

**F** 2-9 | (10-41) TEST DESCRIPTION CONTINUED

(42-53) WORKING LIBRARY TEST ID CY NO. | (54-59) WLT DATE YR / MO / DY | INITIALS | (63-73) TCR NUMBER

**G** 2-9 | (10-21) MASTER LIBRARY UPDATE ID CY NO. | (22-27) MLU DATE YR / MO / YR | INITIALS | (31-41) TEST DESCRIPTION

(42-73) TEST DESCRIPTION CONTINUED

**H** 2-9 | (10-21) MASTER LIBRARY TEST ID CY NO. | (22-27) MLT DATE YR / MO / DY | INITIALS | (31-41) PCO NUMBER

TEST DIRECTOR SIGNATURE | (52-57) DATE YR / MO / DY | *PA SIGNATURE | (68-73) DATE CLOSED YR / MO / DY

*REQUIRED AFTER TURNOVER TO SSEV

— RETEST

SYSTEMS 4614 REV. 8-74

PAGE____ OF____

| S | OFTWARE | | LOG NO: (A) |
| P | ROBLEM | **P** | LOG DATE: (B) |
| R | EPORT | ROBLEM | TIME: (C) |

(D) DEV ☐   INTEG ☐   VAL ☐   ACC ☐ SITE_____    STATUS: (E) | 1 | 2 | 3 | 4 | 5 | 6 | 7

ORIGINATOR: _____ (F)  EXTENSION:

PROBLEM WITH: (G)   ROUTINE ☐   DATA BASE ☐   DOCUMENT ☐

| ROUTINE/ELEMENT/SS: (H) | MOD: (I) | TAPE: (J) |
| DATA BASE: (K) | DOCUMENTS: (L) |
| TEST CASE: (M) | HARDWARE UNIT: (N) |

PROBLEM DESCRIPTION/IMPACT: (O)

NOTES:

(P)

3-18-74

## Software Problem Report (Continued)

| PARAMETER | KEY | PARAMETER DESCRIPTION |
|-----------|-----|------------------------|
| LOG NO. | Ⓐ | A unique SPR number assigned by Configuration Management (CM). This number may have an alpha prefix to denote additional information. (e.g., a development prefix to distinguish these SPRs from problems documented during a parallel maintenance phase of an earlier version of the same software.) Numbers are sequential. |
| LOG DATE | Ⓑ | The date the problem is logged by CM. |
| TIME | Ⓒ | This is the date and time of day the problem was discovered. |
| TEST PHASE | Ⓓ | Test phase during which the problem was discovered.<br><br>DEV - development test<br>INTEG - integration test<br>VAL - validation test<br>ACC - acceptance test<br>SITE - operational problem |
| STATUS | Ⓔ | Status is a dynamic indicator maintained in the CM records. It is on the SPR for use by developers and testers in tracking and reporting latest status to CM. Codes indicate the following:<br><br>1 - The Test Working Group is reviewing SPR to determine appropriate action.<br><br>2 - SPR has been assigned to a developer for correction.<br><br>3 - Fix available, has been tested, and is ready for delivery to master program library.<br><br>4 - Master program library has been updated; retest of fix on master program library not complete. |

## Software Problem Report (Continued)

| PARAMETER | KEY | PARAMETER DESCRIPTION |
|---|---|---|
| STATUS (Continued) | | 5 - Test rerun, problem still exists, SMR rejected. |
| | | 6 - Test rerun, fix works, SPR closed. |
| | | 7 - Hold for future closure. Problem is not reproducible, is product improvement, very low priority, etc. |
| ORIGINATOR/EXTENSION | Ⓕ | Name and telephone extension of author of SPR. |
| PROBLEM WITH | Ⓖ | Identification of whether the problem is in a routine, the data base, a document, or some combination of these. |
| ROUTINE/ELEMENT/SS | Ⓗ | Name of the routine exhibiting the problem. If the routine is not known, identify the element or subsystem (i.e., provide the maximum amount of detail possible) |
| MOD | Ⓘ | Modification of routine exhibiting the problem, if known. |
| TAPE | Ⓙ | Master Program Library tape I.D. with the offending routine. |
| DATA BASE | Ⓚ | ID of data base used when the problem was discovered. |
| DOCUMENTS | Ⓛ | CDRL number(s) of document(s) exhibiting errors. |
| TEST CASE | Ⓜ | ID of the principal test case which demonstrated the error. |
| HARDWARE UNIT | Ⓝ | ID of the computer system being operated when the problem was discovered. |

## Software Problem Report (Continued)

| PARAMETER | KEY | PARAMETER DESCRIPTION |
|---|---|---|
| PROBLEM DESCRIPTION/IMPACT | Ⓞ | Detailed description of the symptoms of the problem and, if possible, a description of the actual problem. Impact of the problem on future testing, on interfacing software, documentation, etc. should also be provided. |
| NOTES | Ⓟ | Working area for status keeping, additional information, etc. |

PAGE _____ OF _____

| **S** OFTWARE | **M** ODIFICATION | LOG NO: (A) |
|---|---|---|
| **M** ODIFICATION | | LOG DATE: (B) |
| **R** ECORD | | TIME: (C) |

ORIGINATOR: (D)      SS: (E)    ROUTINE: (F)

RESPONSE TO SPRS: (G)

RESPONSE INCLUDES: (H)   ROUTINE MOD ☐   DOC. UPDATE ☐   DATA BASE CHG ☐   EXPLANATION ☐

RESPONSE: (I)

APPROVAL: (J) _____

MODIFICATION:   CODE TYPE: (K) I/Ø ☐   COMP ☐   LOGICAL ☐   DATA HAND ☐

ROUTINE: (L)     OLD MOD: (M)     NEW MOD: (N)

REF DATA BASE: (O)    DBCR: (P)    REF DOCUMENT: (Q)    DUT: (R)

| HAS FIX BEEN TESTED? (S) | YES NO N.A. | YES NO N.A. | YES NO N.A. | YES NO N.A. | YES NO N.A. |
|---|---|---|---|---|---|
| REMARKS: | ELEMENT | SS | SS INTEG. | VALID. | OPERATIONS |

WAS PROBLEM CORRECTLY STATED ON SPR? (T)    YES ☐    NO ☐

REMARKS: (U)

PROBLEM SOURCE: (V)   SYS SPEC ☐   DEV SPEC ☐   PROD SPEC ☐   DB ☐   CODE ☐

ESTIMATED RESOURCES: (W)    MANHOURS _____ COMPUTER TIME _____

3-18-74

## Software Modification Record (Continued)

| PARAMETER | KEY | PARAMETER DESCRIPTION |
|-----------|-----|----------------------|
| LOG NO | Ⓐ | A unique SMR number assigned by CM upon receipt of the modification. |
| LOG DATE | Ⓑ | Date the SMR is logged by CM. |
| TIME | Ⓒ | Time the SMR and the delivered modification are available to CM and logged. |
| ORIGINATOR | Ⓓ | Author of the modification (generally the closer of the SPR(s)) |
| SS | Ⓔ | Subsystem affected by the modification being delivered. |
| ROUTINE | Ⓕ | Name of the routine for which the modification is being delivered (This field is a repeat of field Ⓛ) |
| RESPONSE TO SPRs | Ⓖ | SPR number(s) being totally or partially closed by the delivery. If an SMR partially closes a problem, a P is appended to the SPR number (e.g., 1234(P)) |
| RESPONSE INCLUDES | Ⓗ | Identification of elements in the delivery; e.g., a routine modification, document update or data base change or a combination of these. If the SMR effects closure of a problem with an explanation this is indicated. |
| RESPONSE | Ⓘ | Detailed description of the correction being made to the software. In the case of a document update or data base change, the document update transmittal (DUT) and data base change request (DBCR) numbers, respectively, are referenced with the description of the necessary change in Ⓟ and Ⓡ. |
| APPROVAL | Ⓙ | Signature of appropriate manager. |

## Software Modification Record (Continued)

| PARAMETER | KEY | PARAMETER DESCRIPTION |
|---|---|---|
| CODE TYPE: | Ⓚ | Type(s) of source code involved in the routine modification.<br><br>I/O - input, output, or formatting statements, etc.<br><br>COMP - computational code<br><br>LOGICAL - code that establishes branches in the program.<br><br>DATA HAND - code that moves data from place to place, stores data, etc. That is, data handling code. |
| ROUTINE | Ⓛ | Name of routine being modified, document being changed, or data base being altered. In the case of an explanatory SMR the name given on the SPR is repeated. |
| OLD MOD<br>NEW MOD | Ⓜ<br>Ⓝ | Identification of old routine modification to be altered to produce the new routine modification. |
| REF DATA BASE<br>DBCR | Ⓞ<br>Ⓟ | If a data base change is in order, this supplies the data base identifier to which the changes delivered by the data base change request are to be applied. |
| REF DOCUMENT<br>DUT | Ⓠ<br>Ⓡ | If corrective action also requires a change to a document, the title of the document to be changed is given and the document update transmittal (DUT) delivering the change is referenced by number. |
| HAS THE FIX BEEN TESTED? | Ⓢ | Testing of a modification made to a routine must be completed at appropriate predetermined levels prior to delivery of a modification. Element, subsystem, integration, validation, and operational testing, if applicable, will be indicated. Remarks indicating test success are invited. |

## Software Modification Record (Continued)

| PARAMETER | KEY | PARAMETER DESCRIPTION |
|---|---|---|

**PARAMETER**  **KEY**  **PARAMETER DESCRIPTION**

**WAS PROBLEM CORRECTLY STATED ON SPR?**  Ⓣ Ⓤ  Indication of accuracy of the problem statement is to be given. An accurate restatement of the problem is to be given in the remarks section.

**PROBLEM SOURCE**  Ⓥ  Identification of the source of the Problem.

    System Specification - requirements document

    Development Specification - preliminary design document

    Product Specification - detailed design document

    DB - data base

    CODE - source code only

**ESTIMATED RESOURCES**  Ⓦ  Resources required to close the problem in manhours of work and minutes of computer time.

## DESIGN PROBLEM REPORT

CONTROL NO: _____

DATE: _____

DOCUMENT: _____

REVIEWER/AGENCY: _____ APPROVED: _____

PAGE/SECTION/FIGURE: _____

PROBLEM/RECOMMENDATION:

ACTION/CATEGORY:

1 ☐

2 ☐

3 ☐

ACTION ITEM NO._____ 4 ☐

DISPOSITION:

CLOSED ☐
8-17-73

```
┌─────────────────────────────────────────────────────────────────────────────┐
│ ┌──────┐                                            │ SCMO CONTROL.          │
│ │ SPR  │ TO:  CONFIGURATION MANAGEMENT              │ NUMBER _____     │
│ ├──────┘                                            │                        │
│ │ FROM:                                             │ DATE                   │
│ │    NAME _____ DATE _____  │ LOGGED _____     │
│ ├───────────────────────────────────────────────── │                        │
│ │ DISTRIBUTION:                                     │ CMO CONTROL            │
│ │                                                   │ NUMBER _____     │
└─────────────────────────────────────────────────────────────────────────────┘
```

| SPR | TO: CONFIGURATION MANAGEMENT | SCMO CONTROL. NUMBER _____ |
|---|---|---|

FROM:
  NAME _____ DATE _____   DATE LOGGED _____

DISTRIBUTION:   CMO CONTROL NUMBER _____

TEST PERIOD: ☐DEV ☐VAL ☐ACC ☐INTEG. ☐OD | PRIORITY: ☐HIGH ☐MED ☐LOW

CONFIGURATION: SST _____ AMTID _____ TEST ID_____

DATA BASE ID _____ DBRT REEL NO. _____

PROBLEM WITH: ☐ROUTINE ☐DOCUMENT ☐DB ☐COMPOOL

ROUTINE NAME _____ WID _____ MOD _____

DOCUMENT TITLE _____ IDENT_____

PROBLEM DESCRIPTION:




EFFECTS:


COMMENTS:


DEVELOPMENT SOLUTION:
MTM NO_____ CCR NO_____ DBCR NO_____ DUT NO._____
ROUTINE_____ MOD_____
REMARKS: